Dear Mrs Sayre — I
think you will love
this book. I am
simply wild about
it.

Scott

The Diary of Otto Braun (New York: Knopf, 1924). Inscription traced over by unknown hand. Bruccoli Collection.

FITZGERALD/HEMINGWAY ANNUAL 1974

Edited by

Matthew J. Bruccoli

University of South Carolina

and

C.E. Frazer Clark, Jr.

Microcard Editions Books
An Indian Head Company
A Division of Information Handling Services

Editors:

MATTHEW J. BRUCCOLI
Department of English
University of South Carolina
Columbia, South Carolina 29208

C. E. FRAZER CLARK, JR.
1700 Lone Pine Road
Bloomfield Hills, Michigan 48013

Editorial Assistants: Linda Berry
                       Margaret M. Duggan

Address all editorial correspondence to the editors.

Address orders and inquiries to Microcard Editions Books,
5500 South Valentia Way, Englewood, Colorado 80110

Library of Congress Catalog Card Number: 75-83781
ISBN: 0-910972-49-4

Printed in the United States of America.

To Zane Knauss

CONTENTS

F. SCOTT FITZGERALD

Zelda Fitzgerald's Tribute to F. Scott Fitzgerald   3

Letter to Brooks Bowman   9
    F. Scott Fitzgerald

The Fitzgerald Revival, 1941-1953   11
    Malcolm Cowley

Sleeping and Waking — The Literary Reputation   15
    of *The Great Gatsby,* 1927-1944
    Andrew Crosland

John O'Hara's Remarks on the Silent *Gatsby*   25

The Better Fathers: The Priests in   29
    Fitzgerald's Life
    Joan M. Allen

F. Scott Fitzgerald's Associations with Norfolk   41
    and Virginia Beach
    William W. Seward, Jr.

The Discarded Ending of "The Offshore Pirate"   47
    Jennifer McCabe Atkinson

The Intricate Pattern in *The Great Gatsby*   51
    Bruce R. Stark

Perfect Marriage in *Tender is the Night:* A Study in the
Progress of a Symbol   63
Louis K. Greiff

An Interview with Theodora Gager, Fitzgerald's
Private Nurse   75
William Katterjohn

"The Camel's Back" and *Conductor 1492*   87
Alan Margolies

The *F. Scott Fitzgerald and his Contemporaries*
Correspondence   89
William Goldhurst

Gatsby's Bluff and Fitzgerald's Blunders   95
Sterling K. Eisiminger

Fitzgerald and Horace McCoy   99
Richard Layman

****

Interview with Allen Tate   101

The 1920's in American Life and Literature   115
James T. Farrell

****

HEMINGWAY

American Red Cross Reports on the Wounding of
Lieutenant Ernest M. Hemingway — 1918   131
C. E. Frazer Clark, Jr.

Metempsychosis in the Stream, or What Happens in
"Bimini"?   137
Francis E. Skipp

Ernest Hemingway and the Arts — a Necessary
Addendum   145
Hans-Joachim Kann

Contents

The Nick Adams Stories: Fiction or Fact?   155
    Bernard F. Rodgers, Jr.

Hemingway: The Function of Nostalgia   163
    Stephen L. Tanner

Notes on the Manuscript, Date, and Sources of
    Hemingway's "Banal Story"   175
    Philip R. Yannella

Hemingway's "Banal Story"   181
    Wayne Kvam

5000 Grand: The Plagiarism Suit Against Hemingway   193
    Frank M. Laurence

Echoes from the Sea: A Hemingway Rubric   201
    Richard E. Braun

The Man Behind the Masks: Hemingway as a Fictional
    Character   207
    William F. Nolan

"A Sound Basis of Union": Structural and Thematic
    Balance in "The Short Happy Life of Francis
    Macomber"   215
    James Gray Watson

The Valley of Baca and *A Farewell to Arms*   229
    John Unrue

Hemingway in French   235
    David J. Wells

Is Custer a Model for the Fascist Captain in *For Whom
    the Bell Tolls?*   239
    David McClellan

Hemingway on Dialogue in "A Clean, Well-Lighted Place"   243
    George Monteiro

REVIEWS

The Great Gatsby: A Facsimile of the Manuscript, ed.
  Bruccoli   247
    Budd Schulberg

F. Scott Fitzgerald's Ledger, ed. Bruccoli   253
    Bryant Mangum

Apparatus for F. Scott Fitzgerald's The Great Gatsby
  [Under the Red, White, and Blue], Bruccoli   257
    David J. Nordloh

Bits of Paradise, ed. Smith & Bruccoli; *The Basil and*
  Josephine Stories, ed. Bryer & Kuehl   261
    Kenneth Eble

Hemingway at Auction, ed. Bruccoli & Clark   265
    William White

Ring Around Max, ed. Carruthers   269
    Richard Layman

BIBLIOGRAPHICAL MATERIAL

Bruccoli Addenda II   275

Reprintings of Fitzgerald   285
    Margaret M. Duggan

Fitzgerald in Translation II   313
    Linda Berry

Fitzgerald Checklist   317
    Margaret M. Duggan

Hemingway Checklist   323
    Margaret M. Duggan

General Checklist   331
    Margaret M. Duggan

ANNOUNCEMENTS

FITZGERALD/HEMINGWAY ANNUAL 1974

F. Scott Fitzgerald

During the last World War, many cosmic destinies were strung together on the loom of tragic gallantry and courage to the purpose of ending written tradition the dramatic and pictorial tempos to which the age had fallen heir. Fights of men at this time included shivering to death in box cars over the lost frontiers of lonely foreign provinces, drowning in mudand smothering in submarines. Many had learned too much of painful and even exotic ways to die so that life presented itself by contrast in less agonizing if more immutable terms than before the troubles in Europe.

This era assisted at the nursing of a badly shell-shocked logos back to some semblance of tenability on the dreary and

ZELDA FITZGERALD'S
TRIBUTE TO
F. SCOTT FITZGERALD

This 8-page holograph document was probably written shortly after Fitzgerald's death. The manuscript is now in the Princeton University Library.*

During the last world war, many cosmic destinies were strung together on the tone of tragic gallantry and courage to the purpose of binding within tradition the dramatic and pictorial tempos to which the age had fallen heir. Habits of men at this time included shiverring to death in boxcars over the lost frontiers of lonely foreign provinces, drowning in mud and smotherring in submarines. Many had learned too much of painful and even exotic ways to die so that life presented itself by contrast in less agonizing, if more immutable, terms than before the trouble in Europe.

This era assisted at the nursing of a badly shell-shocked logos back to som semblance of tenability on the drear and dusty sun parlours

*Published here with the generous approval of Scottie Fitzgerald Smith. All publication rights to this writing remain the property of Mrs. Smith; and it cannot be reprinted without the permission of Harold Ober Associates.

3

orchidaceous elevators whirring to [8
plaintive deaths, the gilded aspiratories
of a vigilant and protesting age, taxis
sumptuously afloat on deep summer nights —
such Fitzgerald made into many
tragic tales; sagas of people compelling life into some more commensurate and compassionate measure
His meter was bitter and ironic and
spectacular and inviting: so
was life. There wasn't much
other life during those times
than to what his pen paid tribute
of poetic tragic glamour and
offered the reconciliation of the
familiarities of tragedy.

Rest in Peace.

of chateaux converted to convalescent hospitals and entered a failing social structure from personal necessities of survival.

A few facetious gestures: dancing with the dead at Chambrai, the painting of the Portughese leavened the four year spectacle and diverted some of the spiritual casualties from despair to bitterness — perhaps the easier to bear.

When nobody could think up any more mathematical formulas for destruction and no further ways for forwarding the plot, the war was declared to be a political inconvenience, and ended Through the disorientations resultant from many distrusted and uncondoned experiences the soldiers looked toward home as the right of a long and hard earned holiday. People that had been spared active participation in the gala débacle converted themselves into a grand pleasure chorus as effectively as possible and deadicated the decade to reconstituting the shatterred illusions of those who had served in France with, perhaps, more verve and courage than judgment.

The United States greeted the returning young men with appropriate tragic and ecstatic pathos, and compensatory dramatics but still the erst-while dough-boys languished, and werent quite able to take up the thread on the same attenuate pitch as before.

It was past time for whatever had been scheduled to have happened and people were worn out with long abeyant attendance

The prophet destined to elucidate and catalogue these pregnant and precarious circumstances was F. Scott Fitzgerald. The times exacted a dramatization compelling enough to save its protagonists from sleep-walking over the proscenium in the general doesnt-matter suasion of the letdown; and splendidly tragic enough to turn the barbarism of recent war experiences into drama. Fitzgerald was the first and always the most indicative of authors to persuade the desperate latent flaire of these souls so tolerantly and self-abnegatively pursuing policies of "qui en-faire" to attitudes of a better masterred Olympian regret. He endowed those years that might have been so garishly reckless with the dignity of his bright indicative scene, and buoyed the desperation of a bitter day with the spontaneity of his appreciation.

Fitzgerald's heroines were audacious and ingenuous and his heroes were fabulous strangers from lands of uncharted promise. His tragedies were hearts at bay to the inexorable exigence of a day whose formulas no longer worked and whose ritual had dwindled to less of drama than its guignol. His pathos was the pressure of inescapable necessities over the keeping of a faith. His poignancy was the perishing of lovely things and people on the jagged edges of truncate spiritual purpose. These were the themes that transcended the crassness and bitterness which so easily betrays the ironic pen and leads the conviction of tragedy too frequently astray in the briars of scathing invective

Fitzgerald seized, from the nebulous necessities of an incubating civilization, the essence of a girl able to survive the new, and less forbearing, dramas and presented in poetic harmonies the tragicly gallant stoicism so indispensible to traversing that troubled and turbulent epoch between world wars.

As the era is absorbed by its category and lost in its platonic sources, one remembers romanticly the figure who so ingratiatingly reconciled his readers to the diminution of individuality and rendered more tangible those movements which he affectionately and indulgently humanized: "youth movements, sufferage drives, temperance objectives," and many no-matter how-dearly-bought subscription to any dominant idea which carried the promise of salvation by rote.

As promisorily as the least tractable wellings of the soul are curbed to the poet's pentameter, as surely as the most unique of cadets is lost on the line of march, so does each generation yield to the thematic persuasions of the day. The meter being waltz-time which moves nostalgic twilights to their rendezvous, the world believes again in sentiment and turns to fairy tale; whereas those years haunted by the more aggressive sadnesses of march time produce a more dynamic, tragic spiritual compensation. Thus the manners and aspirations that were not too long ago recut and polished in the staccato relevance of "This Side of Paradise" and "The Beautiful and Damned" have been able to defend themselves with a better perfected hardi-hood and by means of a faith in *technique* from the heart-break and subsequent ruthless purpose of the nineteen-twenties.

Fitzgeralds books were the first of their kind and the most indicative. If his people didn't have a good time, or things come out well at the end, the scene of their activity was always the arena of some new philosophic offensive, and what they did was allied with many salient projects of the era. The plush hush of the hotel lobby and the gala grandeur of the theatre port-cochiere; fumes of orchidaceous elevators whirring to plaintive deaths the gilded aspirations of a valiant and protesting age, taxis slumberously afloat on deep summer nights — —

Such Fitzgerald made into many tragic tales; sagas of people compelling life into some more commensurate and compassionate measure His meter was bitter, and ironic and spectacular and enviting: so was life. There wasnt much other life during those times than to what his pen paid the tribute of poetic tragic glamour and offerred the reconciliation of the familiarities of tragedy.

Rest in Peace.

LETTER TO BROOKS BOWMAN

1307 Park Avenue,

Baltimore, Maryland,

January 16, 1935.

Mr. Brooks Bowman,

    c/o The Triangle Club,

        Princeton University,

            Princeton, New Jersey.

Dear Mr. Bowman:

        As one of those who considers this year's performance the best in ten years and also as one of those who consider your achievement both as actor and composer the brightest spot in it, I take the liberty of addressing this suggestion to you. For a long time there has been the lack of any new Princeton songs, either suitable to stadium or to senior singing. Several people have spoken to me about it recently on the basis that I used to write the lyrics and a greater part of the shows back in '15, '16, '17 and was a former officer of the club.

        My suggestion is this: that your song "East of the Sun" with a few changes in the lyric could

-2-

be made a fine piece for senior singing. The general
line would be:

> "East of the sun, west of the moon
>
>   Lies Princeton,
>
> South of the south, north of the north
>
>   Lies Princeton,
>
> Here in my heart etc. etc.
>
>   Lies Princeton."

The idea being, of course, that Princeton
to Princeton men lies outside of time and space. It's
an over-sentimental conception but perhaps might mean
something to the older alumni. If practical, you might
try it out with the Glee Club quartet.

Again congratulations to all of you for
a really fine show which indicated that there's life in
the old girl yet, as I had begun to doubt.

yours

F. Scott Fitzgerald

'17

The 1934-35 Princeton Triangle Club show, *Stags at Bay,*
introduced "East of the Sun" by Brooks Bowman '36—easily
the most popular Triangle song. Old grad Fitzgerald wrote to
Bowman suggesting that "East of the Sun" be converted into a
school song.

THE FITZGERALD REVIVAL,
1941-1953

It is true that Fitzgerald died in something close to popular and critical neglect. Max Perkins once told me that, contrary to Fitzgerald's own belief, his books were still in print when he died. In other words, there were copies of them in the Scribner warehouse, as of December 1940, but nobody was buying them. Edmund Wilson worked more effectively to revive his reputation than anyone else in the wide, wide world. First he arranged for the garland of tributes that appeared in *The New Republic* in the winter of 1941. (I was out of the office on a leave of absence and had asked Edmund to take my place for three months, just as I had taken *his* place ten years before.) Then he was given charge of Fitzgerald's papers and prepared his unfinished novel, *The Last Tycoon*, for publication in a 1941 volume that also contained five of the best stories and *The Great Gatsby*. Then finally he edited *The Crack-Up*, which Scribners decided not to publish, to their lasting regret, and which New Directions published in 1945. The book aroused very wide interest and the Fitzgerald revival was under way.

Wilson then dropped out of the parade, after leading the band. I have a question about Wilson's part in it. In later years did he feel that Fitzgerald was being praised too highly and unreservedly? I don't know, I don't know, but Wilson didn't join in the later chorus.

Who persuaded the Viking Press to do a Portable Fitzgerald in 1945? That may have been Dorothy Parker, who made the

11

selections, but didn't supply an introduction. John O'Hara was the logical man to write this, since his stories were carrying on the social-history side of the Fitzgerald tradition. *The Portable Fitzgerald* was No. 14 in the series and its early sale was considerably less than that of the Hemingway (No. 6), but rather more than that of the Faulkner (No. 18). The book was published under a five-year lease from Scribners, and—to Viking's sorrow—the lease was not renewed when it ran out in 1950. "We want to bring Fitzgerald's books under one roof," Scribners explained.

Until that time Scribners had shown something less than an all-absorbing interest in Fitzgerald. They had chosen not to publish *The Crack-Up* and they had allowed Arthur Mizener's biography, *The Far Side of Paradise*, to go to another publisher. I don't know when Mizener started working on the book; perhaps it was as early as 1946. He published extracts from the Fitzgerald papers (*Furioso*, 1947; *Kenyon Review*, 1948). By the time his biography was finished, in 1950, Budd Schulberg had published a best-selling novel, *The Disenchanted*, in which everybody recognized Fitzgerald as the alcoholic hero. *The Disenchanted* was dedicated to Arthur and Rosemary Mizener. While it was still being widely read, *The Far Side of Paradise* was being serialized in *The Atlantic Monthly*, then summarized in an article for *Life*. The book was extraordinarily successful when it appeared in the spring of 1951; I heard that it had sold more than fifty thousand copies in the first year.

So one can mention Wilson, Schulberg, Mizener as leaders of the Fitzgerald revival, the latter two because they made the story accessible. It was a story that appealed to something deep in the American psyche. "Success" and "failure" had been two weighted words for generations. "Will I be a success?" young Americans had kept asking themselves; and then, "Mightn't it be better to be a failure, that is, to fall from some dizzy height and yet in the end to be better than those who kept on rising?" By 1950 Scott and Zelda had become the hero and heroine of an American legend.

In that same year Scribners decided to put his books back into print, and they asked me, as a beginning, to make a selection from his magazine stories. I took the assignment seriously, read everything in print, and worked among the Fitzgerald papers at Princeton, which at that time were opened freely to scholars. I had been writing about Fitzgerald for a long time—actually since I reviewed *All the Sad Young Men* in 1926—and now I wanted to bring everything together. *The Stories of F. Scott Fitzgerald* appeared in the spring of

1951. It contained twenty-eight stories—not enough; I wanted to include at least ten more, but the publishers said there wasn't space for them—besides a long introduction, parts of which had appeared in magazines. The book was very well received and continued to have a sale year after year.

In the Princeton Library I had also come across the copy of *Tender Is the Night* that Fitzgerald had revised and rearranged in the hope that it would be republished. "Let him have his wish," I said to Scribners, and they agreed to issue the new edition. Whether his second version of the novel is better than the first is a question that has been debated since that time. In 1951 the weight of critical opinion was on the side of the first version, but it seems to me that the weight has been shifting in recent years. I prefer the second, for reasons explained in the introduction, but with the proviso that neither version is the perfect novel that Fitzgerald wanted to write; both are flawed, but deeply appealing.

Still later, in 1953, I prepared a new edition of *Gatsby*, with an introducition that contributed to the critical discussion. Except for some further work on the stories, which went into the only collected edition of Fitzgerald—the one published in London by Bodley Head—that has been my complete share in the revival. It was doubtless a real share, but later and less than Wilson's or Mizener's. Isn't it wrong, moreover, to explain the revival by putting the emphasis on critics and biographers rather than on Fitzgerald himself; on his life, on his writings? He dramatized an age and its aftermath, and his books can also be read—I wrote long ago—"as the intimate journal of an author whose story, observed with his own sharp eyes and judged by his conscience, is more impressive than any book about him that others can write."

ANDREW CROSLAND

Sleeping and Waking—
The Literary Reputation of
The Great Gatsby, 1927-1944

Would the 25-cent press keep Gatsby *in the public eye—or* is the book unpopular? *Has it* had *its chance? Would a popular reissue in that series . . . make it a favorite with classrooms, profs, lovers of English prose—anybody?*

F. Scott Fitzgerald, 1940[1]

It is a commonplace that *The Great Gatsby*, after receiving good initial reviews, sank into a kind of literary purgatory and remained there until the Fitzgerald revival brought its resurrection in the late '40's. A survey of critical reference to the novel between 1927 and 1944—the period of its supposed obscurity—indicates that this view is little more than a half-truth. While studies published in these years tend to be cursory, they are surprisingly numerous and are often admiring.

At least thirty-six articles and book chapters containing reference to the novel appeared during the eighteen-year span, but none has been located for 1930, 1936, 1938, and 1939.[2] *Gatsby* is frequently called Fitzgerald's best work. It is praised for its craftsmanship, and for its insight into American life and the Jazz Age. Still, some critics are careful to voice reservations so that their final estimates are at best lukewarm. Only three commentators seem to place themselves squarely in the anti-*Gatsby* camp.

Victor Llona published his French translation of the novel in 1926, and two articles on it appeared in French journals the next year. Both are brief. One, by Marius Boisson, is a general discussion of Fitzgerald and *The Great Gatsby*. In the other, Llona explains why he translated the work.

The 15 July 1928 issue of *Mercure de France* contains a study of contemporary American literature by Regis Michaud. One short paragraph in the thirteen-page article deals with Fitzgerald. He is called the chronicler of the Jazz Age and described as something of a reporter of the eccentricities of his time. *Gatsby* is said to be his finest chronicle. While Michaud's remarks are complimentary, they are not very perceptive.

In 1929, Rebecca West, writing for *The Bookman*, noted that "*The Great Gatsby* was surely a remarkable novel," a "superb imaginative vision of the gaunt fringes of New York." She carries her analysis farther than Michaud did, briefly discussing the various characters and asserting that the work not only describes the Jazz Age but offers interpretation of it. Her conclusion is that "this novel has not been superseded in the common mind by better books: simply by more books."

October of 1931 brought publication of two discussions of *The Great Gatsby*. In *The Bookman*, Gorham Munson stated that the most influential post-World War I American novelists were Theodore Dreiser, Sinclair Lewis, F. Scott Fitzgerald, and Ernest Hemingway. Of these, he sees Fitzgerald as the most promising artist, and *Gatsby* as his best work. Indeed, Munson writes "there is more art in *The Great Gatsby* than there is in the whole shelf of Mr. Dreiser's works." He describes the novel as a "sinister romance" written "with intensity, with intelligence, and with skill," and hopes it and Fitzgerald's other writings may encourage young authors to abandon stultifying realism and naturalism. This article is certainly laudatory and generally perceptive, though it makes no attempt to come to terms with specifics in the novel. The other 1931 study, James Gray's "Let Scott Fitzgerald Not Rest on Laurels Acquired in Jazz Age," appeared in the *St. Paul Dispatch* and is less significant, commenting on *Gatsby* only as part of a broader discussion of Fitzgerald's depiction of the Jazz Age.

One article treating the book appeared in 1932. In *Hound & Horn*, Lawrence Leighton criticizes the American novel of the

1920's, focusing on the work of Hemingway, Fitzgerald, and Dos Passos. The author notes that Fitzgerald is the best of the three and "deserves more serious imitation." He praises him for the economy of expression evident in *The Great Gatsby*, saying that its second chapter "is worth the whole of a Dos Passos novel in the exposition of the dreariness of American life." While Leighton cites the novel as Fitzgerald's best work and as one of the better books of the period, he indicates that it has two major imperfections. The characterization is too superficial, for the author demands "a greater emotional load than his characters will bear." Fitzgerald is also criticized for a defect of imagination—a tendency to report rather than create in his portrayal of the Jazz Age. Thus, like Munson, Leighton believes Fitzgerald and his novel compare favorably with other authors and works of the period. But Leighton is far afield in his assertion that *Gatsby* lacks imaginative power.

Lawrence Gray made the only reference to *The Great Gatsby* to appear in 1933. Writing for the *St. Paul Dispatch*, he called it "a skillful, wise and affecting book." This observation is made in the context of a review of Fitzgerald's career that accompanies the announcement of the forthcoming publication of *Tender Is the Night*.

The Great Gatsby was reprinted in 1934 with a new preface by Fitzgerald. His remarks in this Modern Library edition evoked comment in the *New York Times* and the *New York Herald Tribune*. John Chamberlain of the *Times* generally agrees with Fitzgerald's complaints about critics—especially Marxists—who write him off because of his subject matter. But the reviewer believes Fitzgerald's criticism is ultimately too harsh, for "many critics have been extremely discerning and loyal about 'The Great Gatsby.' " The author's statements are called illogical by P.I.M. in the *Herald Tribune* commentary. This evaluation is based on a low opinion of the book which relegates it to the status of a "brilliant ephemeral novel, written by, for and of a particular period." The reviewer makes no attempt to justify his condemnation of the book with reference to specifics, showing as little insight as he does foresight.

Tender is the Night was also published in 1934, and Chamberlain mentions *Gatsby* in his 13 April review of the later novel. He praises the earlier work as being "so perfect in its feeling and its symbolism, such a magnificent evocation of the spirit of a whole decade," as being the best book of the 1920's.

Harry T. Moore, writing "The American Novel Today" in the

March 1935 *London Mercury*, describes *The Great Gatsby* as "a novel about trivial people that was almost a great novel." He feels that it is one of the best American books of the '20's but has a low opinion of that literature. Unlike P.I.M., Moore thinks the novel has some capacity to survive. Harlan Hatcher's book, *Creating the Modern Novel*, was also published in 1935. In it, *Gatsby* is called Fitzgerald's "best piece of work." Hatcher believes it will last and speaks of "its proportion and firmness of structure, its vividness of character-drawing, its feeling for rhythm, its mastery of the material furnished by the Long Island smart set of the mid-twenties."

While nothing was published on *The Great Gatsby* in 1936, two books and two articles discussing it appeared in 1937. In *Modern Fiction: A Study of Values*, Herbert Muller praises the novel for its technique which he sees as similar to that of the novels of Conrad. He concludes that "although *The Great Gatsby* . . .is tinged with the flippancy, hard-boiled sentimentality, and cock-eyed idealism of the period, it is on the whole honestly, soberly, brilliantly done." In another book published the same year, *Books and Battles of the Twenties*, Irene and Allen Cleaton call the novel "a thrillingly beautiful" work which contains "enough lovely phrases to equip a poet for a lifetime." They disagree with Muller's inference that the novel is a period-piece and see it as a departure from the literary fashions of its time.

James Gray, writing for the *Saturday Review of Literature*, names *The Great Gatsby* Fitzgerald's "finest piece of work." He focuses his attention on Nick and Gatsby, calling the narrator "a good Minnesota boy among New York vulgarians" and the protagonist "a Prohibition Croesus who longs hopelessly for the unattainable security that he believes to be the gift of a graceful and long-established social tradition." Gatsby's aspirations, he adds, "become increasingly . . .pathetic as the reader is made to see how lightly, yet how firmly, the narrator has his hands upon those social values which Gatsby can never have." John Peale Bishop's article, "The Missing All," was also published in 1937. Bishop, too, examines Gatsby's character, describing him as "the Emersonian man brought to completion and eventually to failure; he has returned to the East; the conditions which could tolerate his self-reliant romanticism no longer exist."

Aside from the many passing references to the novel appearing in newspaper obituaries for Fitzgerald printed late in 1940,[3] the only comment on *Gatsby* made that year is found in Carl Van Doren's

The American Novel 1789-1939. In it, he describes *The Great Gatsby* as "a short realistic novel about a romantic bootlegger that remains one of the brilliant books of a brilliant decade."

More discussion of *Gatsby* was published in 1941 than in any other single year between 1927 and 1944. This burst of interest can best be explained in terms of a response to Fitzgerald's death in December of 1940 and to the publication of *The Last Tycoon Together With The Great Gatsby and Selected Stories* in 1941.

The *New Yorker* for 4 January 1941 contains an obituary for Fitzgerald. In it, the book is described as "one of the most scrupulously observed and beautifully written of American novels." About a month later, Margaret Marshall, in *The Nation*, predicted that *Gatsby* would be the author's only enduring novel because it portrays so well the essence of its period.

Several articles on Fitzgerald appear in the 17 February *New Republic*. John Dos Passos criticizes the press for discussing Fitzgerald in terms of fads and fashions and says, "For a man who is making his living as a critic to write about Scott Fitzgerald without mentioning 'The Great Gatsby' just means that he doesn't know his business." Writing in the same issue, Glenway Wescott argues that the novel will last: "I love 'The Great Gatsby.' Its very timeliness, as of 1925, gave it a touch of the old-fashioned a few years later, but I have reread it this week and found it all right; pleasure and compassion on every page. A masterpiece often seems a period-piece for a while; then it comes down out of the attic, to function anew and to last."

In the 3 March *New Republic*, John O'Hara writes simply, "By the time . . .'The Great Gatsby' appeared, the man could do no wrong." Bud Shulberg's memories of Fitzgerald are in the same issue. He refers to *Gatsby* as "that amazing little book that seems to catch and hold more of the spirit of that time in two hundred pages than do all the almanacs and Mark Sullivans." On 15 November, Clifton Fadiman published a review of *The Last Tycoon* in the *New Yorker*. He feels that it is a better book than *The Great Gatsby*, but finds the latter novel "unexpectedly re-readable."

Oscar Cargill's 1941 book, *Intellectual America*, contains discussion of *The Great Gatsby* that is more provocative than perceptive. The novel is described as a minor contribution to literature, an attempt to please unsophisticated readers with "speed and . . .hard surface polish." Cargill then goes on to say that the book sentimentalizes Gatsby as a gangster and thus becomes the "fount of a kind of degeneracy." In his 1932 *Hound and Horn* article, Lawrence Leighton had said that *Gatsby* established the fashion of the "racketeer or 'big shot,'" but, unlike Cargill, he did not condemn the novel because of it. Both critics, however, are wide of the mark in these assertions, for Gatsby's shadowy criminal activities are not sentimentalized by Fitzgerald. Indeed, the protagonist's failure to win Daisy and his inability to gain Nick's complete loyalty may be attributed, at least in part, to the way he has made his money. The novelist de-emphasizes Gatsby's criminality, makes it vague, and concentrates on his romantic idealism.

Peter Quennell published an analysis of *The Great Gatsby* in 1941. His article in the *New Statesman and Nation* examines Fitzgerald's portrayal of Tom Buchanan and Jay Gatsby as rich men during the American boom. J. Donald Adams, reviewing *The Last Tycoon* in 1941 for the *New York Times*, makes this comment on *Gatsby*: "Excellent as [it] was, capturing as it did in greater degree than any other book of the period the feel of the fantastic Twenties, one closes it with the thought that Fitzgerald had not himself quite gotten outside the period." An anonymous article in *Time*, "Fitzgerald Unfinished," also appeared the same year. It refers to *Gatsby* as one of Fitzgerald's "remarkable prose movies," a good novel because the author stood "off from his generation" in his portrayal of it.

Alfred Kazin studied *The Great Gatsby* in some detail in his 1942 *On Native Grounds*. He sees the novel as a lasting work and Fitzgerald's best effort, then raises the question of the author's detachment which Adams and *Time* had examined the year before. Kazin believes Fitzgerald's sympathetic, virtually subjective, approach to Gatsby is what gives the book its greatness. Thus one critic says lack of detachment weakens the novel; another says it strengthens it, while a third sees the author as removed from his material. Perhaps "detachment" is such an elusive concept that consideration of it in this sort of context is meaningless.

Stanley Kunitz and Howard Haycraft included an F. Scott Fitzgerald entry in their 1942 edition of *Twentieth Century Authors*. They damn the writer with faint praise but refer to *Gatsby* as "his finest novel." James Thurber also discussed the work in an article, "Taps at Assembly," which appeared in the *New Republic* in 1942. His observations are very general and very complimentary. Thurber speaks of "the flawless final writing of 'The Great Gatsby,'" of its "sure form and sure direction," and of the way it makes "something that lies between your stomach and your heart quiver a little."

A more extensive commentary on the novel was published in 1943 in Maxwell Geismar's *The Last of the Provincials: The American Novel 1915-1925. Gatsby* is viewed in the context of Fitzgerald's earlier work by Geismar, who points to elements of setting, character, and situation in the book which had previously appeared in the author's writings. The critic asserts that *Gatsby* "prefigures the eloquent and mature Fitzgerald" and explains its superiority to what he had written before in these terms: "While the development of the craft is a factor . . .there is also the development of a point of view that makes the craft possible. While Fitzgerald has blocked out the discordant areas in his own temperament [the social insider and the outsider] and objectified them in terms of the characters and groups of characters who form the novel's tension, he himself has gained serenity and perspective that are remarkable." Geismar also discusses Gatsby as the hero of a cultural legend based on the American dream of success.

Two articles and one book pertaining to *The Great Gatsby* were published in 1944. J. Donald Adams, in *The Shape of Books to Come*, praises the work, saying Fitzgerald caught "the feverish atmosphere of the period" better than any other writer, but was only "able to write about it with some degree of detachment [in] *The Great Gatsby*." Charles Weir, Jr., writing for the *Virginia Quarterly Review*, agrees with Adams. He says that the author's "greatest weakness . . .was that he was so completely of his time and of his country," so completely taken with the surfaces of behavior that he could not plumb the sources. Yet Weir thinks Fitzgerald managed to overcome this limitation in *The Great Gatsby*, "putting . . .material into a form which was truly significant and expressive." Again, the critics expend energy on the non-issue of detachment.

The third examination of the novel in 1944 is by far the most hostile. In a *College English* article entitled "The Essence of F. Scott Fitzgerald," Leo and Miriam Gurko attempt to write Fitzgerald off as "the fictional embalmer" of the Jazz Age, a "minor writer" inferior to Lewis, Hemingway, and Dos Passos. The Gurkos say Fitzgerald uses essentially the same hero in all five of his novels, pointing out that each character is in "virtually the same state of emotional unease, rooted in their creator's belief that happiness is a romantic sensation felt in extreme youth, a sensation that comes to a rapid bloom and vanishes early and forever. . . . Jay Gatsby spends almost the whole of his short life searching for a sublimated love which, when found, crumbles in his hands."

The Gurkos were wrong in adding Fitzgerald to their list of minor authors, and the revival that firmly established his reputation was to begin the next year with publication of *The Crack-Up*. While serious analysis of the novel was not undertaken on any large scale until after the revival got underway, it is a mistake to think *Gatsby* had been forgotten during the years between its 1925-26 reception and the mid-century "renewal" of interest in it.

Commentator after commentator, writing between 1927 and 1944, named *The Great Gatsby* Fitzgerald's best work. And critics often asserted that it compared favorably with the novels of other major American writers. *Gatsby* was most frequently discussed as portrayal of the Jazz Age; but the question of influence on other writers, the study of the protagonist's character, and the author's craftsmanship in writing the book were also topics repeatedly considered. Another question raised several times was that of whether *Gatsby* would be of lasting importance.

Thus, several major approaches to the study of the novel were explored during this period, but it still may be said that the criticism was somewhat cursory. Nevertheless, *Gatsby*, though not studied well, was by no means forgotten, and, though frequently misunderstood, did not go without praise.

University of South Carolina—Spartanburg

---

[1] *The Letters of F. Scott Fitzgerald*, ed. Andrew Turnbull. New York: Scribners, 1963, p. 288.

[2] Anonymous. "Fitzgerald Unfinished," *Time*, XXVI (27 January 1941), 72-74.

————. "Notes and Comment," *New Yorker*, XVI (4 January 1941), 9.

Adams, J. Donald. "Scott Fitzgerald's Last Novel," *New York Times Book Review*, 9 November 1941, p. 1.

————.*The Shape of Books to Come*. New York: The Viking Press, 1944. Pp. 88-90.

Bishop, John Peale. "The Missing All," *Virginia Quarterly Review*, XIII (Winter 1937), 106-21.

Boisson, Marius. "F. Scott Fitzgerald et son *Gatsby le magnifique*," *Vient de Paraître*, VII (janvier 1927), 598-99.

Cargill, Oscar. *Intellectual America*. New York: The Macmillan Company, 1941. Pp. 342-46.

Chamberlain, John. "Books of the Times," *New York Times*, 13 April 1934, p. 17.

————. "Books of the Times," *New York Times*, 20 September 1934, p. 21.

Cleaton, Irene and Allen. *Books and Battles of the Twenties*. Boston: Houghton Mifflin, 1937. Pp. 232-34.

Cowley, Malcolm. "Of Clocks and Calendars," *New Republic*, CIV (17 March 1941), 376-77.

Dos Passos, John. "Fitzgerald and the Press," *New Republic*, CIV (17 March 1941), 213.

Fadiman, Clifton. "Books," *New Yorker*, 15 November 1941, 87-89.

Geismar, Maxwell. *The Last of the Provincials: The American Novel, 1915-1925*. Boston: Houghton Mifflin, 1943. Pp. 287-352.

Kunitz, Stanley J. and Howard Haycraft. *Twentieth Century Authors*. New York: H. W. Wilson, 1942. Pp. 460-62.

Gray, James. "Let Scott Fitzgerald Not Rest on Laurels Acquired in Jazz Age," St. Paul *Dispatch*, 20 October 1931, p. 8.

_____ . "The Minnesota Muse," *Saturday Review of Literature*, XVI (12 June 1937), 3-4, 14.

Gurko, Leo and Miriam. "The Essence of F. Scott Fitzgerald," *College English*, V (April 1944), 372-76.

Hatcher, Harlan. *Creating the Modern American Novel*. New York: Farrar & Rinehart, 1935. Pp. 79-82.

Kazin, Alfred. *On Native Grounds*. New York: Reynal & Hitchcock, 1942. Pp. 315-23.

Leighton, Lawrence. "An Autopsy and a Prescription," *Hound & Horn*, V (July-September 1932), 519-39.

Llona, Victor. "Pourquoi j'ai traduit *Gatsby le magnifique*," *Nouvelles Littéraires*, 12 fevier 1927, p. 6.

Marshall, Margaret. "Notes By the Way," *The Nation*, CLII (8 February 1941), 159-60.

Michaud, Regis. "La Littérature americane d'aujourd'hui," *Mercure de France*, CCV (15 juillet 1928), 310-23.

Moore, Harry Thornton. "The American Novel Today," *London Mercury*, XXXI (March 1935), 461-67.

Muller, Herbert J. *Modern Fiction—A Study of Values*. New York: Funk & Wagnalls, 1937. Pp. 384-85.

Munson, Gorham. "Our Post-War Novel," *The Bookman*, LXXIV (October 1931), 141-44.

O'Hara, John. "Certain Aspects," *New Republic*, CIV (3 March 1941), 311.

P.I.M. "Turns With a Bookworm," *New York Herald Tribune Books*, 7 October 1934, p. 22.

Quennell, Peter. *"The Great Gatsby,"* *New Statesman and Nation*, n.s. XXI (1 February 1941), 112.

Shulberg, Budd, Jr. "In Hollywood," *New Republic*, CIV (3 March 1941), 311-12.

Thurber, James. "Taps at Assembly," *New Republic*, CVI (9 February 1942), 211-12.

Van Doren, Carl. *The American Novel 1789-1939*. New York: The Macmillan Company, 1940. Pp. 326-27.

Weir, Charles, Jr. "'An Invite with Gilded Eagles,'" *Virginia Quarterly Review*, XXI (Winter 1944), 100-13.

Wescott, Glenway. "The Moral of Scott Fitzgerald," *New Republic*, CIV (17 February 1941), 213-17.

West, Rebecca. "A London Commentary," *The Bookman*, LXVIII (January 1929), 519-22.

[3] These obituaries, though numerous, offer little significant analysis of the novel and so are not examined here. Many are difficult to obtain. Jackson R. Bryer's *The Critical Reputation of F. Scott Fitzgerald: A Bibliographical Study* (Hamden, Conn.: Archon Books, 1967) contains an annotated list of them on pages 202-208.

John O'hara's
Remarks on the Silent *Gatsby*

Twenty-two years ago, as the decades fly, I made a rather pathetic attempt to buy *The Great Gatsby* from Paramount. I acted through a paid emissary, but I had done some investigating on my own before opening negotiations. I had learned, for instance, that Paramount did not even have a usable print of the F. Scott Fitzgerald novel, film version. I had also learned that a well-known dramatist had done a talking-picture script that Paramount did not like, and that Paramount considered the property unsuitable for further development, and therefore presumably would let the story go for a price I could pay. I had allowed myself to be encouraged in the project as a result of a conversation with Clark Gable, who I thought (and still think) would make a perfect Gatsby. And I had been told that Paramount would be willing to sell the rights.

But as soon as I, or my emissary, made what was later to become known as a film offer, the price was not doubled; it was quadrupled. I was knocked back on my heels, but I made one more effort to do business: I went to 20th Century-Fox, which was not then, as it is now, my home lot, but where I had a connection, and tried to get a man there to buy *The Great Gatsby* from Paramount. No cigar.

Thus ended my only effort to engage in writing-producing. Paramount, as you may recall, did make a talking-picture version of

The shirt scene: Lois Wilson and Warner Baxter.

The Great Gatsby, starring Alan Ladd, but I never went to see it, and not entirely because I was bitter. Mr. Ladd may have given a good performance in "Shane," but it only convinced me that I was right in not wanting to see him do Gatsby.

The reason I wanted to write a talking-picture version of the Fitzgerald novel was that I had seen the silent version and had admired it enormously. Warner Baxter was a good, if not a great, Gatsby, and Bill Powell as the garage-keeper gave a performance that made his later successes in the Thin Man series seem like kid stuff, which they were. Others in the cast were Lois Wilson, Neil Hamilton, and Hale Hamilton. All good. But even now I can remember my exultation at the end of the picture when I saw that Paramount had done an honest job, true to the book, true to what Fitzgerald had intended. My favorite Fitzgerald novel had not yet been written, but the movies had done right by Our Boy with the best he had written to date. Roughly ten years later I was sure that I could do an even better job through the new camera techniques and audible dialogue.

—*"Novelist Likes the Film Translation,"*
New York Herald Tribune (18 May 1958).

The Plaza scene: Lois Wilson (Daisy), Warner Baxter (Gatsby), Hale Hamilton (Tom), Neil Hamilton (Nick).

JOAN M. ALLEN

THE BETTER FATHERS:
THE PRIESTS IN FITZGERALD'S LIFE

Everyone who is familiar with the important influences in Scott Fitzgerald's life knows about Monsignor Cyril Fay. Their meeting at the Newman School, the Catholic preparatory school in Hackensack, New Jersey, which Fitzgerald attended in the two years before he entered Princeton, and their friendship which developed in subsequent years until Fay's death in 1919 have been noted and documented by every major Fitzgerald biographer. Not so well known to Fitzgerald students are four other priests who significantly touched his life. Heretofore in discussing his religious affiliation Fitzgerald's biographers have tended to emphasize the fact that he left the Catholic Church as a young man and to ignore, neglect, or discount the importance of the early years.

Fitzgerald was raised largely by devoutly religious convent-educated women both in his schools and at home, while his father, a universally acknowledged failure, apparently willingly abdicated his authority in this matriarchy. All of the implications of this fact of biography for Fitzgerald's psychology and emotional and religious life are the subject of a whole other discussion, but one result and the concern of this essay is Fitzgerald's periodic attraction, probably in reaction to his father's inadequate example, to dynamic male models among the priests he met in the course of his life.

29

The earliest evidence we have of such a relationship is a 1905 entry in Fitzgerald's Ledger which refers to a priest who was the pastor of a church in Buffalo, "He fell under the spell of a Catholic preacher, Father Fallon, of the Church of the Holy Angels."[1] The boy of seven apparently had discerning taste, for the Reverend Michael Fallon was no ordinary parish priest. A native Canadian, he had studied at Ottawa University which is run by the Oblates of Mary Immaculate, the order in which Father Fallon would serve as the first Provincial of the Eastern American Province in Buffalo. Apparently marked for leadership by his order, he was sent to Rome for post-graduate study. Here he earned the degree of Doctor of Sacred Theology and was ordained by the Cardinal-Vicar of Rome in 1894.

Upon his return to Ottawa, Fallon taught English at the University. The sermons that later would mesmerize the young Fitzgerald were produced by a man skilled in the uses of rhetoric, one who could support a moral point with patristic allusions and passages from the great English poets. This is not typical Catholic fare, and neither was Fitzgerald's reaction to it typically childish. As later he would be attracted to and instructed by the erudition of Edmund Wilson and John Peale Bishop, so at seven perhaps he intuitively knew that Fallon was the rare Catholic preacher, one who delivered a message of learning and substance with dramatic flair.

Fallon's career was distinguished in every way. A Catholic pastor's measurable success is determined largely by the number and size of the buildings he erects. In 1901 the young priest went to the Holy Angels Church in Buffalo in the dual role of pastor and Provincial, and in his nine years there he was responsible for the building of the Oblate House near Catholic University in Washington, D.C., and the Holy Angels School. Fallon joined the hierarchy in 1910 when, at the age of forty-three, he was appointed Bishop of London, Ontario. His career there was marked by two notable accomplishments; the establishment of St. Peter's Seminary in London, one of the few English seminaries in Canada, and the establishment of training schools for bi-lingual teachers. Fallon opposed the bi-lingual schools in his diocese because of the incompetent preparation of the teachers and the resultant inadequacy of the students' knowledge of both English and French. The matter of language was and still is a hotly partisan issue in Ontario, and Fallon's criticism of the schools brought him under the fire of the French-Canadians. He persisted in his view, however, and persuaded the government of Ontario to provide the training schools which effected great improvement in language instruction in both English and French.[2]

Fallon was known as an educationalist, an excellent English scholar, and as a distinguished preacher and public speaker both in Canada and in the United States. It is clear why this tall, handsome, magnetic man with a voice perfectly suited to oratory was the object of Fitzgerald's admiration.

* * *

In the spring of his second year at the Newman School, Fitzgerald went to Norfolk to visit a member of his father's family, his first cousin, Cecelia Taylor. The important thing about this trip was his visit to her brother, Thomas Delihant, who was attending the Jesuit seminary at Woodstock in Maryland. Just how deeply impressed Fitzgerald was by this visit he indicated in a 1924 magazine article in which he listed some of his heroes; in a catalogue that includes Theodore Roosevelt, Admiral Dewey, James J. Hill, and Garibaldi he mentioned a "certain obscure Jesuit priest" whom he did not name.[3] The only Jesuit Fitzgerald seems to have known was Thomas Delihant.

This visit would produce "The Ordeal" and "Benediction," two of Fitzgerald's overtly Catholic pieces. Apparently the sixteen-year-old Fitzgerald's exposure to the special sort of tranquility of a religious community and to Tom Delihant at the time of his most momentous decision deeply affected him. We cannot know if the character of the novice in "The Ordeal" and his spiritual crisis are accurate representations of Delihant and his state just before his ordination. Perhaps Fitzgerald built upon the hint of apprehension he must have seen in Delihant facing his life's decision, or perhaps Fitzgerald, who had chosen Father Fay as a model and was beginning to speculate about the priesthood for himself, was considering what his own feelings would be in this situation. Surely Delihant's ordination was not a precipitous affair, for the eighteen-year course of preparation for entry into the Society of Jesus is the longest and most rigorous of the Catholic orders.

Delihant grew up in the area and atmosphere that had produced Edward Fitzgerald's ante-bellum sensibility, a factor which must have figured in his attraction for Fitzgerald. Delihant was born in Chicago in 1878 and when he was thirteen came East with his family where he lived in Maryland for a time and then Georgetown in Washington. He finished his sophomore year at Georgetown University, where

Fitzgerald's father had studied, before at age nineteen he entered the Jesuit order at Frederick, Maryland. Here he spent four years in the study of poetry, rhetoric, and philosophy before he was sent to teach mathematics at Holy Cross High School in Baltimore and at St. Joseph's College in Philadelphia. In 1909 he went to Woodstock where he spent the next three years in his final theology course before his ordination to the priesthood by James Cardinal Gibbons in June, 1912. Then he went on to teaching assignments at St. Andrew's in Poughkeepsie and at Loyola College in Baltimore.

Delihant took his final vows in 1914 and then spent three years on the Mission Band, a group of itinerant preachers who either serve areas where there is no parish priest or supplement the Sunday Mass schedules of small churches, and one year as a service chaplain. After a four-year stay in Baltimore as a parish priest, he went to his final assignment at St. Ignatius Church in New York City, where he remained for twenty-one years before being retired to Inisfada on Long Island. Two years later he died after an extended illness and was buried at the novitiate in Wernersville, Pennsylvania.[4]

This was not an especially distinguished career; there is certainly nothing particularly heroic in the bare facts of Delihant's life to have recommended him to the company of Roosevelt and Garibaldi in Fitzgerald's pantheon. Probably his spirituality and gentleness, noted by all who knew him, most impressed Fitzgerald, fresh from the tutelage of Father Fay.

The official Jesuit obituary-eulogy for Delihant written by an old friend and colleague reveals something of the character and personality of the man. It notes a predisposition to nervousness and headaches, an inability to concentrate and to acquire and coordinate knowledge, his ineptness with scholastic philosophy, and his distaste for teaching. That Delihant could remain a Jesuit with these liabilities is testimony to the strength of his positive qualities—his finely honed intuitive powers, his gift for getting close to all sorts of people, and his ability to move and engage people in his sermons.

The very rich were his friends, a fact that certainly interested Fitzgerald, and he was an enthusiastic horseman and sailor when the indulgence of his wealthy friends allowed him to be. The novitiate at Wernersville was donated to the order by a wealthy layman who said he gave it to express his gratitude for Father Delihant's attention and service to his family. On the other hand, for the twenty years he worked in New York, he was drawn to and absorbed by the problems of the very poor of his parish.[5] He was possessed of a great humanness, the sweetness of the priest Keith in "Benediction," that made him the good priest Fitzgerald admired.

Although he had been born in Chicago and his father was a born Irishman, the transplantation of the young Delihant in Maryland had taken well, and, nurtured, he grew into a Dixie man of ante-bellum sentiments. He was proud of his kinship to Francis Scott Key, and he told a friend that when he meditated on Heaven he imagined himself asked by General Lee to carry dispatches for him.[6] This romanticism and deep sympathy for the lost cause of the South were things Fitzgerald admired, and it is clear that he identified Delihant with those qualities of Edward Fitzgerald of which he was most fond and proud.

* * *

One of the "fireside group" at the Newman School, an informal periodic meeting of selected "old boys," Father Fay, and Shane Leslie, the English writer whom Fay had brought to Newman to teach after he became its headmaster, was Fay's assistant, Father William Hemmick. Father Fay had made Fitzgerald see the Church as a "dazzling, golden thing," a glamorous international Church that had nothing to do with the provincial experience of the typical American Catholic. William Hemmick with his cassocks tailored in Paris, silver-buckled pumps, and urbane air was an incarnation of this brand of Catholicism. Fitzgerald knew him at Newman and later, during his Army service, carried on a correspondence with him, but certain knowledge of the breadth and character of this relationship is lost to us, for Shane Leslie reported in 1958 that Hemmick had destroyed Fitzgerald's letters.[7] It is regrettable that apparently Hemmick's profound disappointment at Fitzgerald's failure to become the American Robert Hugh Benson, the English novelist and son of the Archbishop of Canterbury who had first been an Anglican priest and after his conversion to Catholicism a Catholic priest, as he, Fay, and Leslie had urged, outweighed his sense of responsibility to the world of letters.[8] We do know, however, that Father Hemmick joined Shane Leslie in counseling Fitzgerald in matters of religion and in his reading whenever Father Fay was abroad.

William Hemmick was born in Pittsburgh in 1886. His father, Roland Hemmick, was an officer in the United States Foreign Service, which accounts for his son's European education and life-long preference for things Continental. The high point of the senior Hemmick's career was service as consul general in Switzerland. Father Hemmick received his undergraduate education at the Jesuit

College in Feldkirch, Austria, and he studied for the priesthood at the American College in Rome and at Catholic University in Washington where he met Father Fay. Hemmick spent only a few years in America before his permanent expatriation began with his service as an Army Chaplain in France during World War I. He remained in Paris for the next decade, and there he was visited by prominent American Catholic travelers, and often by Leslie who had returned to England.

Hemmick was made a monsignor and was called to Rome in 1932, and after a time he became the first American priest to be named a Canon of St. Peter's Basilica. Here he served as ecclesiastical attaché to the embassy of the Sovereign Order of Malta, a post that gave him diplomatic status and kept him in touch with ambassadors and their aides. He continued to receive visitors in Rome as he had in Paris, until his residence became an obligatory stop for many American tourists. At the time of his death in September, 1971, Monsignor Hemmick had been living for many years in the Doria Palace located in the center of Rome, a home which was owned by a family of old Roman nobility. Hemmick was known for his fluency in several languages, his great store of Vatican anecdotes, and the fact that the Swedish princess who later became Queen Astrid of Belgium was among his many converts.[9]

Monsignor Hemmick was a society priest, a rarity among American clergy, and the part of Fitzgerald that tended to be impressed by the appearances of wealth was drawn to this anachronistic practioner of the old Church art of ministering to aristocracy.

* * *

After his marriage in 1920, which was performed by a priest at St. Patrick's Cathedral in New York, and the Catholic baptism of his daughter a year and a half later in St. Paul, Fitzgerald left the Church. Monsignor Fay, who had come to love Fitzgerald as a son, had tried through several avenues of appeal not only to keep Fitzgerald in the Church, but to convince him that he would be most happy if he were to combine a writing career with a priestly vocation. Fay had profound influence over Fitzgerald when he was near, but his own foreign travels and Fitzgerald's Army career somewhat dissipated his power to affect Fitzgerald's religious and spiritual condition. Zelda Sayre had begun to supplant Fay in Fitzgerald's emotions even before Fay's death. Subsequently their intensely emotional courtship once and for all dispelled the priesthood from Fitzgerald's consideration, and, shortly after their marriage, he resolved his growing ambivalence toward Catholicism by terminating his formal association with the Church.

Whenever Fitzgerald returned to St. Paul, during his 1916 Sabbatical from Princeton, in the summer of 1919 when he was writing *This Side of Paradise*, and in the period in 1921-1922 when the Fitzgeralds went home for the birth of their daughter and to give domesticity a trial, one of the people Fitzgerald saw regularly was Father Joseph Thomas Barron, the last priest in his life.

Fitzgerald's acquaintance with Father Joe Barron had begun years before when Barron's parish priest brought him to meet the influential McQuillans, Fitzgerald's mother's family. Barron, Fitzgerald's senior by eight years, became a close friend of Philip McQuillan, Fitzgerald's uncle and Godfather, and through this association came to know Fitzgerald in later years.[10]

Barron came from a typical family of St. Paul, a predominantly Catholic city which had been built up by the migration of working-class Catholics from the East. His father, John Barron, had left Prince Edward Island for Minneapolis in the mid nineteenth century, as many young people before him had gone to the St. Paul area either to study for the priesthood or to join the Carondelet of St. Joseph, a teaching and nursing order of nuns who were then important and powerful in St. Paul Church life. It was a tradition that vacationing clergy brought back with them more young Canadians to carry on their work. John Barron knew several of the priests, and they influenced his move, but he did not enter the priesthood. His father had been a farmer, and with his move West, congruent with the growing spirit of industrialism, John Barron left the land for employment with a wholesale grocery firm in St. Paul, a branch of commerce dominated by Irish Catholics which had been the source of the McQuillan prosperity.[11]

In Minneapolis, John Barron met Anne Boulger, a native Minnesotan, and a few years after their marriage they moved across the Mississippi River to St. Paul where they raised their seven children in a deeply religious home. Joseph Barron did not come from a long line of clergy; he was the first priest in his family. A brilliant student, he was soon noticed by his pastor for whom he served Mass, and his parents were approached with the suggestion that he enter St. Paul Seminary. None of the Barrons had even remotely considered the possibility, but they were not opposed to the idea, and apparently Joe had a genuine vocation.[12] He studied at St. Thomas College and the Seminary in St. Paul, and when he was consecrated by Archbishop John Ireland in 1912, he was just twenty-four, the youngest priest ever to have been ordained in that diocese. Barron was immediately named Dean of Students at St. Paul Seminary, and thus began his distinguished academic career which took him to Catholic University where he earned the degree of Doctor of Sacred Theology and eventually joined the faculty. At his untimely death in 1939, Barron was Dean of Sacred Theology and was known as one of the most brilliant students and teachers contributed to Catholic University by the Diocese of St. Paul, which had been instrumental in the establishment of the school.[13] One of his three books, *The Elements of Epistemology* (1931), has become a standard theology text widely used in Catholic seminaries and universities. His other titles are *The Idea of the Absolute in Modern British Philosophy* (1929) and *Supplement to Turner's History of Philosophy* (1930).[14]

When he was in St. Paul, Barron frequented the Kilmarnock Bookshop, the headquarters of the local and visiting literati. The shop was owned by Thomas Boyd, a novelist and editor of the *St. Paul Daily News* book page, who had helped to keep Fitzgerald before the public early in his career. Fitzgerald repaid him by personally delivering Boyd's war novel, *Through the Wheat*, to Scribners. Boyd provided a properly rumpled and untidy, dark and slightly dirty meeting place for friends and writers in the back room of the shop where a fire constantly burned. Joseph Hergesheimer was a regular visitor, and Fitzgerald came here each day during the year he lived in St. Paul with his wife and daughter and often met Father Barron.

When Fitzgerald was home from Princeton in the winter of 1916, he often visited Father Barron, who was then a curate at St. Paul Cathedral. These visits were renewed in 1919 after his disappointing experience in New York where he had gone to make a fortune to impress Zelda Sayre, whom he was trying to persuade to marry him. John Briggs, who later became headmaster of St. Paul Academy, and Donald Ogden Stewart, an aspiring young writer whom Fitzgerald had encouraged in his work and introduced to the works of the Catholic writers Compton MacKenzie, R.H. Benson, and Huysmans, often accompanied him to see Father Barron.[15] Stewart, who was experimenting with mysticism after reading the works Fitzgerald suggested, would throw a snowball against the window of Fitzgerald's room at midnight, they would call for John Briggs, and together they went to engage Barron in "a small hours discussion as to the ascetic ideals of the thirteenth century"[16] and other religious and literary subjects. They went out to Barron's rooms in Loras Hall at St. Paul Seminary where he was professor of philosophy, and they discussed, among other things, Fitzgerald's writing. It was probably then that Barron gave "Benediction" his imprimatur, as Fitzgerald later told Shane Leslie.[17]

Barron was alarmed as Monsignor Fay had been by Fitzgerald's spiritual instability, but his approach was gentle scorn rather than the emotional appeals the older fatherly priest had made. Barron was more nearly Fitzgerald's contemporary, and his natural response to Fitzgerald's iconoclasms was a quiet "Scott, quit being a damn fool."[18] Still Fitzgerald went back for more, for he was impressed with Barron's keen intelligence, the breadth and depth of his knowledge, and his idealistic devotion to his students and teaching. The tall, athletic priest, who with his Irish good looks, blue eyes and wavy red hair, was handsome in the style of the Arrow collar advertisements of that day, was a great favorite with the seminarians. Not only was he a brilliant and stimulating teacher, but his disciplining of students was tempered by his delightful sense of humor. He was extremely proud to have received a facial scar, quickly healed, while playing hockey with his students, and he wore the plaster on his cheek like a decoration.[19] Fitzgerald, the thwarted football hero, was naturally attracted to this personality.

In 1921, even though he was about to leave the Church, at his mother's suggestion, Fitzgerald arranged to have his daughter baptized at the Convent of the Visitation in the Chapel of the order of nuns that Fitzgerald's maternal grandfather had been instrumental in bringing to St. Paul.[20] Father Joseph Barron was both the celebrating priest and Scottie's Godfather. The Fitzgeralds spent several social evenings with Father Barron during their year in St. Paul, and the priest liked Zelda, though they disagreed on most points.

In the 30's, when Fitzgerald's parents had moved to Washington and the younger Fitzgeralds were living in the area, Father Barron was teaching at Catholic University. He visited Fitzgerald at Ellerslie in Wilmington and in Baltimore, but the old easy relationship was spoiled by Fitzgerald's pathological drinking and erratic behavior. Barron was afraid to say too much to Ftizgerald because he thought that he might turn on him.

Barron continued to think, however, that Fitzgerald's intelligence and early training would lead him back to the Church, and he kept track of his career and whereabouts.[21] In 1937 Fitzgerald received a letter from Hyatt Downing, a minor Catholic novelist and native of St. Paul, who told Fitzgerald that he had seen Barron and that he had talked about Fitzgerald and told Downing that he could be reached in Hollywood.[22] For all of Barron's concern and interest and contrary to his prediction, Fitzgerald died three years later outside the Church and was denied her final comfort.

* * *

[1]*F. Scott Fitzgerald's Ledger* (Washington: Bruccoli Clark/Microcard Editions Books, 1973).

[2]Vicar-General Andrew P. Mahoney, Oblates of Mary Immaculate, London, Ontario, to Joan M. Allen, 14 December 1971.

[3]F. Scott Fitzgerald, "Wait Till You Have Children of Your Own," *Woman's Home Companion* LI (July 1924), 105.

[4]Hugh A. Kennedy, S.J., to JMA, 3 December 1971.

[5]T.B. Chetwood, S.J., "Father Thomas J. Delihant, S.J., 1878-1949," *Woodstock Letters* Vol. 78 (1949), 351-354.

[6]*Ibid.*

[7]Shane Leslie, "Memories of F. Scott Fitzgerald," *Times Literary Supplement* (21 Nov. 1958), p. 673.

[8]*Ibid.*
Fitzgerald probably would not have been very disturbed by Hemmick's ultimate rejection of him. In a conspiratorial tone Father Fay wrote his response to Fitzgerald's classification system of types in this statement of qualification.
"I should take as the first type ourselves; the second class Leslie; third class Father Hemmick; fourth class Mr. Delbos [the successor to Fay as Headmaster of the Newman School] .... "
C.W.F. to F.S.F. 4 October 1917; Fitzgerald Papers, Princeton University Library (hereafter cited as FP).

[9]*New York Times,* (21 September 1971), II, p. 40.

[10]Irene C. Barron to JMA, 27 March 1972.

[11]I.C.B. to JMA, 11 December 1971.

[12]I.C.B. to JMA, 11 September 1971.

[13]James Michael Reardon, *The Catholic Church in the Diocese of St. Paul* (St. Paul: North Central, 1952), p. 243.

[14]"Funeral Services Are Held Here for Dr. Joseph Barron," *St. Paul Catholic Bulletin* (22 April 1939), p. 1.

[15]Donald Ogden Stewart, "Recollections of Fitzgerald and Hemingway," *Fitzgerald/Hemingway Annual 1971* (Washington, D.C.: Microcard Editions, 1971), p. 177.

[16]F. Scott Fitzgerald, "Reminiscences of Donald Stewart," *F. Scott Fitzgerald in His Own Time: A Miscellany*, ed. Matthew J. Bruccoli and Jackson R. Bryer (Kent, Ohio: Kent State, 1971), p. 232.

[17]Andrew Turnbull ed., *The Letters of F. Scott Fitzgerald* (New York: Scribners, 1963), p. 378.

[18]Andrew Turnbull, *Scott Fitzgerald* (New York: Scribners, 1962), p. 98.

[19]Monsignor Lawrence O. Wolf to JMA, 9 September 1971.

[20] Sister Margaret Mary Burke to JMA, 7 September 1971.

[21] Turnbull, *Scott Fitzgerald*, p. 252.

[22] Hyatt J. Downing to FSF, 14 December 1937, FP.

The Fitzgeralds at the pool of the Cavalier Hotel, 1927. Keystone Photo.

WILLIAM W. SEWARD, JR.

F. Scott Fitzgerald's

Associations with

Norfolk and Virginia Beach

The handsome young man from St. Paul began what turned out to be a permanent love affair with Norfolk after he came East to college. In those days F. Scott Fitzgerald was a remote and glamorous figure. Indeed, even when he was a youth, people were aware of him wherever he went. He engendered a kind of excitement, quite apart from his good looks, that made anything he did a happening. Always having had a greedy zest for life, Fitzgerald represented himself as a romantic—a vain, slightly malicious, intelligent, and quick-witted playboy.

It has been pointed out that Fitzgerald was imbued with the romance of the lost cause of the South.[1] He also developed nostalgic feelings about Norfolk and Virginia Beach as places associated with Cecilia Delihant Taylor, his beloved Cousin Ceci.

Fitzgerald's periodic visits to the Norfolk area stemmed from his closeness to Cecilia, at whose wedding he served as ribbon holder in April 1903. His early visits were made during the Easter holidays of his Newman and Princeton days, partly because of the distance home to St. Paul, but mostly, it seems, because he was so devoted to Cousin Ceci, a young widow then living in Norfolk with four daughters ranging from seven to ten at that time. The girls—Sally, Cecilia, Elizabeth, and Virginia—were called affectionately by their

41

Princetonian cousin: Sally, Little Cecilia, Tommy, and Gigi respectively. Three of the sisters married (Mrs. Charles Abeles, Mrs. J. Hume Taylor, and Mrs. Conrad Little) and still reside in and around Norfolk. Miss Virginia Taylor now lives in Richmond.

When Fitzgerald first started coming to Norfolk, he was seventeen or eighteen. The Taylor girls were nearer their young cousin in age than their mother was, "but miles away in all other respects."[2] One of the sisters, Sally Abeles, recalls: "We were terribly impressed with him. He was a very handsome man and wore beautiful clothes. He was very sweet and kind to his young cousins."[3]

Then she added: "We probably knew Scott during the happiest time in his life. He was lighthearted, gay, and amusing. He hadn't had any big troubles yet. The only thing that worried him was whether or not he would make the club at Princeton or if he would make the football squad."[4]

A first cousin on Fitzgerald's father's side of the family, Cecilia Taylor was sixteen years older than the young author, making her of another generation. Contrary to Arthur Mizener's assertion, it appears to the daughters that Cecilia could hardly have been a woman "with whom he later fell in love."[5] In truth, he adored her as a kinswoman more than any other blood relative except his daughter, Scottie. This fact is verified by all of Cecilia's daughters and attested to "uniquivocally" by Scottie Fitzgerald Smith, herself.[6] According to one of her daughters, the mother, during Fitzgerald's Princeton period, was not as Nancy Milford reports "a pretty woman," but "really beautiful, as like him in appearance as a sister, and comparatively young."[7] Cecilia Taylor, of course, was to become Clara in *This Side of Paradise.*

During one of Fitzgerald's early visits with his Cousin Ceci, an acquaintance in the military service gave him his first drink in Norfolk. Fitzgerald never forgot this episode, which is the obvious reason why he was so concerned about his daughter when she visited their relatives in the area while she was in her teens. In June 1935, he wrote Cecilia: "By now the Result-of-an-Irresistible-Impulse will be among you. I am enclosing a check with which I hope you will buy her as much gayety as she deserves. Don't let her go out with any sixteen-year-old boys who have managed to amass a charred keg and an automobile as their Start-in-Life. Really I mean this . . . . I mean that about any unreliable Virginia boys taking my pet around. I will never forget that it was a Norfolk number (later drowned in South American swamps) who gave me my first drink of whiskey."[8]

Fitzgerald visited only relatives in Norfolk, having no other friends in the area. Virginia Taylor says, "I don't believe he had any friends to speak of in Norfolk. My feeling is that he didn't want to bother."[9] The Taylor sisters attribute Fitzgerald's initial trips mainly to his adoration of Cecilia. He was never very close to his own mother or to his only sister. The boy's mother seems to have irritated him by over-protectiveness with such repeated admonitions as, "You look tired; go upstairs and rest."[10] As late as August 1940, the author wrote Cecilia: "I was fond of Aunt Annabel and Aunt Elise, who gave me almost my first tastes in discipline, in a peculiar way in which I wasn't fond of my mother who spoiled me."[11] This babying no doubt played a role in developing his hypochondria, which eventually reached proportions of the ludicrous.

On one visit when the Taylor girls were still not too young to be dazzled, Fitzgerald wrote a little play for them. With prideful enthusiasm the sisters acted out the parts of this drama which its author called "The King Who Wanted an Appetite." According to those who participated, the occasion was rewarding for all. No one knows where a copy of this play is today.

Apparently this same trip to the South was notable for a visit to Cecilia's only available brother, Thomas Delihant, then a novice at the Jesuit seminary in Woodstock, Maryland. Although Cousin Tom could have been the young writer's father, the two developed an almost brotherly rapport in many ways. However, Fitzgerald could not accept Catholicism, expressing his views quite candidly to his Jesuit kinsman whom he had come to admire.

Tom Delihant, who died in 1949, was a spectacular man—Fitzgerald called him a "personality" while referring to himself as a "personage."[12] Cousin Tom was at Georgetown with John Barrymore, and like Barrymore was himself an actor, charming and handsome. According to relatives, he was a generous man who came to be a great money-raiser for the Jesuits. His magnetism drew personal gifts from all kinds of people. Once a bootlegger friend gave him a boat. He came to Norfolk occasionally, but seldom were he and Fitzgerald there together. On one trip, however, they and Cecilia drove in Tom's car up to southern Maryland on a nostalgic mission to find old family places.[13] There is no secret that Fitzgerald wrote the short story "Benediction" with Cousin Tom in mind. One of the relatives has characterized this remarkable Jesuit priest as "an *important* man—Scott was really not in his class."[14]

In 1927, the Cavalier Hotel, which was to become famous, opened its doors for the first time. Among its guests in July of that year were the Fitzgeralds. As time passed, this Virginia Beach landmark became a favorite hotel of the novelist. This was no accident, for the Cavalier symbolized an entire era to Fitzgerald—its baroque and prestigious atmosphere, its beach and cabana club featuring the famous big bands of the 1920's and 1930's, and its location by the sea. Epitomizing the new romance of the South, the Cavalier beckoned Fitzgerald when he came to Virginia. Evidence of this can be found in widely publicized photographs of the author and his family taken while they were guests at the hotel.

During a visit to Norfolk in the early 1930's, Fitzgerald stayed downtown in the Monticello Hotel. He was drinking then and had come in a car—one of those big, powerful, ornate automobiles about which he knew nothing. All in all, this was not a happy time for Fitzgerald. But one day he asked his Cousin Virginia Taylor to come over to the hotel during her lunch hour so he could dictate a preface to *The Great Gatsby*. According to her: "It was the first of his books to be reprinted, and I imagine it was quite a thrill. I remember his being tremendously meticulous about the smallest grammatical point, and punctuations. There was nothing casual about the preface!"[15] This preface appeared in the Modern Library edition of *The Great Gatsby* in 1934.

One of the stories about Fitzgerald that still circulate in Norfolk has to do with a visit with his relatives some time after publication of *Tender Is the Night*. Arriving by train, he was to have been met by an in-law. But because of an illness in the family, his cousin's husband sent a friend, a superficial young man with social connections, whom I shall call Ed Martin.

The two men had never met before. Driving up Main Street heading for the home of the author's cousin, Martin remained silent. Fitzgerald tried unsuccessfully to start a conversation. No doubt disappointed over the poor sales of *Tender Is the Night* but happy with the generally favorable printed reviews, the novelist seemed to be full of himself. He spoke with pride when talking about his latest novel. Still no comment from Martin, even after Fitzgerald's extended lecturing about his works and his stature as an author. Almost in desperation the novelist finally exclaimed, "Haven't you read any of my books!"

"Not unless you wrote *Black Beauty*," replied Ed Martin without enthusiasm.

As time passed in the mid and late 1930's, Fitzgerald's trips to coastal Virginia became more sporadic. As Scott Donaldson has pointed out, the author retreated to Virginia in order to dry out or refresh himself.[16] Of these years Mrs. J. Hume Taylor observed: "Scott got drunk every time he came to Norfolk during his adult life. He was a wild kind of person later in his life. Our husbands would get terribly irritated at him."[17]

"Of course, Scott was a drunk," Elizabeth Little commented. "We all know that, but he was perfectly, ravingly beautiful all his life. He and Zelda were this gorgeous blond couple who became a household word. He came back from the Riviera with sky-blue flannel trousers and sky-blue sweaters, and that was when men didn't wear light colors. With golden hair and blue eyes, he was strikingly handsome and so was she."[18]

Elizabeth Little then expressed her views of Zelda: "She was not an easy person to get to know. She was a completely schizophrenic case. Hers wasn't just a case of nerves or a little too much liquor. It was truly a mental breakdown off and on all her life.

"They drank like fish, were gay as they could be, spent money like water and then when they suddenly gave out of money, they went abroad because the exchange was better. When he needed money, he would write trashy little pieces for the *Saturday Evening Post* and get $5,000 for them."[19]

Sally Abeles remembers her cousin's enthusiasm for swimming in the ocean at night. She also remembers an incident which she believes to be typical of his impulsiveness and his affection for her mother. In the 1930's, Fitzgerald was staying with Mrs. Abeles' family at a cottage at Virginia Beach. On the spur of the moment, he phoned a photographer in Norfolk to come down and take a picture of Ceci and himself.

Although Fitzgerald did not visit Virginia in his last year, thoughts of the Tidewater country remained very much in his consciousness. Writing from Hollywood to Cecilia Taylor, 14 August 1940, he concluded his letter with these words: "I wrote Scottie to stop by and say hello to you on her way South to see her mother next month. I would so like to see you all myself. Gigi wrote me such a nice letter from Richmond."[20]

Obviously Fitzgerald's associations with Norfolk and Virginia Beach over the years do not constitute a major facet of his career as a writer, but they certainly contributed to his own dream of himself. The evidence seems to suggest that much of his lighthearted gaiety was peculiarly associated with his Cousin Ceci and her daughters, as well as with the two Virginia cities by the sea. And it hardly seems an accident that his favorite hotel was named the Cavalier, for he was one of the very few writers of his generation to project the kind of romance suggested by the word "cavalier." To a new generation, F. Scott Fitzgerald has become a symbol of a lost romantic age—an image of "the last really good time."

Old Dominion University

---

[1] Scott Donaldson, "Fitzgerald's Romance with the South," *Southern Literary Journal*, V (Spring 1973), 3.

[2] Letter from Mrs. Conrad Little, 15 July 1973.

[3] Interview with Mrs. Charles Abeles, 13 September 1973.

[4] *Ibid.*

[5] Arthur Mizener, *The Far Side of Paradise* (Boston: Houghton Mifflin, 1949), p. 9.

[6] Interview with Mrs. C. Grove Smith, 13 May 1974.

[7] Letter from Mrs. Little, 15 July 1973.

[8] Andrew Turnbull, ed., *The Letters of F. Scott Fitzgerald* (New York: Scribners, 1963), pp. 417-418.

[9] Letter from Virginia Taylor, 9 March 1974.

[10] Interview with Mrs. Abeles, 13 September 1973.

[11] *Letters*, p. 419.

[12] *Ibid*, p. 453.

[13] Letter from Miss Taylor, 9 March 1974.

[14] Interview with Mrs. Conrad Little, 6 March 1974.

[15] Letter from Virginia Taylor, 19 July 1973.

[16] Donaldson, 14.

[17] Interview with Mrs. J. Hume Taylor, 19 May 1974.

[18] Interview with Mrs. Little, 6 March 1974.

[19] *Ibid.*

[20] *Letters*, p. 420.

JENNIFER McCABE ATKINSON

The
Discarded Ending
of "The Offshore Pirate"

F. Scott Fitzgerald became a client of the Paul Revere Reynolds agency in October 1919. At the beginning of his relationship with Reynolds and Harold Ober, Fitzgerald was sometimes tentative in his opinion of the marketability of a story, though his confidence in himself as a writer grew rapidly as the agency had success placing his stories. The early correspondence from Fitzgerald reflects both his confidence: "I'm just finishing up a really excellent story, the best I have done" (30 December 1919)—and his uncertainty: "About Myra Meets His Family—I'm afraid its no good and if you agree with me don't hesitate to send it back" (30 December 1919).[1] The most striking case of his asking for critical appraisal of a story involved "The Offshore Pirate."

On 27 January 1920, Fitzgerald sent the story (then entitled "The Proud Piracy") to Reynolds with the statement: "Enclosed is a very odd story. If you think the end spoils it clip it off. I'll leave that to your judgment. . . . Personally I like it as it is." The ending was deleted. Fitzgerald revised the story, and it was published by *The Saturday Evening Post* as "The Offshore Pirate" (29 May 1920).

The discarded ending survives among Harold Ober's papers with a note in his hand reading: "file Scott Fitzgerald last page of The Proud Piracy". The holograph revisions on the typescript are not in

47

... .rdita's eyes opened slowly. It was very dark and quiet and she realized that it must be quite late. her **book** had fallen from her

(38)

lap, but in her hand she still clutched the remains of a sucked lemon. She stretched herself and yawned and listened as she heard steps on the ladder and her uncle's panting as he climbed.

"Did you buy me a bathing suit, Félice?" she called.

Her maid's voice rose from the ladder.

"Ah no, ma'moselle. The store said he had no call for La'moselle's kind."

then Mr.Farnam,

Mr. Farnam's head appeared, and after him Félice. He nodded at her coldly.

"You won't need a bathing suit;" he said, "we're starting north right away."

suggested

"Oh, shut up!" said ardita from sheer force of habit. She turned to her maid.

demanded

"Félice," she said, "was it you who told me you'd seen a wonder-

vaudeville   Black

ful act last spring called Curtis Carlyle and his Six brown Buddies?"

"Yes -- La'moselle, ah, it was truly marvelous --"

eagerly

'Tell me," interrupted ardita, "was Curtis Carlyle a dark-haired young man with blue eyes - very good looking?"

"Oh, no, La'moselle. Oh, no! He is small and ugly as sinning. He has grey hair and his legs they are bow-legged."

"Hm," remarked ardita thoughtfully. "It's a darn funny world, isn't it, Felice?"

agreed

"Oh, yes," replied Félice, "It's a darn funny world."

Fitzgerald's hand or Harold Ober's. However, the handwriting for these revisions resembles Zelda Fitzgerald's; if so, they were certainly made with Fitzgerald's concurrence.

Either Reynolds or Ober advised Fitzgerald to delete the ending and revise the story. There is even evidence that George Horace Lorimer of *The Saturday Evening Post* recommended altering the story. In a 21 February 1920 letter to Ober, Fitzgerald wrote: "I think you'll see if you read this from the beginning that I've put the required Jazz ending on it and I don't doubt they'll buy it. . . . The last line takes Mr. Lorimer at his word. It's one of the best *lines* I've ever written."

That Fitzgerald was wise in accepting the advice given him appears clear when the two endings are compared. In the original ending Fitzgerald uses the commonplace dream device, and uses it badly. Ardita awakes when her uncle and the maid, Felice, return to the yacht. The kidnapping took place in Ardita's dream. To explain the dream, Ardita asks Felice if she hadn't mentioned once having seen "Curtis Carlyle and his Six Black Buddies". The ending is further weakened by the ironic information that the actual Curtis Carlyle was the physical opposite of the handsome Curtis Carlyle in Ardita's dream. The story then trails off with a vague remark by the still petulant Ardita and agreement from Felice—no zing, no spirit, no flair.

The revised story deletes Felice, and it makes the piracy the act of an imaginative young man in conspiracy with Ardita's uncle. In the new ending, Ardita is won over by the dash and daring of the unexpectedly romantic Toby—a young man she refused even to meet at the beginning of the story. The escapade is carried out with style, and Toby is rewarded by the acquiesence of a charmed Ardita. The "Jazz ending" is there, and a poor story has become a good one. The line which Fitzgerald thought at the time was the best he'd ever written is: " 'Perhaps I can guess the other one,' she said; and reaching up on her tiptoes she kissed him softly in the illustration."

---

[1] For other correspondence pertaining to the sale of the story see *As Ever, Scott Fitz--*, ed. Matthew J. Bruccoli and Jennifer McCabe Atkinson (New York & Philadelphia: Lippincott, 1972).

BRUCE R. STARK

THE INTRICATE PATTERN

IN

The Great Gatsby

Victor A. Doyno has provided several examples of patterning on all size levels within F. Scott Fitzgerald's *The Great Gatsby*.[1] Indeed, he found this patterning so well-worked out and so systematic that he concluded "a knowledge of the ways in which the novel is 'intricately patterned,' from minor details up to large structural units, partially explains how Fitzgerald created a novel that is 'something extra-ordinary and beautiful and simple'."[2] I quite agree with Mr. Doyno and would like to extend some of his examples of patterning a bit more, to add some others that I have found, and to suggest just exactly how the patterning of details allowed Fitzgerald to create a verbal artifact that is simultaneously simple and intricate. Like Mr. Doyno, I will consider the smaller verbal elements first and then look at the patterning of such larger structural units as characters and scenes.

One of the details that Doyno points out is Tom's purchase of a pearl necklace, or, Nick guesses, new cuff buttons, when Nick sees him for the last time (pp. 214-216).[3] As Doyno suggests, the necklace implies that Tom has already found a new mistress so that one is led to believe that he has not been affected in any way by the deaths of Myrtle, Wilson, and Gatsby nor by his part in them. As a consequence, we may assume that the cycle of dalliance, careless brutality, and death that began with the accident on the Ventura Road continues unabated and unreflected upon. This brutality may have an even darker tone because Tom's cuff buttons may also reflect Wolfshiem's "Finest specimens of human molars."

Whatever the precise implications of the cuff-buttons may be, the pearl necklace creates several specific internal links between Tom and three other females: Daisy, Myrtle Wilson, and Myrtle's puppy. Taking Daisy first, Arthur Mizener first pointed out and Doyno later emphasized that the pearl necklace becomes "the symbol of Daisy's surrender to Tom's world."[4] This surrender is underscored by the sharp contrast between Tom's necklace and Daisy's letter to Gatsby. When Jordan went to fetch Daisy for the bridal dinner, Daisy was drunk and wanted to return the pearls to "whoever they belong to," but she hung on to a letter until it "was coming to pieces like snow." We are not told to whom this letter is addressed but can infer that it was a "Dear John" to Gatsby which Daisy later rewrote and sent to him at Oxford (p. 182). Daisy's attempt to return Tom's necklace coupled with the passive destruction of the letter indicate a weak attempt to reject Tom and remain loyal to Gatsby. But when Daisy walked out of her bedroom with "the pearls . . . around her neck" and then "married Tom Buchanan without so much as a shiver," we have a very concrete image of Daisy's submission to her social milieu and her bondage to Tom's wealth. The "string of pearls valued at three hundred and fifty thousand dollars" is in effect an expensive collar that Tom has fastened around Daisy's neck in order to have and to hold her.

Two other expensive gifts define Tom's relationship to Myrtle Wilson in a similar but coarser way. The first is the overpriced mongrel (pp. 32-33) that resembles Myrtle in several ways. First of all, they are both females, or, as Tom bluntly says of the dog, " 'It's a bitch' "; secondly, the dog looks like Myrtle because she is in a "brown figured muslin" when Tom buys her the dog,[5] and it has a "brown washrag of a back" that is described like a garment, i.e. " 'Look at that coat. Some coat. That's a dog that'll never bother you with catching cold.' " The brown "coat" of this part Airedale would further resemble Myrtle's "brown figured muslin" because the coats of Airedales have a black saddle-shaped figure over a brown background.[6]

Because both Myrtle and the dog are females, because both are dressed in figured brown, and because both have been bought and kept by Tom, they are metaphorically equivalent. As a matter of fact, Tom makes this association directly when he says that Gatsby " 'ran over Myrtle like you'd run over a dog' " and that when he " 'saw that damn box of dog buscuits sitting there on the sideboard, I sat down and cried like a baby.' " What all of this indicates is that Myrtle is Tom's "bitch"; it also suggests that Daisy, who puts Tom's string of pearls around her neck and is kept by a wealth that "imprisons" as well as "preserves," is his expensive, well-bred house pet.

The metaphorical equivalence between Daisy, Myrtle, and a mongrel bitch is not as tenuous as it might seem at first glance because these relationships are realized in several other very specific verbal patterns. During the course of her blurred party Myrtle lists a number of things that she plans to buy the next day. Among them are "a collar for the dog" and "a wreath with a black silk bow for mother's grave that'll last all summer." The close juxtaposition of the collar with a funeral wreath is portentous because just as we see Myrtle at her most brilliant, an image of her death appears; for, even though she is named for an ever-green, Myrtle Wilson does not last out the summer.[7]

This indicator of Myrtle's imminent death is reinforced by the similarity between the color of her third dress and the car that kills her. While Myrtle thinks over her shopping list, she is dressed in her third "costume" of the day: "an elaborate afternoon dress of cream-colored chiffon." Gatsby's car, the one that kills Myrtle, is described by Nick as "*a rich cream color*, bright with nickel, swollen here and there in its monstrous length with triumphant hat-boxes and supper-boxes and tool-boxes, and terraced with a labyrinth of wind-shields that mirrored a dozen suns." Gatsby's car, like Myrtle's dress, is not only "cream-colored" but also quite obviously "elaborate." The mention of a funeral wreath plus the similarity between the color of her dress and the car that kills her foreshadow Myrtle's death at the very moment we see her at the zenith of her pomp and pride.

The dog's collar points to Myrtle's death in a second way because it is the key link in the chain of accidents that leads to her death. The collar leads to Myrtle's death as well as to Wilson's and Gatsby's, because when Wilson finds it, he finally realizes that Myrtle is up to something "funny." Referring to the "small, expensive dog-leash, made of leather and braided silver," he tells Michaelis that " 'I found it yesterday afternoon. She tried to tell me about it, but I knew it was something funny.' "[8] Acting on this sudden insight, Wilson locks

Myrtle up and makes plans to leave for the West. It is partly Myrtle's desperate attempt to escape Wilson that causes her to rush "out into the dusk, waving her hands and shouting" toward Gatsby's car and to her death.

Wilson's discovery of the expensive leash also precipitates the general "holocaust"; for, after Wilson mistakenly assumes that the person who gave Myrtle the collar also ran her down, he sets out to kill him. And after Wilson is told by Tom that it was Gatsby who owned the death car, Wilson finds him, kills him, and then shoots himself. Thus it is Tom's expensive gift to Myrtle that deprives Gatsby of his life just as it was his expensive gift to Daisy that robbed Gatsby of his beloved. Tom's wealth buys gifts that bind his women to him like expensive pets; his physical power demoralizes his weaker rival, Wilson, and his brutal malice shatters the stronger one, Gatsby.

We now have several very specific patterns of equivalent elements that relate Daisy to Myrtle and both of them to Myrtle's dog. First, Daisy's string of pearls is equivalent to the dog's expensive leash and to the second pearl necklace that Tom is about to buy when Nick last sees him; second, Myrtle's brown dress, her sex, and the fact that she was run down "like a dog," relate Myrtle to the bitch; third, the close juxtaposition between the funeral wreath, the cream color of Myrtle's party dress, and the dog collar foreshadow the chain of events that leads to Myrtle's death by Gatsby's elaborate cream-colored car. Finally, we may infer from the first two patterns that Tom's women are bound to him by expensive necklaces and collars like pets so that Myrtle is his bitch whereas Daisy is his better-kept but somewhat neglected lap dog.[9]

It is useful to isolate the specific features in a pattern of images because once isolated, they can then be used to explicate larger and more complex units within a particular discourse. To be specific, the brown, female, and pet features that relate Myrtle, the dog, and Daisy can be used to explicate a rather enigmatic scene in which a Mr. Sloane, Tom, and a woman ride up to Gatsby's house one Sunday afternoon. This short scene appears to be somewhat loosely connected to the rest of the book but can be placed within the novel's verbal pattern when we note that the woman is "in a brown riding-habit" and had been to Gatsby's house before. Using the features isolated above, we may infer that since we again have a female dressed in brown, this woman is probably Sloane's mistress. The fact that she had been to Gatsby's before supports the inference because the reputation of all the women who had been to Gatsby's parties was dubious: Catherine, Myrtle's sister, is described as "a slender, *worldly girl* of about *thirty*" who lived "with a girl friend at a hotel"; Jordan Baker, who is "dishonest" in many ways and became so, Nick supposes, in order to "satisfy the demands of her hard, jaunty body" moved freely "between hotels and clubs and private houses."[10]

Taken by itself, the fact that Sloane has what Catherine would call a "sweetie" is of minor importance, but within the context of this scene it becomes significant for several reasons. The news that Gatsby, a man whom Sloane's girl friend knows and is obviously quite strongly attracted to, claims to know Daisy provokes two reactions in Tom. First, his false prudery is revealed when he exclaims, " 'By God, I may be old-fashioned in my ideas, but women run around too much these days to suit me. They meet all kinds of crazy fish.' " Of course, Tom's "old-fashioned" ideas do not prevent his running around with Myrtle and others, nor his associating with Sloane and his girl-friend. Secondly, and much more importantly for the narrative, Gatsby's acquaintance with Daisy causes Tom to begin his own investigations into Gatsby's real background. For unlike the "ambitious young reporter" who came out " 'to see' " (p. 117), but did not, Tom squeezes a great deal of useful information about the "material" Gatsby out of his friend, Walter Chase.[11] Tom's information is useful because he wins back Daisy with it during the crisis at the Plaza.

Tom's interest in Gatsby's true background and his ability to "see" make him very much like Nick. But since Tom's insights are badly distorted and quite limited, one of Nick's principal tasks is to counter Tom's misrepresentations, as well as his guests' misconceptions, by setting the record on Gatsby straight. For the narrative pattern the important thing about this scene with Slaone's sweetie is that Tom is alerted to the danger to his marriage and therefore goes out to get the information necessary to defend it. Whatever one may think of Tom, he is not, like the other characters, "blind"; like Nick, he "sees."

Thus far we have examined some of the smaller verbal patterns in *The Great Gatsby* and the ways in which features extracted from them serve to integrate an anomalous scene into the novel's narrative sequence. Next, I would like to consider the striking place a much larger unit has in this sequence—the story of Gatsby's five-year stint as Dan Cody's factotum. The fact that Gatsby told Nick about Dan Cody the morning after Myrtle's death, near the beginning of Chapter VIII, but Nick retells it to us after Gatsby's reunion with Daisy, at the beginning of Chapter VI, poses the obvious structural question: why has the Dan Cody story been shifted out of sequence? There are, of course, all sorts of possible answers: external ones (the influence of Joseph Conrad), psychological ones (the Cody story prolongs Gatsby's reunion with Daisy within the reader's mind), internal ones (Nick's desire to explode the first wild rumors about Gatsby's antecedents). But none of these answers give a specific structural reason for the shift of the Dan Cody story to the particular place in the narrative sequence that we find it, i.e., just after Gatsby is reunited with Daisy and just before the scene with Sloane and his sweetie. If *The Great Gatsby* really is "intricately patterned, from minor details up to large structural units" there should then be a specific, structural reason for the Dan Cody story being placed where it is in the novel's sequence of narrative units.

There are several clues as to why Fitzgerald shifted this story forward from Chapter VIII to Chapter VI. The first has to do with its thematic content. In general, the Dan Cody story deals with three matters: (1) Gatsby's real background and unique education, (2) his experience as Cody's factotum, and (3) his betrayal by Ella Kaye. We shall now examine how each of these fits into the book's semantic system.

Gatsby's real background fits into the novel's semantic system by contrasting point for point with both Nick's own background and Gatsby's fantasy past, the one he told Nick during their drive to New York. Although both were Middle Westerners, Gatsby's real parents were "shiftless and unsuccessful farm people," whereas Nick's parents had been "prominent, well-to-do people in this Middle Western city for three generations" (p. 3); in Gatsby's imagination, however, he was "the son of some wealthy people in the Middle West." Because his parents did not suit his imagination, Gatsby "had never really accepted them as his parents at all," whereas Nick is obviously quite proud of his "clan." Setting aside his two weeks at St. Olaf's, Gatsby had little education, whereas Nick had gone to prep school in the East and graduated from Yale as his father had before him; Gatsby told Nick that he had been " 'educated at Oxford, because all my ancestors have been educated there for many years. It is a family tradition.' " In other words, Gatsby's real background was far below Nick's, whereas his imaginary one was somewhat above it; in either case, the basis of the contrast is Nick's education, family background, and his self-conscious identity with them, things that Gatsby lacked and tried to make up for with his imagination.

Even if Gatsby's background and education lacked the quality of Nick's, or of Tom's, and therefore ill-prepared him to deal with men like them, it had nevertheless prepared him well for his role as the Trimalchio of West Egg.[12] For surely his parties should be seen as up-dated versions of the "savage violence of the frontier brothel and saloon" that Dan Cody brought to the Eastern seaboard—some of the excitement of Gatsby's parties is derived from what he learned as Cody's "steward, mate, skipper, secretary . . . ."

Gatsby's work for Cody did not, however, complete his education. It is only after we hear of Ella Kaye that we are told that Gatsby "was left with his singularly appropriate education." Gatsby's five years with Cody prepared him for his role as the producer of brilliant, rather wild parties, but how, one wonders, was his experience with Ella Kaye "singularly appropriate?" Gatsby's run-in with Ella Kaye was appropriate because it not only previews his encounter with Daisy but also foreshadows his inability to understand it—his inability "to see."

Nick tells us that by some legal device which Gatsby "never understood" Ella Kaye tricked him out of his twenty-five-thousand-dollar inheritance from Cody. But Gatsby learned absolutely nothing from this betrayal, nor any others, because he was betrayed by Daisy at least four times. First, she marries Tom instead of waiting for him as she had promised to do. Second, during the crisis at the Plaza, she loses her nerve again and turns back to Tom a second time, even though she had promised to leave him and marry Gatsby. Third, she apparently does not tell Tom that she was driving Gatsby's car and, what is worse, allows Tom to let Wilson believe that Gatsby was driving the death car. As a result, Daisy contributes in an indirect but substantial way to Gatsby's death. Finally, after Gatsby is killed, she deserts him completely for the fourth and final time by not coming to his funeral. But just as with his betrayal by Ella Kaye, Gatsby neither saw nor understood Daisy's corruptness: unlike Tom and Nick, Gatsby does not "see"; he is one of the "blind."

In addition to being a vivid emblem of her apparent innocence and purity but inner cowardice and corruption, Daisy's name clinches, I believe, her connection with Ella Kaye as the second of Gatsby's female betrayers. Mrs. Buchanan's "real" name, as far as Gatsby is concerned, *Daisy Fay*, is phonologically equivalent to *Ella Kaye*.

Note the following phonological equivalences between /déziy féy/ and /éllə kéy/:[13] (1) *Fay* and *Kaye* rhyme; (2) their rhyming vowel /ey/ is repeated in *Daisy*/deyziy/ and is similar to the /e/ in *Ella*/ellə/; (3) both *Daisy*/déy-ziy/ and *Ella*/él-lə/ are dissyllabic with the strongest stress on the first syllable; finally (4) both *Fay* and *Kaye* are monosyllables so that when said with their pre-names they form phonological phrases that are exactly alike: *Daisy Fay*/déy-ziy féy/ and *Ella Kaye*/él-lə kéy/.[14] All of this specific phonological equivalence between the names of the only two women in Gatsby's life whose names we know indicate that Ella Kaye is the analogue of Daisy Fay so that her betrayal of Gatsby and his lack of understanding of it foreshadow his betrayals by Daisy and his complete unawareness of them.[15]

The parallelism between Ella Kaye and Daisy Fay not only integrates the Dan Cody story into the novel's thematic pattern, it also accounts for its specific place in the novel's narrative sequence. For, if one accepts the thematic parallelism between these two women, then the placement of the Ella Kay story just after Chapter V is a very deft touch, since it is at the end of this chapter that Gatsby re-wins Daisy. And right after Nick goes "out of the room and down the marble steps into the rain, leaving them there together," he tells us the Dan Cody-Ella Kaye story. Thus, just as Gatsby has recaptured his dream, Nick tells us the story of Ella Kaye's betrayal, which he "never understood." Just as with Myrtle, the shadow of Gatsby's fall is cast over him at the precise moment that his fortunes seem to have reached their zenith. This shadow immediately becomes substance because it is just after we hear of Ella Kaye's betrayal that Tom rides up to Gatsby's house with Sloane and becomes suspicious when Gatsby tells him "almost aggressively" that " 'I know your wife' "; once Tom is alerted, he comes to Gatsby's party and then digs up the information that will win back his wife and destroy Gatsby. It is thus for these specific, structural reasons that the Dan Cody-Ella Kaye story is placed where it is in the novel's sequence of narrative units.

The suggestion that Gatsby's downfall at Daisy's hands is foreshadowed at the precise moment that he re-wins her is reinforced by another verbal detail—the "rain" that pours down intermittently during the day of their reunion. In addition to creating the comic situations that deflate Gatsby and his reunion with Daisy,[16] this rain is fateful because the only other rain in the book falls on the day of Gatsby's funeral.[17] On that day the rain begins as a "drizzle" but then increases to a "thick drizzle" so that the hearse looks "horribly black and wet"; finally, the drizzle becomes a rain that "poured down Owl-eyes' glasses and is referred to in the blessing of Gatsby. The occurrence of rain on these two days in conjunction with the placement of the Ella Kaye story is not accidental but an important element in the network of verbal relations linking Gatsby's funeral to his reunion with Daisy, since this reunion is not the start of a new life, but is the beginning of the "holocaust" that reduces him to ashes and dust.

I would like to conclude with a brief remark about the notion "intricately patterned." As I have tried to show here, the words in *The Great Gatsby* participate in a multitude of complex patterns that link images, anomalous minor scenes, and even rather large units to one another in a variety of complex and subtle ways. The small dog's collar, the color of Myrtle's dresses, the sounds and colors of Daisy's name, the rain that falls on Gatsby's funeral are not just empty signs that refer to external meanings, nor merely pleasing verbal ornaments, they are elements in an extremely complex and unified system of internal, nonreferential meanings. As such, the novel's words are concrete exemplifications of Northrop Frye's assumption that "a poem's meaning is literally its pattern or integrity as a verbal structure. Its words cannot be separated and attached to sign-values: all possible sign-values of a word are absorbed into a complexity of verbal relations."[18] When this absorption is as completely realized as it is in *The Great Gatsby*, the result is a unique verbal artifact whose words ressonate with one another in an ever-widening circle of internal signification. It is this multiple use of a few elements that makes *The Great Gatsby*, like a successful poem, at once simple and yet complex, and it is this complex simplicity, this meaning that is *in* the book's web of words, that makes it extra-ordinary and beautiful and simple.

University of Wisconsin—Milwaukee

---

[1] Victor A. Doyno, "Patterns in *The Great Gatsby*," *Modern Fiction Studies*, 12 (Winter, 1966-67), 415-426.

[2] *Ibid.*, 426.

[3] F. Scott Fitzgerald, *The Great Gatsby* (New York: Scribners, 1925). All quotations are from this first edition; all the emphases within the quotations are mine.

[4] Arthur Mizener, *The Far Side of Paradise* (Boston: Houghton Mifflin, 1965), p. 189, and Doyno, 417.

[5] When we meet Myrtle at the garage she is dressed in "a spotted dress of dark blue crêpe-de-chine"; for the trip to New York she changes into the brown muslin; at the apartment she is in "an elaborate afternoon dress of cream-colored

chiffon". The color of this last dress is also important as we shall see.

[6] *The American College Dictionary* (New York: Random House, 1958) says the Airedale has "a rough brown or tan coat which is black or grizzled over the back."

[7] Myrtle's name has a number of interesting lexical features. The *American College Dictionary* tells us that the *myrtle* is the generic name of an evergreen that "is used as an emblem of love and was anciently held sacred to Venus"; in addition, the South cultivates a species of this plant called *crape myrtle*, a name that reminds one of the "wreath . . . that'll last all summer."

[8] Wilson uses the word "leash" rather than "collar," but it is fair to assume that the leash includes a collar.

[9] I do not mean to imply by these metaphorical identifications that Tom had no feeling for Myrtle or Daisy; he quite clearly did. But his relationship to them was brutalized as indicated by his physical violence: he breaks Myrtle's nose and bruises Daisy's little finger; in addition, he is a party to a chambermaid's broken arm.

[10] Jordan Baker's function in the novel, her "dishonesty," her affair with Nick, and her attempt to make him do the "honorable" thing by her have been neglected by the critics. This is unfortunate because the contrast between Nick's rejection of Jordan, which allows him to return to the West and write his book about Gatsby, and Gatsby's complete acceptance of Daisy, which makes him want to "repeat the past" with her, is, I believe, the cornerstone of the novel's basic thematic pattern.

[11] A link between Walter Chase and an anecdote by Wolfshiem furnishes another telling example of how intricately patterned this book is. On page 161 Tom tells Gatsby that " 'Walter could have you up on the betting laws too, but Wolfshiem scared him into shutting his mouth' "; on page 84 Wolfshiem tells Gatsby that he told Katspaugh: " 'All right, Katspaugh, don't pay him a penny till he shuts his mouth.' He shut it then and there." On the basis of Wolfshiem's threat and the similarity between "shutting his mouth" and "shuts his mouth," it is just possible that *he* in Wolfshiem's story is Walter Chase.

[12] Fitzgerald considered such titles as "Trimalchio in West Egg" and "Trimalchio," among others, before finally deciding upon, very uncertainly, "*The Great Gatsby*"; see John Kuehl and Jackson R. Bryer, *Dear Scott/Dear Max: The Fitzgerald-Perkins Correspondence* (New York: Scribners, 1971), pp. 80-85 and 94-96.

[13] The system of phonological representation used here is based on George L. Trager and Henry Lee Smith, Jr., *An Outline of English Structure*, Studies in Linguistics: Occasional Papers 3 (Washington: ACLS, 1957), pp. 11-52.

[14] In his article "Conrad and *The Great Gatsby*," *Twentieth Century Literature*, 1 (1955), 7, Robert Stallman notes that "Jay Gatsby is tricked by two women, both having names that rime on his—Daisy Fay and Ella Kaye" but draws no conclusions from this observation.

[15] Both of Daisy's names are symbolically rich. Like the flower she is named for, Daisy is white on the outside (her clothing, her white roadster, her "white girlhood" but yellow within (she is a coward because "she lost her nerve and turned back" to run down Myrtle, just as she turned back to Tom after "whatever intentions, whatever courage she had had were definitely gone." She

is attached to wealth which is symbolized by gold and, in fact, a stream of yellow pours out of her because "her voice is full of money"; she is deadly—she drives the yellow car that kills Myrtle). The same white-without/yellow-within symbolism also relates her to the book's many eggs and suggests that she is really not a "daisy," nor a "day's-eye," but a "rotten egg" because she does not contain the seeds of life but of death. Her maiden name, *Fay*, suggests not only *fay* 'fairy' and 'faith' but also *fey* which is defined as "fated to die soon; full of the sense of approaching death" and as "appearing as if under a spell; enchanted; touched" by *The American Heritage Dictionary* (New York: American Heritage, 1969). Most of these meanings are found in the probable source of *Fay*, i.e. the two lines from John Keat's "Ode to a Nightingale" that Fitzgerald left out of his epigraph to *Tender is the Night*: "and haply the Queen-Moon is on her throne,/cluster'd around by her starry Fays." Daisy is most certainly one of the Queen-Moon's "starry Fays" for several reasons: (1) Fitzgerald loved Keat's poetry and this poem in particular; (2) Daisy is strongly associated with the moon (not the sun, Tom is the hot one) all through the book; (3) and she says, somewhat wistfully after Tom's call from Myrtle, "its very romantic outdoors. There's a bird on the lawn that I think must be a nightingale come over on the Cunard or White Star line." On Fitzgerald's use of Keat's poetry see, Richard L. Schoenwald, "F. Scott Fitzgerald as John Keats," *Boston University Studies in English*, 3 (Spring 1957), 12-21 and the essays by John Grube and William Doherty in Marvin J. LaHood, editor, *Tender is the Night: Essays in Criticism* (Bloomington, Indiana: Indiana University Press, 1969), pp. 179-189 and 190-206.

[16] The tea party at Nick's is in ironic contrast to Gatsby's carefully staged and "gorgeous" parties. That Gatsby had naively hoped Daisy would "wander into one of his parties, some night" and not only be dazzled by their wealth and brilliance but also see him under the most glamorous and flattering circumstances is quite obviously the fantasy of an imaginative seventeen year old. But Gatsby is seen at his very worst at Nick's party so that it is a kind of "anti-party" when compared to Gatsby's productions. Note too that Daisy, like the "two rows of brass buttons on her dress," is distinctly "brazen" when she goes over to Gatsby's house, exclaims at its "huge" size, takes up his brush "of pure dull gold" to smooth her hair, bursts into tears at the sight of Gatsby's shirts, and exclaims "you never told me you had a pomadour—or a yacht." Daisy is clearly captivated by Gatsby's conspicuous display of wealth.

[17] There is a minor reference to rain on p. 70 where Jordan Baker "left a borrowed car out in the rain with the top down, and then lied about it."

[18] Northrop Frye, *The Anatomy of Criticism* (Princeton: Princeton University Press, 1957), p. 78.

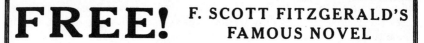

LOUIS K. GREIFF

PERFECT MARRIAGE
IN *Tender is the Night:*
A STUDY IN THE PROGRESS
OF A SYMBOL

In F. Scott Fitzgerald's *Tender Is the Night*, the union between Dick and Nicole Diver is a most complex human relationship and one, apparently, of considerable symbolic force. As a symbol, however, the Diver marriage yields up no single clear-cut meaning but rather suggests or implies a multitude of possibilities. Thus it has been studied from divergent points of view and given a wide variety of interpretations by critics of the novel. It has, for example, been seen as representing the defeat of a vital male at the hands of his wife, a selfish and typically destructive American child-bitch. From another standpoint, it has also been viewed as the surrender of imagination to money, the collapse of Dick Diver, in spite of all his talent, under the weight and pressure of the Warren millions.[1]

A less grim but perhaps more intriguing possibility is that the Diver marriage may be symbolic of something positive rather than destructive, even though it eventually ends in tragedy and failure. It involves, after all, a distinct union of opposites, and such a union always hints optimistically at synthesis or at the creation of some new and "higher" reality. More specifically, this key relationship in *Tender Is the Night* involves a coming into harmony, at least for a time, of two figures who reflect basically opposed value-systems and styles of life: the imaginative and idealistic, on one hand, and the

63

purely materialistic on the other.

Dick Diver, the husband in this improbable marriage, is Fitzgerald's idealistic spokesman. Ever the dreamer of perfection, he aspires " 'to be a good psychologist—maybe to be the greatest one that ever lived,' " and, in the thick of failure, refuses to abandon the unfinished (and unfinishable) book that he hopes some day will prove his worth.[2] Ever the imaginative creator as well, Dick maintains the delicate sanity of many of his friends by spinning bright illusions for them, illusions which successfully ward off despair. This, again, he persists in doing well past that point in the novel when his own life, like theirs, has begun to fall apart.

In contrast to her husband, Nicole Diver emerges as Fitzgerald's representative of the non-ideal or material realm. Her internal, imaginative, resources have never been strong, so that she comes to depend on Dick for the whole of her intellectual and emotional life. Rather than "spiritual," then, the assets which Nicole brings to her marriage are of the real or visible variety—her sexuality, her unique physical beauty, and, of course, her fortune.

Thus, when these two extreme beings join forces in *Tender Is the Night*, they seem to establish a symbolism, not of compromise nor of loss, but of transcendental aspiration. Brought into accord by marriage, Dick and Nicole Diver apparently stand for Fitzgerald's effort as a writer to reconcile the ideal with the real, to merge them through his central characters in the expectation that contrary elements will yield a new and perfected whole. Given such a "Romantic" approach to the Diver marriage, Fitzgerald's *Tender Is the Night* in its entirety can be viewed as a test of the human potential for ideal synthesis. By exposing his brave pair of opposites to the novel's many difficulties, that is, Fitzgerald seeks to determine whether "the higher reality" can actually come about in an imperfect world; likewise, he seeks to determine whether the original union itself can permanently endure.

If synthesis is, after all, what Fitzgerald is attempting through the Divers, then certainly he reveals his roots in the classical tradition of American literature. It immediately comes to mind, for example, that Whitman was also much concerned, in *Leaves of Grass*, with reality that had been suffused and elevated by the ideal. Yet it is Emerson, even more than Whitman, who appears to be Fitzgerald's literary ancestor with regard to this matter of union. In his key essay "Nature," especially, Emerson characterizes matter (designated by the terms "NATURE" or the "NOT ME") and spirit as the isolated halves of a perfect yet potentially attainable universe.[3] Throughout the work he calls for their merger as man's surest hope for his own redemption. "Nature [the essay announces] is made to conspire with spirit to emancipate us" (p. 28). Nearer to the close of Emerson's basic manifesto, he makes even more explicit his belief that the world's realities and the invisible ideal share one substance, and thus can be reconciled by an enlightened human race: "Man and woman and their social life, poverty, labor, sleep, fear, fortune, are known to you. Learn that none of these things is superficial, but that each phenomenon has its roots in the faculties and affections of the mind" (pp. 41-42).

Thus a hopeful Emersonian image is surely formed when Fitzgerald marries a beautiful and rich woman to an imaginatively wealthy man—when he unites, as he points out many times, the millionaire's daughter and the clergyman's son. The transcendental aspect of the Diver relationship is stressed yet more strongly by Fitzgerald's insistence, early in *Tender Is the Night*, that Dick and Nicole have not merely joined forces through matrimony but that they have fused into a single being. It is Rosemary Hoyt who first perceives their apparent synthesis during her initial encounter with them at the French Riviera: "—the only matter of importance to her now [Fitzgerald writes of Rosemary] was that in a few hours she would see the person whom she still referred to in her mind as 'the Divers' on the beach." A more touching detail, expressive of the same sense of transcendental merger, involves the names of Fitzgerald's principal characters. Since marriage, both Divers have written their signatures with the single word "Dicole," a composite of their two appellations which thus implies a oneness of being.

Beyond the suggestion of synthesis, Fitzgerald reveals a further Emersonian twist to the Diver relationship, and one, again, of surprising hopefulness. This is the fact that, by coming together, Dick and Nicole seem to bring into existence a vivid life for themselves, entirely different from what each had separately possessed before. Fitzgerald indicates that, at least temporarily, the Divers' marriage creates an altered world around them, one which generates great happiness, and one which even attracts outsiders who perceive it and are drawn to enter.

In elucidating this, it is again useful to turn to Emerson's "Nature" for the necessary transcendental point of reference. At the conclusion of that essay, Emerson apparently states in expository terms the very same thing that Fitzgerald dramatizes through his symbolic couple—namely, that the union of matter and spirit does indeed engender a heightened reality or bring about a re-created world. The substance of Emerson's final and climactic paragraph in "Nature," for example, reads as follows:

> Nature is not fixed but fluid. Spirit alteres, moulds, makes it. The immobility or bruteness of nature is the absence of spirit; to pure spirit it is fluid, it is volatile, it is obedient. Every spirit builds itself a house, and beyond its house a world, and beyond its world a heaven. Know then that the world exists for you. For you is the phenomenon perfect . . . .Build therefore your own world. As fast as you conform your life to the pure idea in your mind, that will unfold its great proportions. A correspondent revolution in things will attend the influx of the spirit . . . .so shall the advancing spirit create its ornaments along its path, and carry with it the beauty it visits and the song which enchants it; it shall draw beautiful faces, warm hearts, wise discourse, and heroic acts, around its way, until evil is no more seen (p. 42).

"Beautiful faces, warm hearts, wise discourse, and heroic acts"; do not Emerson's exact phrases seem to characterize the Diver milieu during those early, optimistic, days at Gausse's beach? It is then that Dick and Nicole, for a short while, build their own world in concert. And specifically, that world comes about as Dick applies his imaginative spirit to Nicole's material realm—the realm of society and of luxury—and thus elevates it, almost as an artist might, to beauty. Book 1 of Fitzgerald's *Tender Is the Night* is really a celebration of this shining Diver world, written, it seems to me, with no trace of the irony that a different author might provide it. To read Fitzgerald's early descriptions of the Divers, in other words, is to feel that he responds to their transcendent magic as deeply as do the fictional characters, within the novel, who surround them and pay them tribute. What follows, for example, is one of Fitzgerald's many sequences in Book 1 treating a "triumphant" Diver party. As it describes how Dick and Nicole, in their oneness, are able to raise all present to perfect emotional communion, it becomes not merely eloquent, but euphoric—exactly as did the above-quoted climax to Emerson's "Nature":

> . . .the two Divers began suddenly to warm and glow and expand, as if to make up to their guests, already so subtly assured of their importance, so flattered with politeness, for anything they might still miss from that country well left behind. Just for a moment they seemed to speak to every one at the table, singly and together, assuring them of their friendliness,

their affection. And for a moment the faces turned up toward them were like the faces of poor children at a Christmas tree. Then abruptly the table broke up—the moment when the guests had been daringly lifted above conviviality into the rarer atmosphere of sentiment, was over before it could be irreverently breathed, before they had half realized it was there.

But the diffused magic of the hot sweet South had withdrawn into them—the soft-pawed night and the ghostly wash of the Mediterranean far below—the magic left these things and melted into the two Divers and became part of them (p. 44).

In spite of such passages, however, Fitzgerald's euphoria is only temporary, as anyone knows who has read beyond Book 1 of *Tender Is the Night*. Equally temporary is his Emersonian faith in union; for although he is Romantic enough to create the hopeful symbol which unites spirit and reality, he is finally too modern to convince himself that it can succeed. Thus where Book 1 of Fitzgerald's novel celebrates the brave marriage of Dick and Nicole, at its peak of strength, Books 2 and 3 trace its destruction. More specifically, these later sections of *Tender Is the Night* confess that the ideal and the actual are not in fact made for synthesis—that they will inevitably begin resisting one another and pulling apart, until the glowing world created from their union has been split in two. The remainder of my present comments on *Tender Is the Night* will treat this developing failure within the Diver marriage and, thus, the process whereby Fitzgerald negates his own transcendental symbol, a symbol which at first he seemed so optimistically to proclaim.

The earliest indication within *Tender Is the Night* of disharmony between spirit and matter occurs, most aptly, as the beautiful party mentioned above comes to an end. Here, in particular, Fitzgerald provides his first shocking hint that Nicole Diver is insane. Nicole's mental distress, however, does not merely sound a crude warning that she is flawed and thus that her symbolic marriage must fail. Rather, the purposes behind creating a mad heroine, and the meanings implicit within her madness, are far more subtle in kind. By conceiving of one party to the transcendental marriage as insane Fitzgerald raises the possibility that such a marriage only occurs and endures under drastic conditions. In terms of the symbolism here under study, he raises the possibility that the real and the ideal only merge when one of those elements has become susceptible to its opposite through abnormality or distortion.

To test this "possibility" against the hard specifics of Fitzgerald's novel is indeed to discover its truth. Nicole Diver may be an ambassador of the actual within *Tender Is the Night*, but she is also an individual whose normal processes have been severely deranged. Her true materialistic nature, in short, has been undercut by the illusions of madness; and it is precisely those illusions, Fitzgerald implies, that have made her temporarily subject to other illusions—to the ideals, dreams, and constructs of Dick Diver's imaginative world. A more blunt way of putting this is to state that had Nicole Warren been in her right realistic mind from the first—had she been "a sane crook," as she later comes to call herself, instead of "a mad puritan"—her transcendental union with spirit could never have come about (p. 379).

Fitzgerald brings many of these issues to the surface in Book 2 of *Tender Is the Night* when, through flashback, he explores the Divers' odd initial courtship. Here he makes perfectly plain that Nicole encounters her future husband during the crisis of her illness, when delusion has obscured or collapsed the whole of her normal world. In a vacuum of experience, then, what Nicole desperately needs when she meets Dick is to have some sort of world built up around her once again. She is drawn to him, in particular, because he is clearly the perfect man to accomplish this rebuilding. Every inch the ideal psychiatrist, Dr. Diver is always willing to create imaginative constructs for those around him, willing to spin visions of perfect realms into which the desperate can fit themselves and feel secure.

In the light of all of this, it seems no mere accident that Fitzgerald has the Diver love-affair begin with an eight-month exchange of letters rather than with a more direct form of contact. By such a device, Fitzgerald is able to show that Nicole initially responds to the idealistic world-builder in Dick before she responds to the man. Since he is miles away from her, that is, neither his sexuality nor any of his physical attributes act to influence her toward union. Rather, this is all accomplished by imagination—the disembodied but powerful element in Dick's being which reaches Nicole through those letters, and which, in her darkest time, offers reassurance and the vision of sanity restored.

In general, then, Fitzgerald establishes Nicole's abnormality or deviation from "healthy" materialism as a requisite to the transcendental union. Because of this, her reattainment of complete sanity, which occurs late in Book 3 of *Tender Is the Night*, takes on a great deal of significance both with respect to her marriage to Dick, and with respect to the outcome of the novel as a whole. More specifically, a cured Nicole Diver is a "sane crook" once again—an independent realist no longer in need of visionary constructs and no longer even compatible with imagination or the ideal. A cured Nicole Diver, in other words, is a sure signal that the marriage of matter and spirit is about to come to an end and, thus, that the Emersonian symbol has failed.

Ironically, Fitzgerald makes Dick Diver himself the prime agent of Nicole's cure, showing in extreme detail how he expends more and more of his professional energy on her until finally she becomes his only patient. In spite of this sacrifice, however, once Nicole receives the gift of sanity from Dick, she shows herself to be very much Devereux Warren's daughter in her decisive and antithetical response to her husband's kind of world. "Returned to her senses" as a realist, she leaves Dick for another man in short order and thereby separates the amalgam of real and ideal back into its original, opposed, components. The following passage, then, represents a true "watershed moment" within *Tender Is the Night* since it depicts Nicole at the instant of cure, at the instant in which her symbolic bond with spirit becomes undone:

—Nicole relaxed and felt new and happy; her thoughts were clear as good bells—she had a sense of being cured and in a new way. Her ego began blooming like a great rich rose as she scrambled back along the labyrinths in which she had wandered for years. She hated the beach, resented the places where she had played planet to Dick's sun.

"Why, I'm almost complete," she thought. "I'm practically standing alone, without him." And like a happy child, wanting the completion as soon as possible, and knowing vaguely that Dick had planned for her to have it, she lay on her bed as soon as she got home and wrote Tommy Barban in Nice a short provocative letter (pp. 372-73).

By so reversing synthesis and splitting his symbolic couple through separation (and ultimately through divorce), Fitzgerald reveals the truly pessimistic statement at the heart of *Tender Is the Night*. The Great American Dream of union, he proclaims, is finally not to be realized; matter and spirit, instead of cohering, tend to fly apart, and thus to explode any "higher realm" created by their temporary connection.

Fitzgerald underscores his loss of faith in synthesis most heavily as his novel nears its close. For during the final chapters of *Tender Is the Night* he comes to insist that the real and the ideal don't merely separate, as their symbolic marriage ends, but that they polarize, thereby leaving no doubt as to their contrary and irreconcilable natures. In more specific terms, Fitzgerald indicates that, once apart, Nicole and Dick quickly return to opposite and mutually exclusive worlds, despite their many years of deceptive harmony together. While one Diver moves back to an environment of soul-denying materialism, that is, the other enters a purely disembodied realm very much in keeping with his own insubstantial essence, a realm so vague that it finally seems to suggest a counter-denial by spirit of external reality itself.

It is Nicole Diver, of course, who realigns herself with the materialistic world. This is signalled, for example, in the fact that she is joined by her sister, Baby Warren, immediately upon breaking with Dick. By comparison with Nicole, Baby is far more pure an arch-priestess of the real—all dollars and nerve-endings—so that any alliance with her automatically implies a more universal commitment to mammon.

Of more significance than Baby in this regard is Tommy Barban, the man singled out by Nicole to take Dick Diver's place. He most of all, and especially in contrast to Dick, represents the stark values that Nicole now embraces as her own. He supplants Dick's reflective nature, for example, with physical vitality and with a kind of unthinking primitivism. In an ugly twist, Fitzgerald shows that Tommy combines these traits with an ever-active passion for war, a passion which certainly seems to foreshadow the events that were about to engulf Europe just six years after the publication of *Tender Is the Night*. Nicole Warren's first and second husbands, then, are antithetical figures in all possible respects; and Tommy's clear-eyed animality, his passion, and his war-lust provide an accurate résumé of the world willfully chosen by Fitzgerald's heroine after her relationship with Dick. Simply, it is the world of hard facts, upon which Dr. Diver's magical and fanciful trick of "elevation" no longer seems to work.

If Nicole is so thrust into "Reality," once her transcendental marriage is shattered, then Dick is thrust into exactly the opposite sort of realm, and into a fate very revealing of Fitzgerald's sad pronouncement on matter and spirit. More precisely, Dick Diver enters a shadow world after splitting with Nicole and completely disappears as an active character in *Tender Is the Night*. To cancel Dick out, in this way, as the novel terminates is a stroke of genius on Fitzgerald's part; for it provides the hero with a final destiny which, like his wife's, perfectly fulfills the major symbolism of the work. All along, in other words, Dick has played the disembodied role, the role of imagination and idealism, in contrast to Nicole's more substantial nature. Now, as their unsuccessful union comes to an end, and as Nicole rejoins the one world suitable to her materialism, disappearance becomes Dick's only logical option, given his spiritual identity. Pure spirit, cut off from a real realm upon which to project itself, that is, necessarily becomes invisible and ceases in tangible terms to exist.

There is evidence within *Tender Is the Night* that Fitzgerald has anticipated Dick Diver's fate from the very start, that he has planned for his central character to "dissolve" upon being denied the solid basis of Nicole's social world. The following observation about Dick, for example, seems a direct foreshadowing of this; however, when it is made (back, near the very beginning of the novel's lyrical first book) virtually no reader can yet suspect that it will prove true:

But to be included in Dick Diver's world for a while was a remarkable experience: people believed he made special reservations about them, recognizing the proud uniqueness of their destinies, buried under the compromises of how many years. He won everyone quickly with an exquisite consideration and a politeness that moved so fast and intuitively that it could be examined only in its effect. Then, without caution, lest the first bloom of the relation wither, he opened the gate to his amusing world. So long as they subscribed to it completely, their happiness was his preoccupation, but at the first flicker of doubt as to its all-inclusiveness he evaporated before their eyes, leaving little communicable memory of what he had said or done (p. 35).

The prophetic fulfillment of this odd hint is not to come until much later—to be precise, until only three chapters before the end of *Tender Is the Night*. When it comes, though, it proves to be complete; in addition, its moment of occurrence proves to be both predictable, and identifiable to the very paragraph. Dick Diver "evaporates" before all our eyes, as has been made clear, in the instant that he cuts free of material reality by walking away from Nicole for the last time. During the passage which follows, Fitzgerald focuses upon this instant and, in the final sentence especially, leaves no doubt that it represents the symbolic vanishing-point for his champion of the ideal: "So it [the separation] had happened—and with a minimum of drama; Nicole felt outguessed, realizing that . . .-Dick had anticipated everything. But also she felt happy and excited, and the odd little wish that she could tell Dick all about it faded quickly. But her eyes followed his figure until it became a dot and mingled with the other dots in the summer crowd" (p. 401).

Soon after this important juncture, what remains of Dick is not even a dot in the summer crowd, but merely insubstantial words upon a page. The last traces of his being which Fitzgerald describes are the few letters he has written Nicole after their separation, letters which originate from progressively more obscure locations within New York State: Buffalo, Batavia, Lockport, Geneva, and finally Hornell.

That letters from America are the only remaining vestiges of Fitzgerald's hero, as the novel terminates, is a significant fact with regard to the particular symbolism under present study. In the first place, letters are the pure abstractions of a human being, reflecting his essence but not his flesh-and-blood reality. Hence they provide an appropriate device by which Fitzgerald can point to his hero, again at the close, as a symbol of the disembodied ideal. Also, letters allow Fitzgerald to end Dick's relationship with his wife as it began; for this correspondence from New York recalls an earlier one, also addressed to Nicole across long distances by the same phantom-presence.

A final observation to be made about Dick Diver's "parting words" is that they reach Nicole from the American Northeast, thus indicating that his destiny, at the end of *Tender Is the Night*, is somehow tied to that region. In particular, it seems an apt irony that Fitzgerald ultimately loses track of his hero not far from the birthplace of transcendentalism—not far from the source of the unifying dream itself, after that dream has been proved a failure by Dick's own example. Hornell, New York, the place where Dr. Diver's progression stops, might possibly have been selected by Fitzgerald at random. Yet the striking resemblance between the hills surrounding Hornell and those of New England seems significant.[4]

The chapter of *Tender Is the Night* devoted to Dick's last letters from America is the one with which Fitzgerald concludes his work. Yet, in a sense, a more decisive conclusion to the novel has occurred somewhat before this point, with respect to the problem of Emersonian unity. Specifically, Fitzgerald seems to give his final word on the matter back near the end of Book 2, in a sequence devoted to the funeral of Dick Diver's father. During that sequence, Dick returns to America from Europe at the news of his father's death. He accompanies the body from New York to Virginia where it will be buried, and, while at the grave-side, utters the following solitary and singular line: "'Good-by, my father—good-by, all my fathers.'"

This statement can be seen as the "true" conclusion to *Tender Is the Night* in that it provides a compelling terminal comment on the entire transcendental question and on the American Dream of union between reality and the ideal. Clearly, the sad farewell it makes is addressed not only to fathers by blood, but to cultural fathers as well—fathers, for example, of the national literary and philosophical traditions. In this sense, the words come directly from Fitzgerald himself, even though he "speaks" them through the mouth of his central character. They are the author's own farewell to the early optimistic fathers of his craft, and perhaps in particular to Emerson as foremost among them. At the same time, these words are Fitzgerald's farewell to the belief such fathers maintained in the oneness of matter and spirit, a belief he yearns to share with them, but then comes to reject as unworkable and, thus, as tragically untrue.

Alfred University

---

[1] Among other critical works, Kenneth Eble's *F. Scott Fitzgerald* (New York: Twayne, 1963) deals with the money issue within the Diver marriage, while Milton R. Stern's *The Golden Moment: The Novels of F. Scott Fitzgerald* (Urbana: Univ. of Illinois Press, 1970) explores the destructive effect of "the vastly attractive, powerful, energetic, voluptuously affluent Beautiful Bitch" upon Fitzgerald's hero (p. 326). A separate view of the union between Dick and Nicole Diver which brings together the sexual and financial themes is provided by D. S. Savage's article "The Significance of F. Scott Fitzgerald," reprinted in *F. Scott Fitzgerald: A Collection of Critical Essays*, ed. Arthur Mizener (Englewood Cliffs: Prentice-Hall, 1963), pp. 146-56. Other works giving particular attention to the Diver marriage are James E. Miller's *F. Scott Fitzgerald: His Art and His Technique* (New York: New York University Press, 1967), and Eugene White's "The 'Intricate Destiny' of Dick Diver," *Modern Fiction Studies*, 7(1961), 55-62. Both of these treatments stress the transfer of vitality and health from husband to wife during their relationship, with White's article interpreting this as a "deliberate choice" or self-sacrifice on Dick Diver's part (p. 55).

[2] F. Scott Fitzgerald, *Tender Is the Night* (New York: Scribners, 1934), p. 174. Future references to *Tender Is the Night* will appear in the text.

[3] In *The Complete Essays and Other Writings of Ralph Waldo Emerson*, ed. Brooks Atkinson (New York: Modern Library, 1950), p. 4. Future references to "Nature" will appear in the text.

[4] Clayton Mau, *The Development of Central and Western New York* (Dansville: F. A. Owen, 1958), pp. 67-73.

*M. Edgerton M. Sayre / To / 1st Lt. F. Scott Fitzgerald / 654th Infantry / Camp
Sherdian / For-get-me-not / Zelda / 9-13-18 / Montgomery, Ala.* Bruccoli Collection.

WILLIAM KATTERJOHN

AN INTERVIEW WITH
THEODORA GAGER,
FITZGERALD'S PRIVATE NURSE

Interviewer's Note

Miss Theodora Gager, a vivacious and high-spirited lady in her middle seventies, is a retired nurse who worked for over a decade at Johns Hopkins Hospital at Baltimore, Md., where her patients included F. Scott Fitzgerald and Clark Gable. She now resides in a converted stable at Henderson, Kentucky, a small-town community about one hundred and ten miles west of Louisville, on the banks of the Ohio River. Miss Gager daily walks to the Henderson Public Library where she engages the librarians and others interested in discussions centering around F. Scott Fitzgerald and the Jazz Age. She has an uncanny ability for recalling details of the days she served as Fitzgerald's nurse while he lived at "La Paix."

I first sought Miss Gager's company to discuss two Fitzgerald-autographed books she possessed and followed up that visit with another to talk about her working relationship with Fitzgerald. Occasional footnotes have been added, where facts conflict somewhat with the interview.

KATTERJOHN: Where did you first meet F. Scott Fitzgerald?

GAGER: One morning in February, 1932, I was called out to his

75

TENDER IS THE NIGHT

A ROMANCE

By

F. Scott Fitzgerald

DECORATIONS BY
EDWARD SHENTON

NEW YORK

CHARLES SCRIBNER'S SONS

1934

"For Gay ("gloom") Gager from the author F Scott Fitzgerald"

house, "La Paix." He came down to Baltimore and his wife entered Phipps Clinic at Johns Hopkins. The Fitzgeralds were renting the Bayard Turnbull house. I went to the door and knocked; it was a bright and sunny morning and I was struck by the beauty of the house because it was picturesque. Scottie, I think she was twelve, met me at the door. She was very gracious. She was a little girl who spoke French. She took me in and introduced me to her dad. He struck me as being a very handsome young guy, blond hair and blue eyes. A very beautiful face. He was easy to know and gracious and asked me to come on in. Here was this man trying to write with no money. He took to gin and that was his downfall; he was just ambitious in a literary way. Scottie then disappeared and Scott Fitzgerald's butler, Aquila, came up, and I'll never forget Scott's breakfast on that silver tray. Oh, he lived in style. At "La Paix," he never dressed up and always wore four sweaters. He had a tussle with TB one time and was deathly afraid of a recurrence. He was very casual in his manner and spent a lot of time in bed. He'd get up and wander around the house when he became restless. Everywhere he went, he'd have an encyclopedia, even in the bathroom on the john. He had a hunger for facts, for books. He hungered after knowing about things; he never stopped and this hunger or search was with him while I was on duty at La Paix. In most ways, he was a very ordinary man, sweet and appealing until he became intoxicated and then he was wild.

KATTERJOHN: Why did Fitzgerald require a nurse?

GAGER: I had to take his gin and cigarettes away from him, and he was terribly lonely, with Zelda in Phipps Clinic. At night he was a poor sleeper and would eventually get out of bed and wander about the house. On occasion, we would sit in the library, with me listening to him read the stories he was writing for *The Saturday Evening Post*; he got about $5,000 for each story. He would interrupt his reading and write a little, pleading with me to give him some more gin. The tension was great, because I was there to discipline the man and I admired him so. He would drink until he fell asleep.

KATTERJOHN: How long were you on duty as Scott's nurse?

GAGER: I was at La Paix for about a month, until Zelda came home. Scott spent something like $40,000 on her at Switzerland, just to get her well but to no avail. Zelda kept him financially strapped. He told me about her; it ruined his life.

KATTERJOHN: Was Scott sensitive toward other people?

GAGER: Yes. Very, in his dealings with other people.

KATTERJOHN: Did Scott adopt any names for you?

GAGER: Oh, when he was very happy, he would call me "Gaga" and when he was only moderately happy, he would call me "Gay" and then when he would drink and get depressed, he would say, "Gloom, come in here and let me read to you."

KATTERJOHN: What was your first impression of Scott?

GAGER: My first impression was that here was a brilliant young man drinking and going to the dogs. He needed help. And he really needed help. He was not the strongest man in the world. He was weak.

KATTERJOHN: When would Scott write?

GAGER: Whenever the mood struck him, day or night, and usually both. He wasn't writing a novel then, just short stories for the *Post*[1] I met his mother, too. He should have been a Catholic, but he veered away from the church and I can't hold that against him. He was the last of the Jazz Age. Night and day meant nothing to him. He would get up and wander around in the middle of the night, and if he was in the mood, he'd start to write. But he had his secretary, you know, and he would dictate to her. His secretary came out to "La Paix" every morning and worked there during the day. Scott always attracted worthwhile beings to him. I came out to the Turnbull house week after week and got to know Scott quite well. He'd have a thing about having his hair washed. He'd sit in front of the sink with those sweaters and towels, and I managed to do a good job of washing that beautiful blond hair. Oh, I kissed him. It wasn't anything; his mind didn't run that way. I was just a nurse to him and he thought I was pretty wonderful, and he kissed me several times. Oh, his breakfast consisted of two slices of buttered toast, a glass of orange juice, coffee—he was very particular about his coffee and two-and-a-half-minute boiled eggs. If the eggs were over or under, he'd send them back. I asked him why they had to be cooked to the minute, and he said, "That's the way I like them, but you'll never know why, Gaga!"

KATTERJOHN: He was writing short stories for *The Saturday Evening Post* at that time?

GAGER: Yes, and he was finding it more and more difficult to do all the time. And more difficult to sell them. His mind was sort of . . .he wasn't too popular at that time; he was an alcoholic.

KATTERJOHN: Did he say why the stories were getting more and more difficult to write?

GAGER: No. But I could realize that he felt it very keenly. But he wasn't up to par.

KATTERJOHN: He thought so himself?

GAGER: He did. He realized he wasn't up to par. He was grabbing for straws and thought he was sinking under the influence of liquor. And Zelda was like a ball and chain around his neck.

KATTERJOHN: Did Scott mostly typewrite?

GAGER: He wrote with a pencil on big yellow paper. His handwriting wasn't great.

KATTERJOHN: Could Scott work well without drinking?

GAGER: No. Zelda and Scott, when they were at "La Paix," were very uncomfortable with each other. They didn't communicate.

KATTERJOHN: Did Scott ever test any of his characters on you?

GAGER: Occasionally he would read them to me. He'd say, "What do you think, Gaga?" And I'd say, "Well, listen, I just think you're wonderful." But that was his specialty, that was his line, he would tell me, putting words down onto paper. He just ruined his life drinking. See, he wanted to grow up in the world. He wanted to make a name for himself. I think like Edgar Allan Poe. He was a great man. People felt so darned sorry for him. He drank, didn't he?

KATTERJOHN: Did Scott and Zelda live in the same part of "La Paix" when Zelda came home from Phipps Clinic?

GAGER: They didn't communicate with each other. She had her bedroom; it was to the back of the house and she had a nurse. It was tragic. And of course Scottie would come home and see this. And one time he was drunk and I saw him throw an inkwell at that child. He would make up to her and she would say she understood. And she did; she was a wonderful child. He was very ambitious for her; he wanted her to be bright and smart and make a good marriage and do all things that girls do.

KATTERJOHN: When Scott wrote in bed, what would he do to break the routine?

GAGER: He would write for about an hour and then he would throw the sheets onto the floor and I would pick them up for him. He couldn't concentrate for more than an hour or two at the most and then he would get up from the bed and go walking. Occasionally, he would go down to the kitchen and pick around on the floor. And then he would go outside and walk. He was melancholy and moody.

KATTERJOHN: Did Scott ever express which of his books or short stories were his favorites?

GAGER: He told me he thought *This Side of Paradise* would put him down in literary history.

KATTERJOHN: While you were on duty at "La Paix," who were some of Scott's visitors?

GAGER: He didn't have any visitors at "La Paix." Scott Fitzgerald was sort of a loner.

KATTERJOHN: Did Scott write to many people while you were on duty?

GAGER: No, he didn't. He wasn't able to unless his secretary took that over and did it for him. I know that he had an old automobile and his butler's name was Aquila. Aquila was an old-fashioned Negro, elderly at the time. Scott Fitzgerald took Luminol at the time. That's a type of phenobarbital. When he got, what do you call it, soused? Well, when he got that way, he would take some wild smelling stuff.[2] Anyway, would he smell! He wanted to down it, anything to go to sleep. He wanted to go to sleep. He liked sleep. He wanted to get away from things. He was running.

KATTERJOHN: From whom or what was he running?

GAGER: Himself. And his bitternesses and disappointments and most of it was due to his wife, I think. The utter disillusionment that came over the marriage when they were so young. She just worried the socks off him when she was around. He couldn't stand it, for her to be around.

KATTERJOHN: Did Scott have any girlfriends he mentioned?

GAGER: Oh, no. He didn't. At "La Paix," he managed to get gin in a demijohn. I think it held two gallons. He drank it straight and he drank it not because he liked it, but because it soothed him. You see, it was a fool's paradise. It made him, for the time being, feel better. I said to him one time, "Aren't you afraid you'll get cirrhosis of the liver?" And he'd say, "Oh, Gaga, I don't think about that."

KATTERJOHN: Did Scott mention Ernest Hemingway while at "La Paix?"

GAGER: Yes, he did. He said he thought he was in Ernest's class. He generally didn't talk about people. That was a beautiful turn about him. Scott would try to get ahead, but he got himself mixed up with liquor. That was the downfall of his life, really. He'd be living today . . . I last heard from him in 1934.

KATTERJOHN: How often did you see or meet Scott after you left his duty?

GAGER: Not often. You see, after Zelda left Phipps, he got an apartment on Park Avenue. It's not like Park Avenue in New York. It's a modest street, strictly residential and high grade. But in 1934, I began to see him less and less. Sometimes, he would come down to the hospital and sit in the dispensary just to get material to write about. He had a thing about hospital life; he liked it. He would watch the patients that came in, because it was a different life and he wanted to get right down to how their lives were, their sadnesses and their joys. He knew all phases of life; he had seen it all.

KATTERJOHN: Did Scott have occasion to meet Clark Gable while at "La Paix?"

GAGER: I don't think . . .wait, it was back in 1939, that I knew Clark Gable. I used to give him occasional back massages. He said I was a darned good back-rubber. He was just down-right he-mannish. One night I tried to help put his pajamas on and he said, "Miss Gager don't you know it's wonderful to sleep without pajamas on?" I told him I would just take his word for it. He slept in the nude, that's all I know about him.

KATTERJOHN: Who did the Fitzgerald family cooking while at La Paix?

GAGER: Aquila. He was the family's cook, butler, and chauffeur.

KATTERJOHN: What was Scott's favorite meal?

GAGER: Breakfast. You see, by this time he had had some sleep and needed his bacon and eggs. That silver tray was really handsome. He lived in style. I remember about his eggs, two-and-one-half-minutes . . .I didn't time the eggs, Aquila did. When they would come up, if they weren't just right, Scott would send them back down. Then, I would try my hand and take them back upstairs to Scott and tell him, "Now, Scott, I've timed them by my watch." Oh, he was sweet, but no one would have married the man; he was too wild, too disconnected, too disjointed. And he was spasmodic.

KATTERJOHN: What kind of relationship did Scottie and Zelda have with each other?

GAGER: You mean mother and child? Oh, nothing. She was her father's child. Scott always had her interest at heart, and looked after her.

KATTERJOHN: Did Scott ever mention wanting to get a divorce from Zelda?

GAGER: No, no. Never. He never mentioned it. Oh, I think he did on one occasion.

KATTERJOHN: Did Scott mention why he was so loyal to Zelda when she had apparently caused him so much anguish?

GAGER: Oh, he had high ideals. I think his idea of disrupting the marriage and getting a divorce and marrying someone else wasn't his style of life. He would say that he'd rather their marriage last. He wasn't too virile a man. You know some men just live for sex, but Scott Fitzgerald didn't. I could see that distinction.

KATTERJOHN: Why did you cease being Scott's nurse?

GAGER: He was going to move to town (the apartment on Park Avenue, Baltimore) and he was going to Asheville, North Carolina.

KATTERJOHN: At the time you left La Paix, do you remember what project Scott was working on?

GAGER: He was still writing those stories for *The Saturday Evening Post* and getting less and less for them, and he was less good at writing them. That broke his heart. He said he was mortally humiliated. He just couldn't think of the words to say; he said he couldn't pull himself together. That's what made him so sad.

KATTERJOHN: What type of books did Scott read?

GAGER: Classics; he had about 500 volumes in his library. He'd have a hunger for the nicer things that were written. He did not have a dirty, low, down-in-the-mud mind. He just wasn't that type. Scott had trouble sitting and staying quiet long enough to read a novel. He'd read mostly encyclopedias and he didn't dress up much. He wore an old shirt and a couple of mufflers around his neck and he'd shave anytime during the day that the mood struck him. The front room at "La Paix" opened up into a bathroom. He'd go in there and say, "Gaga, don't you want to wash my hair again?" And I told him, "I just washed it yesterday, but if you like, here we go!"

KATTERJOHN: Have you heard from Scottie since your tenure at La Paix?

GAGER: No, no. Listen, nurses ran in and out of their lives. He had about half a dozen nurses while at "La Paix," and we would compare notes, and he didn't ever make a mad dash for any of us.

KATTERJOHN: How would you contain Scott when he had been drinking?

GAGER: It wasn't hard. He wasn't brutal. He was very easy to manage. I'd take him by his arm and we'd walk a bit. And I'd put compresses on his head. And I'd rub his back. And I did everything I could in a legitimate way to help him quiet down because I felt sorry for him. He'd like compresses on his head. He didn't wear glasses, and he had all of his teeth. He had nice habits, but when he was sober, he would say, "Gaga, couldn't I have a drink?" And I said, "Well, we'll shove it (the drinking timetable) up a few minutes; will that make you feel better?"

KATTERJOHN: Did Zelda speak to you often?

GAGER: She didn't like me, and I didn't like her. I was a nurse and she didn't like nurses. Here was a man who should have been at the prime of life, but he wasn't interested in that sort of thing. The last day I worked for Scott Fitzgerald, he gave me a five-dollar gold piece and said, "Gaga, save this in case you're ever broke."

---

[1] Work on *Tender Is The Night*, is believed to have started in either June or July 1932.
[2] Probably paraldehyde, a sedative.

Fitzgerald and Cornelius Vanderbilt, Jr. judging a Woodbury soap beauty contest in 1929. John Barrymore was the third judge.

"THE CAMEL'S BACK"
AND *Conductor 1492*

During the summer of 1973, at the Museum of Modern Art in New York, I attended a screening of *Conductor 1492*, a film whose existence many Fitzgerald buffs have wondered about. In his *Ledger*, Fitzgerald had indicated that he had sold the rights of "The Camel's Back" to Warner Brothers and that the film's title was *Conductor 1492*. But searches over the years of reviews and film indexes failed to show any connection between the film and the short story. Reviews suggested a plot completely different from the original story and none of the indexes linked the novelist with the film. Fortunately, one film collector had retained a copy of *Conductor 1492* and, in 1973, loaned it to the Museum for its Warner Brothers' retrospective.

Conductor 1492, a 1924 comedy-drama, was directed by Charles Hines and Frank Hines; the story was credited to Johnny Hines. In the film that I viewed, there was no mention of Fitzgerald or "The Camel's Back." The cast featured Johnny Hines as Terry O'Toole, an Irish immigrant who becomes a trolley conductor and eventually marries his wealthy boss's daughter. O'Toole's father some years before had purchased two shares in the company. When the present owner vies with another faction for control of the company, O'Toole comes up with the missing stock. Minor plot incidents include

O'Toole, early in the film, saving the life of the owner's young son, and, later, saving his own father in a fire.

What does all this have to do with "The Camel's Back"? Actually, very little. At one point in the film Johnnie confronts a drunk going to a roller skating carnival and costume ball and the two go in a camel's costume, Johnnie in the front, the drunk in the rear. The camel dances and roller skates, generally entertaining the crowd. But the scene is merely a comic interlude and is interrupted when a shady character shows up with some counterfeit stock which is to be used to enable the opposition to control the trolley company. Other than this scene, there is no similarity between the film and the short story. Terry is not jilted at first by his sweetheart as is Perry Parkhurst at the beginning of "The Camel's Back." And there is no mock wedding that turns out to be the real thing as occurs at the ending of Fitzgerald's story. The similarity begins and ends with two men in a camel costume going to a masquerade—and even the two parties are different.

John Jay College of Criminal
Justice—CUNY

WILLIAM GOLDHURST

THE *F.Scott Fitzgerald and His Contemporaries* CORRESPONDENCE

During the years 1959-62 I was involved in the process of researching and writing my dissertation—a study of F. Scott Fitzgerald, with an emphasis on the personal and professional relationships he had had with literary friends. The main thesis was that vibrations from these friendships eventually left their mark on his fiction, the cases in point being Fitzgerald's associations with Edmund Wilson, H. L. Mencken, Ring Lardner, and Ernest Hemingway.

Early in the project I had written to Wilson and others for information about FSF; after the dissertation was completed and had been accepted for publication by World, I wrote to a number of Fitzgerald's associates and other individuals asking for permission to quote letters and other materials; and finally, after the book appeared I had World send copies to persons I assumed would be interested, several of whom wrote me their impressions. Thus I acquired correspondence in three stages: letters answering queries, letters denying or granting permission to quote, and letters expressing a reaction to what I had written.

I must immediately dispel the notion that this is a rich or extensive collection. In the first phase I received one short letter from Edmund Wilson, one short letter from Thornton Wilder, one short letter from Charles Angoff (who had been Mencken's friend and editorial assistant back in the days of the *American Mercury*), a letter from Burroughs Mitchell at Scribner's, and full and detailed letters from two critics, Henry Dan Piper and Maxwell Geismar. In the second stage I received replies from T. S. Eliot, John O'Hara, Thornton Wilder, Gilbert Seldes, Arthur Mizener, Glenway Wescott, Harold Ober, and John Dos Passos. In the third phase I received letters from Edmund Wilson, Mark Schorer, and Mrs. James Branch Cabell. In addition, there are a few items that fall outside these categories, such as a note from Norman Mailer about Ring Lardner, a note from Malcolm Cowley about the sale of Lardner's works at Viking; a letter from Anne Louise Davis informing me of the sudden death of Harold Ober, a brief good-luck letter from Arnold Gingrich, whom I had interviewed at the *Esquire* offices, and a lengthy letter from a graduate student concerning a claim I had made about influences on *The Great Gatsby*. There is also a migraine-producing empty envelope from Edmund Wilson, addressed to me at the University of Puerto Rico (where I taught for three years) and postmarked October 7, 1962 from Boonville, N.Y., the contents of which will remain forever a mystery. Though I have no recollection whatever of what Wilson wrote me on that occasion, possibly his letter contained the information that Zelda had written *This Side of Paradise* and that Maxwell Perkins had served as the model for Hemingway's hero in *To Have and Have Not*.

By any standards this is a minor collection, especially since a few of the letters say little more than sorry, I can't answer your questions; or yes, you may quote me; or no, you may not quote me. On the other hand, I find that I am impressed with this collection of correspondence, however modest it may be, and this for three reasons. First, I had no intention of accumulating a correspondence, but simply sent out stray inquiries as the need arose; considering this casual approach, the returns were substantial. Secondly, scattered throughout the collection are comments, remarks, and recollections that will be of genuine interest to scholars. Thirdly, I am still surprised that I got any replies at all to my letters of inquiry.

In any case, on the assumption that students of Fitzgerald's life and works will appreciate clues to the content of the collection, until such time as they might peruse it at Princeton Library, I shall very briefly summarize what appear to me to be the high points of interest in the correspondence.

The first letter in the collection is from Maxwell Geismar, whom I knew personally and to whom I had written spelling out some of my confusions. Geismar suggested that I adopt a "literary and personal" approach to influences on FSF, which is eventually the emphasis I chose to pursue in my research. Geismar also recommended that I read the novels of Edith Wharton and Henry James for their influence, early and late, on FSF. Dan Piper suggested that Fitzgerald's greatest period of "literary companionship" occurred during and immediately following his years at Princeton. Piper also pointed out specific influences on all of Fitzgerald's novels, from *This Side of Paradise* to *The Last Tycoon*. Edmund Wilson's first letter contains brief references to Fitzgerald's relationships with H. L. Mencken and George Jean Nathan. The letter from Charles Angoff describes the same relationships and adds the information that Nathan had little respect for Fitzgerald's writing ability. The first letter from Thornton Wilder pooh-poohs the idea that he had any influence on FSF and further states that Wilder's meetings with FSF were too "shadowed" by Zelda's illness to permit much shop-talk. Burroughs Mitchell describes the poor sales of Lardner's works and the great demand for Fitzgerald's. All these letters are from the period 1959-1961.

The first letter from the second stage of operations was a TLS from John O'Hara denying permission to quote a letter he had written FSF in 1935. O'Hara says that some years back he got tired of giving out interviews about FSF, and letters fall into the same category at interviews. The T. S. Eliot letter, typed by a secretary on Faber & Faber stationery, grants permission to use a quotation about an early FSF novel and adds that it would be interesting if I would reprint the letter Eliot wrote FSF in 1925 in praise of *The Great Gatsby*. In the margin Eliot has added a hand-written comment to the effect that the letter to FSF has been reprinted in *The Crack-Up*, published by New Directions. The letter from Glenway Wescott is hand-written and grants me permission to use part of the Wescott essay "The Moral of F. Scott Fitzgerald" and asks me to pay attention to the proper spelling of Wescott. The Gilbert Seldes TLS grants permission to quote a letter he wrote to Tristan Tzara introducing Scott and Zelda. Seldes adds information about how he met FSF and how he rated him very low in a poll conducted by the editors of *Vanity Fair* magazine. The Dos Passos reply is written in the margin of one of my typescript pages; it grants permission to quote from a letter Dos Passos wrote FSF following publication of "The Crack-Up" in *Esquire* in 1935. The TLS from Arthur Mizener grants me permission to quote anything at all from *The Far Side of Paradise*. The second letter from Thornton Wilder is an ALS and grants me permission to quote from an early letter Wilder wrote FSF. Wilder adds that he is at present astonished at his "impertinence" in condescending to the authors mentioned in the letter—e.g., Edith Wharton and Sinclair Lewis. All the letters in this second category are dated various months in 1962.

The year following, after the book appeared, Mrs. James Branch Cabell wrote me from Richmond that she found my literary analysis well done and interesting. Mark Schorer, the biographer of Sinclair Lewis, wrote that I had been too literal in my interpretation of his comments on Fitzgerald's Hollywood decline (I had quoted a sentence about Fitzgerald's last years from Schorer's book). He added that he had heard Ramon Guthrie react rather negatively to Budd Schulberg's treatment of Fitzgerald's trip to Dartmouth.

The second Wilson TLS informed me that he had read my book and wished to correct some errors I had made. These concerned details of the FSF-George Jean Nathan friendship and my conclusions about Wilson's view of *The Vegetable*. Wilson added that "The Rich Boy" was written before FSF met Hemingway and thus could not have been influenced, as I had claimed, by an early draft of *The Sun Also Rises*.[1] Wilson ends on a curious note of regret, saying that Fitzgerald's literary friends confused him and diverted him from his original intentions. Michael Bell, a graduate student at Yale, wrote to the effect that his research confirmed and reinforced my thesis that Ring Lardner's story "A Caddy's Diary" had influenced elements in *The Great Gatsby*.

The prizes of the collection, if they may be so called without exaggeration, are the T. S. Eliot letter—for the signature and the marginal comment, representing a moment's extra effort which indicates a still active interest in FSF some twenty years after his death; the first Wilder letter, suggesting by its tone of complete honesty that he was writing to an old friend; the Gilbert Seldes letter, containing heart-felt nostalgia for the period dominated by FSF; and the second Wilson letter with its melancholy and totally unexpected closing comment.

When I was in the early throes of my research in the summer of 1959 I interviewed Budd Schulberg at Princeton and asked him to sign my copy of *What Makes Sammy Run?* On the flyleaf of that novel Schulberg wrote "Good luck with your adventure into the sad and brilliant world of FSF." With great accuracy Schulberg had foreseen that my research project would be an adventure into the 1920's (from which I have never properly emerged), and that letters written to me many years after the death of FSF would reflect a world that was both sad and brilliant.

University of Florida

---

[1] Wilson is confused about his chronology here. FSF met Ernest Hemingway in the spring of 1925 and was still revising the ms of "The Rich Boy" in mid-summer of the same year. See *The Letters of F. Scott Fitzgerald*, edited Andrew Turnbull (New York: Scribner's, 1963), p. 179; also *As Ever, Scott Fitz-*, edited Matthew J. Bruccoli (New York: Lippincott, 1972), pp. 77-80. The influence of EH on FSF at this point, though conjectural, is still possible. For a full discussion see pp. 156-165, *F. Scott Fitzgerald and His Contemporaries* (New York: World, 1963).

AS NEVER BEFORE THERE IS A NEED FOR GOOD BOOKS WRITTEN & PRINTED IN GOOD FAITH AND IN GOOD TASTE

THE PRAGMATIC TEST by H. B. Parkes. Essays on the history of ideas by the author of "Marxism: An Autopsy." $3.00

THE HELMSMAN by J. V. Cunningham. The second of the Poetry Booklets. Limited to three hundred copies. $1.50. Fifty signed special bound copies: $3.00

Coming

THE GRAND PIANO or *The Almanac of Alienation*. A surrealistic novel written by Paul Goodman.

NOTE-BOOKS OF NIGHT. Lyrics and satire by Edmund Wilson.

THE CRACK-UP. Autobiography and letters by F. Scott Fitzgerald with critical appraisals by T. S. Eliot, Paul Rosenfeld, John Peale Bishop, Glenway Westcott, and John Dòs Passos.

POEMS by Hugh MacDiarmid. The first American edition of the great modern Scotch poet.

Colt, Current and Choice

THE WIFE OF MARTIN GUERRE by Janet Lewis. Decorations by Valenti Angelo. "A fascinating tale told with restraint and beauty," Joseph Henry Jackson. Trade edition: $2.50. Limited edition, hand colored, signed by author and illustrator: $5.00

THE COLOSSUS OF MAROUSSI by Henry Miller. The author of "Tropic of Cancer" writes magnificently on modern Greece. $3.50

THE BOYS IN THE BACK ROOM by Edmund Wilson. Essays on O'Hara, Fitzgerald, Saroyan, Steinbeck, and others. Trade edition: $2.50. Limited special bound, signed edition: $5.00

 ## *The* COLT PRESS
617 MONTGOMERY : SAN FRANCISCO

31 January 1942. The Colt Press edition of *The Crack-Up* was not published.

STERLING K. EISIMINGER

GATSBY'S BLUFF AND FITZGERALD'S BLUNDERS

Fitzgerald encountered several problems in creating Jay Gatsby, not the least of which was his character's credibility. After Gatsby lies about his place of birth and background, readers have a difficult time accepting the truth of Gatsby's other autobiographical claims. But Fitzgerald intended for his readers to accept the fact that Gatsby served with the Seventh Infantry, that he was a decorated hero, and that he did attend Oxford for five months after the war where he met the future Earl of Doncaster.

Several days after the party at which Nick met Gatsby, and after Nick has heard several mysterious rumors about his neighbor, Gatsby takes Nick to lunch. Driving into New York City, Gatsby promises to tell Nick the "God's truth" about himself because as Nick deduces, he is "aware of the bizarre accusations that flavored conversations in his halls." Gatsby then lies about his place of birth, his family's status, his family's tradition of attending Oxford, the death of his parents, and his enormous inheritance which permitted him to live like royalty, but the identity of the young man standing on his left in the photograph that Gatsby says was taken in Trinity Quad in 1919 is meant, I think, to be the truth. The young man is identified by Gatsby as one who between 1919 and 1922 became the Earl of Doncaster. Between 1919 and 1922, however, no English peer

95

succeeded to this title. In fact, The Most Noble Sir John Charles Montague-Douglass-Scott, K. T., Seventh Duke of Buccleuch, who also sits as the Earl of Doncaster, was at the time fifty-five years old, father of eight children, and a former member of parliament.[1] This distinguished gentlemen did have two heirs: Walter John and Lord William Walter, who were twenty-five and twenty-three years old respectively in 1919. Either of these young men could have been standing on Gatsby's left in the photograph, but as late as 1929, John Charles was still alive and still the Earl of Doncaster. More than likely this discrepancy is Fitzgerald's error, not Gatsby's, because we know Fitzgerald intended Gatsby's war exploits and decorations to be legitimate, and there is every reason to think Fitzgerald intended Gatsby's friendship with the young English aristocrat to be legitimate.

Another curiousity which I feel is Fitzgerald's mistake is the relation between the Duke of Buccleuch, to whom Nick believes he may be distantly related ("we have a tradition that we're descended from the Dukes of Buccleuch"), and the Earl of Doncaster. The Duke of Buccleuch simultaneously held the title of Earl of Doncaster since before the eighteenth century.[2] (Interestingly, the second Earl of Doncaster was Francis Scott, the Duke of Buccleuch.) Gatsby, of course, has no idea Nick may be descended from the Buccleuchs; and Nick apparently has no idea that the Duke of Buccleuch sits as the Earl of Doncaster, or he would have realized the coincidence. Since really nothing is gained on Fitzgerald's part by manufacturing this relationship, I feel sure it was not intended.

In the same vein is the apparent error involving the Montenegrin *Orderi de Danilo* medal that Gatsby shows Nick. The actual medal cannot be inscribed on either side because of its ceramic coating, yet Nick reads the inscription, "Major Jay Gatsby, For Valour Extraordinary."[3] Fitzgerald apparently chose the name of the medal for its exotic connotations unaware that it could not be engraved. In fact, he wrote to Maxwell Perkins in December of 1924 asking " . . .whether a courtesy decoration given to an American would bear an English inscription . . . ." His description of the medal he felt sounded "horribly amateurish."[4] Clearly, Fitzgerald intended his readers to accept the validity of Gatsby's war heroics. Though Fitzgerald specifically requested Perkins to answer all of his questions, no answer to the medal query has been found.

Finally, there is the matter of Gatsby's war record, which sounds suspiciously like Sgt. Alvin York's. York led a group of men in

Badge of the Order of Danilo I: Gatsby's medal from "little Montenegro down on the Adriatic Sea!" Bruccoli Collection.

advance of the allied lines in the Battle of the Argonne Forest, captured or killed all of a German machine-gun battalion virtually single-handedly, was awarded among other things the Montenegrin war medal, and was promoted to sergeant. York, however, was an instant celebrity; *The New York Times* included over twenty-five articles about him between 1919 and 1925. If Gatsby did all he said he did, his war exploits would certainly have been known. Fitzgerald erred when he made Gatsby a great hero and then expected the reader to believe that no one knew about him.

To be sure, these are minor discrepancies, and they do not detract from the greatness of the book, the title character, or the author. Fitzgerald wanted his reader to believe that Gatsby was a war hero with an Oxford background to substantiate his romantic stature and moral greatness, but several minor errors cause Gatsby to look more dishonest than he is. If we regard the errors as Fitzgerald's, however, the fictional hero emerges unscathed.

Clemson University

---

[1] Arthur Charles Fox-Davies, ed., *Armorial Families: A Directory of Gentlemen of Coat-Armour* (Rutland, Vermont: Tuttle, 1970), II, 1380.

[2] George Edward Cokayne, Vicary Gibbs, et. al., eds., *The Complete Peerage of England, Scotland, Ireland, Great Britain, and the United Kingdom* (London: St. Catherine's, 1936), II, 367.

[3] An example of the medal is in the collection of Matthew J. Bruccoli.

[4] John Kuehl and Jackson R. Bryer, eds., *Dear Scott/Dear Max: The Fitzgerald-Perkins Correspondence* (New York: Scribners, 1971), p. 90.

RICHARD LAYMAN

FITZGERALD
AND
HORACE McCOY

In a letter to New American Library editor Victor Weybright dated 16 April 1948 Horace McCoy, Hollywood screenwriter and author of *They Shoot Horses, Don't They?*, listed his literary debts, concluding:

> Scott Fitzgerald influenced me too, not in my writing, but in my behavior and understanding of people. He was a fine human being, a sweet and wonderful guy—and of all the people who have been in my life and now are gone I think probably I miss him the most.[1]

There is virtually no record of the relationship between McCoy and Fitzgerald; and McCoy's reputation for bolstering his own accomplishments and exaggerating his acquaintances compromises his credibility. But there is some evidence to support McCoy's claims of friendship with Fitzgerald, for in 1939 Fitzgerald was working on a script at Paramount where McCoy was under contract. In February 1973 Sotheby Parke-Bernet Galleries auctioned a presentation copy of *All the Sad Young Men* to Horace McCoy inscribed: "Paramount, 1939";[2] and Lawrence D. Stewart quotes the inscription in a Modern Library reprint of *Gatsby* Fitzgerald presented to McCoy in 1939:

> From Scott Fitzgerald
> (Of doom a herald),
> For Horace McCoy
> (No harbinger of joy)[3]

How close was the relationship between Fitzgerald and McCoy? Does it deserve more examination?

University of South Carolina

---

[1] John Thomas Sturak, "The Life and Writings of Horace McCoy, 1897-1955," Unpub. Diss.; UCLA, 1966, p. 394, n. 76.

[2] Sale Number 68, item 214.

[3] "Scott Fitzgerald D'Invilliers," *American Literature*, 29 (May 1958), 212.

INTERVIEW WITH ALLEN TATE

On 6 March 1973 Allen Tate received the University of South Carolina Award for Distinction in Literature. This interview was recorded at that time, and the transcription has been corrected by Mr. Tate.

M.J.B.

BRUCCOLI: You wrote splendidly about Hemingway in your *Prose** article. Did you have any kind of connection with Fitzgerald?

TATE: I didn't know him as well.

BRUCCOLI: But you did see him in Paris or America?

TATE: A couple of times in New York, but my acquaintance with Scott Fitzgerald was limited really to about four months in 1929 in Paris—in the fall of '29.

BRUCCOLI: That was the bad period while Zelda Fitzgerald was experiencing her breakdown.

*"Miss Toklas' American Cake," *Prose*, III (1971), 137-161.

TATE: Yes, she was going off badly at that time, although I didn't know—only their more intimate friends knew that. I didn't know until later because I hadn't known her before, and couldn't see the difference. But Scott was a very appealing character, I liked him very much. He was warm-hearted and—well, I liked him better than I liked Ernest, although Ernest was wonderful company. Did I write anything in my article about the bicycle races? He came by my hotel one Sunday morning, it must have been late September. He said, "Come on and go to the bicycle races." I said, "Hell, no." I said I liked football. Well, he persuaded me, and so I went every Sunday with him for about three months. I got to be an afficianado in bicycle racing. I was won over by his enthusiasm.

BRUCCOLI: Was this the actual bicycle racing or that sport of pacing he got interested in? Of the man bicycling behind a wind screen?

TATE: There were different forms. I liked that, the demi-bond; it is the most brutal of all and the most dangerous. If the man on the bicycle fell away from the motorcycle, he could get killed. I liked that best.

BRUCCOLI: That is the one he took you to?

TATE: Every Sunday and they had sprints and all kinds of races including the demi-bond.

BRUCCOLI: Donald Ogden Stewart speaks rather bitterly about being dragged to the bicycle races by Hemingway.

TATE: I liked it.

BRUCCOLI: Don said that when Hemingway said come to the bicycle race, you went.

TATE: He was such a strange fellow, you know, in those days. I could never reconcile the later public image with the Hemingway I knew. I remember early in 1930, in January, John Bishop and I went by to see him; he lived down in the rue Ferou—near where I lived in the Place de l'Odeon. *A Farewell to Arms* had just been out a few months. As we were leaving, he called down the stairs and said, "Wait a minute, I want to ask you something. The BBC has asked me to give a broadcast about *A Farewell to Arms*. Do you think it would violate the integrity of the writer to do that?" Four or five years later he was having his picture taken in bed and published in *Look* magazine. What had happened to him? But he went to drinking, you know—the sort of heroic drinking he was famous for. But I never saw him take anything stronger than a glass of dry vermouth. He worked all the time. He'd go off on weekends some place or other. He'd go skiing. One thing I didn't put in my memoir—this is hearsay, so I left it out: John and Katie Dos Passos were to arrive in about a week; so Ernest said, "Come on, you and Caroline come on and go to Switzerland with us and go skiing." I said, "I can't ski. I was brought up in a part of the country that had almost no snow. I can't do it." John Bishop later told me, "It would have been very interesting if you had gone because Ernest always stays on top of the hill with the ladies . . . ."

BRUCCOLI: Can you recall how you first met Fitzgerald?

TATE: Yes, I didn't have that in my article, did I? The Fitzgeralds I think came to Paris in October and the Hemingways had been there for sometime. I first met Ernest in Sylvia Beach's Bookshop in September. Well, anyhow, Margaret Bishop was going to have a dinner party and said the Fitzgeralds were back and she was going to have a party. I can't remember all the people who were there. Pierre le Lanux—Lanux was the first Frenchman to write about the southern states of this country. A book called *Sud*, a very interesting book. Anyhow, a party of 8 to 10 people. And I said to John Bishop, "Where are the Fitzgeralds? You said they were coming." He said, "Never mind, they'll be here; they're always late." Well, they came in and Scott went at once to the kitchen. Zelda came in and was introduced around. She was very charming. She said, "You must have danced with me at Sewanee." I said, "No, that's impossible. I was at the carpetbag institution, Vanderbilt, 80 miles away." She was a prom-trotter. And still Scott didn't appear. He was in the kitchen. So I thought I'd ask John Bishop.

"He's hiding his bottle of gin in the kitchen. He'll have a drink with us then he'll go back and have one on his own." Well, he finally came in. And John introduced us and the first thing he said to me was, "Do you like sleeping with your wife?" I said, "That's none of your damn business." I asked John then what he was talking about. John said he asked everybody that question at their first meeting. He said, "He's got you either way. If you'd said yes, he'd be happy. If you'd said no, he'd be happy too." But a few days later we got together again and we became very good friends. He got into a tangle with Robert Penn Warren, who was at Oxford and came to Paris to see us. At that time there was this tough little Canadian novelist, Morley Callaghan. He turned up in Paris. Have you seen his book?

BRUCCOLI: *That Summer in Paris.*

TATE: Yes. He didn't know Hemingway and Fitzgerald as well as all that. But that's beside the point. The point is that Ernest had to work out every two or three days at a local athletic club. He invited Callaghan to spar with him. Callaghan was about five eight but built of solid granite. Ernest asked Scott to come along to observe it. Ernest had to play up to the gallery, and he began to warm it up a little. In a few seconds Ernest was lying flat on his back. Callaghan had knocked him out. Callaghan rushed straight to the shower, put on his clothes, and rushed to the nearest poste et telegraphe and sent a cable to his publisher: "Just knocked out Ernest Hemingway." Well, Ernest made Scott cable Max Perkins at Scribners denying the whole thing. Scott went on a drunk that lasted three weeks. He'd come around and say, "What a son of a bitch I was to tell that lie." I remember once I took him 3 times to his flat near the Etoile, and 3 times I'd get back to my hotel at Place de l'Odeon and there he'd be in a taxi right behind me. John Bishop had the same experience with him, but finally he sobered up. I don't think that incident has ever been cleared up—the true story ever been told. Carlos Baker doesn't do much with it. It is a very amusing story and very illuminating about the characters of the two men. Because Hemingway bullied Scott. I think his treatment of him in *A Moveable Feast* was outrageous.

BRUCCOLI: You started to tell about Robert Penn Warren and Fitzgerald.

TATE: Well, Red came to Paris. Red, Scott, and I were over in Montmartre one night on a cafe crawl. And along about midnight we were talking at random—Red said, "I admire very much *The Great Gatsby.*" And Scott said, "If you say that again I'll hit you." And

Allen Tate

Red said, "I admire *Gatsby*." He didn't hit him, but he got up and rushed out and took an overcoat that happened to be Red's overcoat, and not his own. It took John Bishop and me two or three days to get the coats exchanged.

BRUCCOLI: It was *Gatsby* that Mr. Warren mentioned, not *This Side of Paradise*?

TATE: Yes, yes—*Gatsby*. Apparently Scott didn't want anybody to like books that he wasn't working on then. He was working on *Tender Is the Night* then. And he seemed to turn against every book in the past. At least I got that impression.

BRUCCOLI: Well, he felt guilty about his inability to complete *Tender*.

TATE: Exactly.

BRUCCOLI: And he didn't want to be measured against *Gatsby*.

TATE: Exactly. He was afraid he couldn't live up to it.

BRUCCOLI: I've interviewed maybe a score of people who knew Fitzgerald, and everyone of them has told me a story of trying to deal with Fitzgerald when he was drunk. But no person has ever spoken with disgust for Fitzgerald. There was always affection.

TATE: They forgave him everything, even when he was absolutely plastered. He was not unpleasant. I liked him much better than I liked Ernest—everybody did. And he had a curious combination of naivety and cunning. I think in my article I describe an evening with Scott at Gertrude Stein's flat. He thought she was wonderful. But I thought that she was a b-i-t-c-h. I couldn't stand her. "I've seen Shelley plain," he said, as we left. But his observations of human character were usually astute. As I said, he was a combination of childishness and cunning.

BRUCCOLI: A number of people, including Gerald Murphy, have told me that Fitzgerald's problem was something like Poe's, in that his system couldn't tolerate alcohol, so he got drunk awfully fast.

TATE: Well, a couple of martinis would throw him, and he'd drink about eight martinis.

BRUCCOLI: Did you ever observe that almost instantaneous shift from being a little tight to being senseless?

TATE: No, I never saw him pass out. Shortly after the overcoat episode, Red Warren and I were in the Brasserie Lipp across from the Deux Magots; it was a rainy, cold afternoon. We were talking and a man came in and sat down by us there—we didn't notice who it was. We were talking about Scott. And as we were leaving, he got up and came over and said, "I heard every word you said about me."

BRUCCOLI: Did you ever see Fitzgerald and Hemingway together?

TATE: Oh, yes. Fitzgerald adored him. He had to have his heroes. Gerald Murphy was one of them. But Ernest more so. He liked Dos Passos but they weren't so close. A lot of this we're talking about comes out in Malcolm Cowley's new book, *A Second Flowering*— essays on Fitzgerald and Hemingway—two long essays on Hemingway. It's a most interesting book, the best thing on the 1920's and that generation I've seen. I think the weak place in the book is the essay on Thornton Wilder—because Wilder was a rather weak character himself. Malcolm's essay on Faulkner is the best thing ever written about him. Curious, you know, that Malcolm, a Pennsylvania Yankee, could get inside Faulkner and understand him so completely. And, of course, the essay on Hart Crane is very fine. There are only two poets he covers in detail—Crane and Cummings. He apologized to me for giving me short space, but to make up for it he dedicated the book to me. I kidded him about that. I said the dedication's only 4 words. Malcolm and I are very old friends— almost 50 years.

BRUCCOLI: Did Fitzgerald ever discuss his writing with you?

TATE: No, he wouldn't do it. He may have discussed it with other people but never, never with me.

BRUCCOLI: He said nothing about the problems with *Tender*?

TATE: He may have discussed it with Ernest or John Bishop. John

Bishop had a peculiar role in the situation. He seldom mentioned it. He read all their work in manuscript, and he was one of the shrewdest critics I ever knew. They paid no attention to him, and John's own writing is very important. He was a very fine poet; his short stories, *Many Thousands Gone*, is a fine book; his one novel, *Act of Darkness*, was neglected for years but now is out in paperback with an introduction by Leslie Fiedler, of all people. But Fiedler seems to understand it.

BRUCCOLI: Fitzgerald came to feel somewhat superior to Bishop.

TATE: Yes, but it was largely because at that time—up until say the middle of the 1930's—John wasn't doing much work. He had completed the book of short stories. I don't think he would have left anything but the stories and early poems if it hadn't been for Red Warren and myself. As I was saying, back in '29 when Red was in Paris we spent a couple of evenings with John, and he read some of his stories to us. I said you've got to publish them, and Max Perkins at Scribners will do it. Also his poems—*Now With His Love*. He was discouraged, and his wife was not sympathetic.

BRUCCOLI: It was her money, I gather.

TATE: Yes. She was the daughter of a banker. The only ungentlemanly remark I ever heard John Bishop make about anything—well, he had to go to Ohio occasionally to visit his wife's family. And I said one day, "John, what do you think about those people in Ohio?" And he said, "I think they all ought to be killed." I was more astonished than shocked. I think that he got along better with Ernest than he did with Scott. I don't know why, but that's my impression.

BRUCCOLI: Their relationship changed from Fitzgerald being tutored by Bishop at Princeton, so to speak, to Fitzgerald enjoying vast success.

TATE: Exactly, and John felt the sting of that a little, and his wife was very ambitious. She wanted him to write a best-seller.

BRUCCOLI: I have seen hundreds of photographs of Zelda Fitzgerald. She does not look like the same woman in any two photos. And in most of them she doesn't look particularly beautiful.

TATE: She wasn't beautiful.

BRUCCOLI: What did she have?

TATE: She was attractive. She had what do they call it today—what is the word?—charisma. I vividly remember the very first thing she said to me: that she must have danced with me. Within 2 or 3 minutes it was as if we were old friends. She had that gift. She had social sense.

BRUCCOLI: I gather that she was much more than a Southern Belle.

TATE: She was very intelligent. Her conversation was terrifically intelligent. Some of her stories are brilliant. But there was competition. She was one of those unhappy women who are jealous of their husbands. She was jealous of his talent. Red Warren's first wife was that way. So was T. S. Eliot's first wife. So I had three friends who had wives who were jealous of them. And it came to disaster in all 3 cases. But Scott was deeply in love with Zelda, there's no doubt about that.

BRUCCOLI: I am told that in public she was very loyal to him, that whenever anyone criticized Fitzgerald they caught it from Zelda.

TATE: Exactly. She was perfectly loyal to him. Well, so was Vivian Eliot. And she was extremely intelligent, too. She did things to the *Waste Land* that improved it. And it was quite remarkable that she would be willing to have that poem published at all, because some of the scenes in it reflect her life with Tom Eliot. The conversation, you know, in "A Game of Chess"—the man and the woman. Frank Morley told me that was right out of Eliot's life.

BRUCCOLI: When was the last time you saw Fitzgerald?

TATE: About 1932.

BRUCCOLI: New York?

TATE: Yes, very briefly. We went out to lunch. A little restaurant where Max Perkins lunched, on East 52nd—Cherio's.

You know, I had one letter from Zelda written after she had returned to her family. It's with my correspondence at Princeton now. It's one of the saddest letters I ever had. She wrote about the past in Paris—this was about 1934 Or 1935—as if it were 50 years ago. It all had the glamour of the past, as though it had taken place in the *remote* past. It was a very curious letter.

BRUCCOLI: Do you have any recollections of the wife Hemingway had at that time, Pauline?

TATE: I knew Pauline very well indeed. In fact, I knew all of them except the last wife, Mary. I knew Hadley, Pauline, and Martha Gelhorn; but I met Hadley years later after she became Mrs. Paul Scott Mowrer. I never met Mary. I liked Pauline very much. Pauline died many years ago. The last time I saw her was in Washington. That must have been, oh, about 1950. Well, I knew one thing that broke up that marriage was Pauline's sister, Jinny. She was a tall, skinny girl from Arkansas; she came to stay with them in Paris, and she got on Ernest's nerves terribly. She seemed to be under foot all the time.

BRUCCOLI: Hemingway and Zelda had hatred at first sight. Do you have any recollection of seeing these two together?

TATE: I saw them together, but I never got that impression. But I know that he hated her. Why, I don't know. Maybe he didn't know, either.

BRUCCOLI: She was one of the few people in Paris who didn't join the Hemingway claque. You know her remark about *The Sun Also Rises*: she said it's about bullfighting, bullthrowing, and bullshit.

TATE: You know that *The Sun Also Rises* is a remarkably good book. And she knew it too.

BRUCCOLI: Do you recall any of those people that Hemingway put into it?

TATE: Well, I knew Harold Loeb; he drove Ford Madox Ford to Tennessee to see me in the early 1930's. I met Duff Twysden. I saw her maybe twice at the Duex Magots. She wasn't with Ernest. I've forgotten who she was with, she may have been with Ford Madox

Ford. Ford knew her, I'm sure he did. She was not a beautiful woman by any means. I was not impressed with her. She talked all the time. Oh now, something else comes back to me: I saw her twice. But with whom the second time I can't remember. I'm so uncertain of this that I must suppress it.

BRUCCOLI: Was Harry Crosby really serious about publishing or was this just dilettantism?

TATE: Dilettantism. He was all right, but he was frivolous and he didn't understand what it was all about.

BRUCCOLI: The Black Sun Press books are lovely things.

TATE: Well, I think Caresse did that. But Caresse—she was the kind of patron of the arts who doesn't know one artist from another. The books were beautiful, but it was just luck that she happened to like Hart Crane and published *The Bridge*. Good luck for Hart. We didn't see much of Hart, and I don't even know if he ever met Hemingway or Fitzgerald. He got into a gang of queers at the Dome. I don't think I saw him in Paris more than 3 or 4 times.

BRUCCOLI: You were close to Ford. What was really the basis of Hemingway's animosity toward Ford?

TATE: Well, he didn't like Ford's personality. He wrote that sketch of him in *A Moveable Feast*: Ford was pulling Ernest's leg about the "English gentleman" business, you see. Ford was quite capable of doing that with a dead-pan. I think it was the fact that Ernest was one of these peculiar people who can't allow themselves to feel grateful to anybody who has done anything for them. Particularly if his benefactor were a writer of fiction. Ernest liked poets—he liked me; he liked John Bishop; and Archie MacLeish was a great friend of his—because they were not competing with him in anything. And part of the strife between Ernest and Scott was just on that basis.

BRUCCOLI: But Ford did have mannerisms.

TATE: Oh yes—and they were exasperating. But you know, Ford knew everything that Ernest was saying about him, and then he wrote that beautiful introduction to the Modern Library edition of *A*

Farewell to Arms. I never heard him say anything against Ernest Hemingway. Ford was an extremely generous and disinterested man. Ernest was a great writer, and Ford knew it, and that was that.

BRUCCOLI: What about McAlmon? Did you know him at all?

TATE: I never knew him at all. I never met him. I don't know how that happened.

BRUCCOLI: Is his work as bad as I think it is?

TATE: Yes, I think it's awful.

BRUCCOLI: His importance is that he published other people as well as himself.

TATE: Well, I thought he was just nothing at all, but now Kay Boyle has tried to revive him and make something out of him.

BRUCCOLI: But the book she revived is *Being Geniuses Together*, which is important as literary history—not as literature itself.

TATE: Yes, exactly. It's pretty good from that point of view. In *A Moveable Feast* there is a sketch of an eccentric old poet, Ralph Cheever Dunning. I knew him very well indeed. He lived at 72-bis rue Notre Dame des Champs, the flat that Pound had had. And when Pound went to Italy he turned it over to Dunning. Dunning was a kind of 1890 character who wore striped trousers and black jackets and usually a wing collar. He'd been on heroin for years but he'd kicked it and he would take a pound of tea and boil it in a quart of water—just boil it—and go on a jag of tea. He had charming manners of a gentlemen of the 1890's, perfect manners. He had a great crush on the poet Leonie Adams who was with us in Paris and Leonie would have nothing to do with him. He was always sad because he was isolated. The only people I know of at that time who were kind to him were Ford and Hemingway.

The first time I met Pound he'd come up from Italy—this must have been in the spring of 29. I met him in the studio of Stella Bowen who was Ford's common-law wife. Ford and Pound of course were great friends. Stella had painted Pound. She's been dead now for years and some of her pictures are lost. Stella was a very fine woman, and Ford deserted her for a rich American woman from St. Louis—she was a chic country club type. Ford went to New York and left a lady with us whose name I will not mention. We had to see her practically every day and take care of her. I always resented that—still do a little, to this day.

BRUCCOLI: I will put one last question to you—which can't be answered—and then leave you to your duties and honors. The unanswerable question is: What made the Twenties? How do you account for this explosion of genius?

TATE: I don't account for it. I've written about it a few times from the point of view of the South, the Southern Renaissance, and I think very much the same thing happened everywhere in the country. There was that crossing of the ways—the old America was gone and the new era was coming in.

BRUCCOLI: As a result of the World War I experience?

TATE: Yes, exactly—I have no doubt at all that it caused the Southern Renaissance. It's perfectly plain because the Southern writing up to that time is mediocre. There were only two: there was James Branch Cabell and Ellen Glasgow, and that was it. And then Faulkner suddenly appeared, and the illiterate state of Mississippi produced more brilliant novelists than any state in the union. Stark Young and Eudora Welty and Roark Bradford and Shelby Foote. Faulkner's not the only one.

THE 1920's
IN AMERICAN LIFE
AND LITERATURE

Duke University, 17 December 1957;
Mr. Farrell has revised his talk for publication.

I said that I was going to speak about the 1920's. I was thinking about those years at dinner and was thinking about them back-stage—the years of the youth of some of us—and it occurred to me that the United States of America, at least in that department of its life that is taken over by the intelligentsia, so-called, is forever growing up. I recall back in the 1920's it was stated that America was coming of age, and all through my literary life I have been hearing again and again, with new generations, that America is coming of age. And we have—it has come of age by looking back on the 1920's. And one of the representatives of this generation—it's a generation of youth—with a little bit of an alderman on his stomach, and a little bit of grey in their hair, but they are still young writers—*Partisan Review* writers and the like—one of them is Leslie Fiedler, who has written a book called *An End to Innocence*—and all previous generations of writers prior to Leslie Fiedler. And today the new generation is no longer innocent and the great theme of American culture today is to write about how finally America has come of age. Along with that, there are interpretations of past decades, the 1920's and 1930's. These usually a matter of cliches. There is a habit in American literary journalism and editing, to lock up each successive decade, to find one or two aspects of the conduct of those ten years and to present that as a defining characteristic of a period of American life and then to assume that in the next ten years everything is different. Along with that, for about ten or twenty years the writers of one decade are attacked and forgotten before they are restored; but they are usually restored to cliches. There are many cliches and many stereotypes repeated at the present time. Particularly some member of the generation that finally is no longer innocent is now making symbolic interpretations of some of the writers in the 1920's. They're finding Christ images and many other types of symbols and images, and all this would have been foreign to the people of the 1920's as it would have been foreign to the writers of that period.

The 1920's in American life is important for more reasons than the fact that it is called the "roaring twenties." It is important for more reasons than the fact that it was the time of prohibition era, and that there were dramatic events and features of the life of the times. It marked a turning point in the history of America, politically, socially, culturally, and economically. The United States became the cheif producer of industrial goods about 1883. After the first World War, in which the United States intervened, America became a creditor rather than a debtor nation. The basic capital investment had been made so that the industrial structure of the country was established. You have undoubtedly read, that is, those of you who are students, of the prosperity of the twenties. It was a prosperity which has been surpassed by the post-war prosperity of the last 12 years, but prior to that, it was perhaps the most prosperous period in the history of America. Along with that, it is believed that because it was so prosperous the entire nation spent its time playing the stock market and watching Babe Ruth hit home runs, which is not quite true.

But, one of the defining differences we can see after the First World War is that we have the beginning of what is now quite clear and apparent, a consumption attitude towards life. The best way for me to indicate that is to refer to a study made by a sociologist of cultures, Leo Lowenthal. He took the popular biographies in magazines, such as *Collier's* and *The Saturday Evening Post* for 1900 and 1945 or 1946. In the biographies of 1900 he found that there were more men of affairs treated, and that there were fewer entertainers than in the later period. The entertainers treated in early periods were more serious. The sense of the articles was that the writer addressed the audience by saying that if *you* can't do it yourself, your son can. The emphasis was on success and acheivement. The content revealed *how* a person became a success. It emphasized personal initiative; it emphasized those personal traits which led to success. In the case of the entertainers, there was more about their technique and less about the way they consumed goods or used their leisure. In 1945 and 1946, the popular biographies were different. The emphasis was on their swimming pools, was on their leisure life, on the kind of goods they consumed, what they did when they had nothing else to do. There were more entertainers and they were less serious in character. There were fewer men of affairs, fewer business men and even they were treated more as consumers of goods rather than as men of affairs or as men who had accomplished and achieved. And usually it was explained that they had become a success by luck, by getting a good break.

The attitude so clearly emphasized and marked in Lowenthal's studies begins to become clearly noticeable in the twenties. In the 1920's there was a considerable investment in what we will call services, culture, and entertainment. And if we look at these sociologically and economically, we can link them together. It was a time when new organizations, new publishing houses and new cultural enterprises, were established and capitalized, sometimes in millions and in hundreds of millions of dollars. The motion pictures expanded, and in addition to their expansion the talking picture came in. Radio became a major communications industry within a period of less than ten years. The Book-of-the-Month Club and the Theatre Guild were founded, a new type of magazine such as *Time* magazine was established.

Writing of the earlier period of American life, in this century and the writing of the 1920's, are somewhat different. One of the defining differences is that the characters of the 20's are presented more in reference to consumption, more in reference to leisure, more in a setting where you see them attempting to enjoy life. There is even a marked difference in this sense in the earlier novels of Theodore Dreiser, and in his book *An American Tragedy*. Theodore Dreiser, in passing, might be described as the American novelist, more than any other, who was influenced by the ideas of social Darwinism. Social Darwinism was a major tendency in American though in the 1890's and the early part of the 1900's. As a matter of fact, there is a very good study of social Darwinism in America by Richard Hofstadter published by the University of Pennsylvania

Press. He described the influence of Darwinism thought in America. But in the 1920's in *An American Tragedy* you can perceive this difference. I mentioned social Darwinism in the connection with Dreiser. The spectacle of gradeur and misery, the sense of survival of the fittest, the contrast of the strong and rich, and the poor and weak, in Dreiser; the dramatization of success, of success and failure, in his early books—is not to be found in *An American Tragedy*. In his earlier book, you can take three characters who were material successes in the world. Sister Carrie, Carrie Meeber, the heroine or chief protagonist of *Sister Carrie* become a famous actress. Eugene Witla, the chief protagonist of his book *The Genius,* published in 1916, becomes a successful artist. And Cowperwood, the hero of his trilogy, *The Titan, The Financier,* and *The Stoic*—the first two of which were published prior to 1920, the last was published posthumously—becomes a financial wizard. And in each case, material success is a consequence of some capacity, some trait which the character has in himself or in herself. In the case of Witla, artistic talent and genius. In the case of Cowperwood, financial wizardry. In the case of Carrie Meeber a warmth and sympathy of nature which helps her to become an actress, and is the basis for her success. This is the underlying reason that she has theatrical talent. But Clyde Griffith, the protagonist or hero of *An American Tragedy,* is not only a failure, but he also cannot use his best talents. His life is a socially abnormal life. He is the son of itinerate religious preachers or missionaries, gospel preachers like those of the Salvation Army. The book opens, as those of you who read it know, with a scene on a street corner in San Francisco, with the hurrying crowds at sunset while the father and mother are preaching, attempting to dent the "apathy of life." That phrase is in the opening of *An American Tragedy.* And there is the boy, Clyde Griffith, sort of bewildered and young, looking out at a world he cannot possibly feel he belongs in. And his entire boyhood is socially abnormal. He does not go to one school steadily; he does not live in one neighborhood. His parents do not have an occupation which is similar to the occupations of boys with a socially normal boyhood, living in one place, going to one school, having some life in the community. His first contact with the outer world where he learns, is in a hotel. Dreiser stresses that. As a matter of fact, you might say that, and particularly for the earlier generations of Americans, there was a kind of hotel culture. The hotel was a kind of a fraternity and country club of the self-made, uneducated men, the salesmen and others. They learned manners, and they got an idea of how the other half lived. And Clyde Griffith, seeing the way money is wasted, seeing how the people who to him are rich and successful live in a hotel, learning this as a bell-boy—he gains a distorted sense of values. But again, it is a distorted sense of values which is a relationship to *spending* money, not to *making* it, to consumption and leisure, not achievement and constructiveness. He meets an uncle who owns a shirt factory in Lycurgus, New York. Clyde is brought to Lycurgus to work in the shirt factory. He still lives his socially abnormal life in the sense that he does not belong with the workers, nor does he belong with his rich relatives, the Griffiths. In the end, there is this tragedy in which he abandons and plans to murder the girl he originally loved, in order to marry a rich girl of the local social set, a girl who treats him as an object of revenge, rivalry and vanity. But, the whole emphasis on success and the treatment of success is success by connection. The treatment of the rich in Dreiser here is almost entirely again of their leisure in terms of their consumption. I'm emphasizing that because we can see today the degree to which this kind of attitude permeates our education and our national life.

If you consider a number of the writers of the twenties, F. Scott Fitzgerald, Ernest Hemingway, Ring Lardner, you will find that these aspects and features of life are the ones mainly treated. If you ask yourself the question, what types of occupations, what types of work are described in the short stories of Ring Lardner, you will find that almost every character who is presented as working, is engaged in a kind of job, or occupation, or profession which caters to the amusement of others—a golf caddy, a song writer, a ball player. You consider the world of Ernest Hemingway—and I am making a descriptive statement—it's the tourists' world, it's Americans in Europe on a vacation, or it's the newspaperman like the "I" of *The Sun Also Rises.* And in the movies, and in the commercial or popular stories, I think you will find the same emphasis. You find that there's a beginning of the change in the conception of and also the representation of the American way of life.

How, that is one of the important features in the 1920's. That has nothing to do with the present interpretation in terms of writers subjecting myths and symbols that are archetypes, that have some universal significance.

A second factor about the 1920's which is important and which is neglected today was the depth and the significance of post-war disillusionment. In 1916, Woodrow Wilson was elected largely because "He Kept Us Out of War." In 1917 the United States became involved in the First World War. The Liberals believed with Wilson that it was a war to make the world safe for democracy. They believed that the war would be *their* war, and that as a consequence of it a more liberal and more democratic world could be established. After the Versailles Treaty of Peace, disillusionment set in. The original studies of the origins of the First World War, the most important ones, were made in the United States. One of the books that influenced the new generation of that time was *The Economic Consequences of the Peace,* which was an attack on the Versailles Treaty. And the generation of writers which had gone to war and the newer generation, both were strongly infected and strongly influenced by a kind of bitterness and a sense of disillusionment. One of the first books of John Dos Passos was the novel *Three Soldiers,* which was a tale of war disillusionment, a novel in which the soldiers were ground down by an army machine. At first Ernest Hemingway was largely interpreted as the novelist expressing post-war disillusionment. When Gertrude Stein said to Ernest Hemingway that "'you are a lost generation"—and he used that as a quotation in the front of his novel, *The Sun Also Rises*—the sense of the lost generation, that it had suffered such spiritual wounds from war, was that it was lost: it was directionless. And it is interesting that with current interpretations of Hemingway, the simple connection of the fact that he uses this quotation as a beginning of his novel *The Sun Also Rises*—it was his first novel—and the "I" of the story is impotent because of wounds of war—that type of symbolism is too obvious and too definitely intended and too simple for the later critics who are inventing meanings and significances in the writers of the 20's. But, writers like Hemingway and writers like Dos Passo were not the dominating writers of the 20's. These were the older generation. The influential voices were Dreiser, Nathan, Mencken, Sinclair Lewis, and Sherwood Anderson; to some degree Carl Sandburg, Edgar Lee Masters and James Branch Cabell. They were writers who had all begun and who had published their first book in the 1910's or earlier, or else between 1910 and 1920. I believe Anderson's first book was published in 1916. And those writers were directly or indirectly also influenced by the 1890's in England, the *fin de siècle* or "the yellow decade" as it was called, that is, the time of the period of the break-up of the Victorian world. In passing, I would remark that there is an excellent study of the period, titled *The 1890's*, by Holbrook Jackson and I believe that this book affords sound insight into the influence and the background of the break-up of the Victorian world as all this affected America. Jackson does not say as much, however, this is my interpretation. But, by understanding the Yellow Decade or the last decade of the 19th century it is more easy to see its influence. In the 1920's, as a matter of fact, some of the writers from England and Ireland, Wilde and Shaw, George Moore, William Butler Yeats became more popular in America. The city became the kind of landscape for the English writers of the 1890's. The city as a significant center for culture—for art, for esthetic experience. Now, in the United States, from the 1890's on, we had the triumph of the town over the country, of the city over the small town and the rural areas. It is interesting in passing that in Theodore Drieser's first novel, *Sister Carrie,* the opening pages, the first chapter, tell us of a country girl from a small town in Wisconsin going to the big city to make her fortune to find more life, to find a better type of life, to find experiences which are impossible for her to have in the small town. What these experiences are she does not know. She is just going to a bigger world, and the city was a bigger world. In the early novels of Dreiser, every town that a character goes to, in particular Chicago—there is a sense of hope, and of growth. And of course Dreiser himself, when he first went to Chicago, felt very strongly the spirit of growth in Chicago. He said that Chicago was singing and that he was singing with it. Now then, by the 1920's, the city had triumphed over the small town and you have an attack on the small town. But there were earlier novels which reflected a kind of disillusionment about the small town. One of them, one of the most significant of American novels, *The Damnation of Theron Ware.* However it is in the 1920's we get a strong revulsion expressed in criticism and in literature of the small town, and of the origins of the writer. Floyd Dell wrote a minor novel, *Moon Calf,* a novel of the small town boy going to the big city. Sinclair Lewis's first success, *Main Street,* was to a considerable extent an attack on the small town. The character, Carol Kennicott, cannot have a more cultured life, cannot have a more significant, personally meaningful life in a small town of Minnesota, that is located, perhaps near Minneapolis. And in *Babbitt,* Zenith the city is actually Minneapolis, but it is presented as though it were a smaller town. At the same time you find revulsion against, in this attack on the small town—the attack is made largely in terms of the way people enjoy life, of what they feel about the good of life. In other words, the emphasis is on leisure and consumption life. In passing, it would be very interesting to compare, say, a salesman in Sinclair Lewis with the salesman, Drouet, the first lover, one of the leading characters of Dreiser's *Sister Carrie.*

Now, along with the small town and with the attack on Puritanism. (I'm just watching the time so that I do not keep you too long.) Mencken and Drieser were two of the ones who led the attack on Puritanism. But we must define exactly what kind of Puritanism they attacked. And of course, in that definition we can readily recognize that they attacked conventions. But, actually, the Puritanism they attacked was mainly a colonial, Victorian Puritanism with an emphasis on sin, a verbal revulsion against sin. It was one which led to an effort to legislate other people's morals, and other people's conduct. Now Puritanism was a much bigger and more complicated phenomenon than that, and the effect of Puritanism in England was different. Particularly, the nonconformist sects. English Puritanism created a moral attitude towards work. It stimulated scientists like Faraday and there was certain constructive, moral feature to English Puritanism which was different from the small-town, rather parochial Puritanism which Mencken and Lewis and Dreiser attacked, and most particularly Mencken. So when we say that Mencken attacked Puritanism we must recognize that you can't accept Mencken's structures as a total dismissal of a movement as profound, as complicated, and as influential, in the history of the human race as was what we call Puritanism. That centers in Calvinism and Presbyterianism.*

Also, Mencken attacked the timidity of college professors. In the 1920's and prior to that, novelists who had written such as I, would not have been invited to speak to a college audience. We would not have been let near a college. Writers like Dreiser and Anderson were not taught in colleges. A fight was made to gain acceptance of those writers. And some of the most distinguished scholars of the time lost all decency, intellectual objectivity, and sense of fair play in their violent and vile and vicious attack on contemporary writers. For instance, one of the most distinguished American scholars, an authority on Plato, the late Dr. Paul Shorey, of the University of Chicago, wrote attacks on Dos Passos, on contemporary writers, which would be laughed at in the most backward colleges of the United States today, and that man was a distinguished scholar. Dr. Paul Elmer Moore was considered one of the literary humanists. He

---

*Cf. *The Protestant Ethic and the Spirit of Capitalism* (1930) by Max Weber and *Religion and the Rise of Capitalism* (1926) by R. H. Tawney.

wrote often with grace and elegance. Particularly for those of you interested in 18th century poetry, I would strongly recommend an essay of his on Thomas Crabbe. But when Paul Elmer Moore wrote about modern writers, such as James Joyce, he was like a backwoods preacher denoucing sin. There was the late Irving Babbitt of Harvard who is the most energetic and thorough-going collector of quotations in the history of the human race. And he collected hundreds and hundreds of quotations to prove that Zola was a romanticist standing on his head, and to prove that every evil of the modern world, including American writing of the 20th century, was the result of the lack of discipline and the lack of control in Jean Jacques Rousseau. The book, *Rousseau and Romanticism,* is—well today, it is an extraordinary scholastic curiosity.* But there were few professors who defended contemporary writing, or who even defended Zola. And the attack of Mencken, particularly, was directed those professors. As a matter of fact, today many of the English and other professors, whom you students have, are those who grew up on Henry Mencken, and those who were students who revolted against the kind of narrowness and restriction that existed particularly in the English departments in the early years of this century, and even in the 1920's to some degree.

Further than that, Mencken's main object of attack was prohibition. Now, Mencken himself recognized that in his attack on prohibition he was also attacking the moral attitude and the attempt to legislate morality of the small towns and the rural areas. In the 1920's, one of the significant facts, then, is the city. The city is, in the 1920's, the center of what is important in American life and it has become important to the extent that rural life is laughed at, that the farm problem and other problems are considered as almost inconsequential. In passing, there's no necessary correlation, but in the 1920's the one group in America who did not actually participate in the prosperity of the country were the farmers. But the emphasis on the city, even the prejudice and bias of the city against the country, is one of the features or one of the aspects of the 1920's.

Also in the Twenties, there was a feeling of zest, the desire for

---

*While I leave this stand, since I said it in my lecture, I think I should add that I was less than fair to Irving Babbitt. I would, in fact, recommend the reading of *Rousseau and Romanticism*. While I do not agree with much in this work, I now realize that in my two readings of it I was stimulated, and I learned from Irving Babbitt.

personal freedom. In so far as there was revolt in the 20's, it was revolt in the name of self-expression. And one of the features of Sherwood Anderson, which made him so important, was that self-expression, that self-realization, was so involved in his writing. His book *Winesburg, Ohio,* published in 1919, was the most influential of his works. It is a series of short stories laid in a small Ohio town in the 1890's. Actually, it is probably Camden, Ohio, near Cincinnati, the town in which he was born. Now, the humor of America had been a humor directed against every kind of oddity, of peculiarity, every type of person who did not fit into a kind of middle-class, Protestant, Nordic, Anglo-Saxon norm. Accent, brogue, the color of your skin, the shape of your nose, the peculiarity that you had feeling and wrote poetry or read books—those were the objects of humor. And the people who were queer were the people who didn't fit this norm. Sherwood Anderson called his book, *A Book of Grotesqueries,* and every one of the characters of Winesburg, Ohio, is queer, is singular in that sense. And the pattern of most of the stories is one in which there is a sudden awakening of a creative feeling, or else of that creative feeling being dammed up. In the latter case, the result is some aberrant, or neurotic, or violent, or aggressive expression or action. The notion of creativity, the creativity, the capacity for creativity applied to everyone. It is central in Sherwood Anderson's work and this aspect of his work was perceived in the 1920's. I have already spoken about the small town and the country. Anderson wrote about the small town and the country in a different sense, without sarcasm, without irony, without attack. He wrote about it with a kind of remembered humanity, and sympathetic feeling concerning frustration of small town characters. Also, he had grown up in the 1890's. The 1890's was a period of great hope of American capitalism. It was a period in the solidification of big and huge monopolies. It was a period in which the factory mushroomed to the small town. It was a period in which crafts began to disappear or even disappeared. And the feeling of craftsmanship was strong in Anderson, and he had an abiding memory of the craftsman, of the changes which had been wrought in American life and with it of the destruction of the craftsman. Sherwood Anderson read very few books and I don't believe he ever read Thorstein Veblen. Thorstein Veblen was one of the most profound and important of American social thinkers, and Veblen's book, *The Instinct of Workmanship* was different from the instinct psychology of the time. It was influenced by men like John Dewey, and I believe

William James. Veblen saw the Instinct of Workmanship really as the need to create, as involving the creativity of man. With that, he saw how the organization of life of man by time, and the development of the factory system, distorted and thwarted human nature. And Sherwood Anderson's stories are a kind of an illustration of the analysis of the effect of industrial civilization, the effect of Time, the effect of the ordering of life and time in our industrial civilization on the nature of man and on the instinct of workmanship as Veblen described it. Now, similarly, Anderson never read the American philosophers, Dewey and George Herbert Mead. Particularly Mead I am thinking of here, the idea of social identity. I mean Mead was influenced by the American sociologist Cooley. Professor Cooley of Wisconsin used the phrase "the looking glass self," in which he said that looking at others, pleple in society, we see ourselves. Mead further developed the idea of "the looking glass self" into a conception of how the self, or the personality, is created in society. Mead's social psychology can be seen relating to the problem of what we will call identity. Now as I said, Anderson sought his own identity, sought it by his own identity in a world that has changed. That Anderson can be read in the same sense as Mead as though it were an illustration of Mead's ideas. Now I think Anderson is significant in this sense for the reason that, with the changes that had been wrought in America, the triumph of big town over the small town, the problem of identity was a significant and an important one. And that is part of the significance and the importance of Sherwood Anderson.

There was an entirely different side to the 1920's. There was a separation between the literary men and the political and philosophical thinkers of the 20's. As a matter of fact, many of the writers and particularly the new generation, Hemingway and Glenway Wescott and F. Scott Fitzgerald and others, did not read much of the political writing. But the other side of the 1920's is very important and it is well described in *The Crisis of the Old Order* by Arthur M. Schlesinger. In it Arthur Schlesinger shows the preparation for the New Deal, the thinking about social problems, the thinking about problems of taxation, about problems of bigness and industry, about problems of social justice and social control. And in all the major universities of the country studying these problems there were professors and students, students who became the shock troops, as it were, of the New Deal. In contemporary images of the 1920's, this side of the 20's is rarely recognized. There was much intense social thought in the 1920's. President Franklin Delano Roosevelt's

New Deal was not merely a concoction. Raymond Moley, more or less, suggests that it was pieced together as kind of a means of being elected, but that is not totally true. Roosevelt finally gathered around him the men who had done new and original social thinking in America, in connection with the changing problems of America. This was reflected very little in the novels of the 20's but it is one of the most important aspects of the intellectual activity.—the New Deal was prepared first in the Twenties. Now to some degree, men like Mencken who could not stand Roosevelt after 1934, helped to create the generation of New Dealers also. Mencken's attack on bigness, his attack on business men, on figures like Coolidge and Harding, helped to prepare New Deal journalists and others. Although Mencken himself was one of the arch critics and most bitter critics of the New Deal, he himself contributed to it.

Now, I've taken there and attempted to present to you various aspects of the 1920's. I do not think that you can take the life of a country, the life of generations through ten years of change, and lock it up in one or two stereotypes. There were many features of the 1920's. The past is not fixed. The past is always changing. Thus we can keep seeing now more of the meaning of the 1920's if we study these years. I have mentioned Sherwood Anderson, the 1890's, the small town, the changes in America in the 1890's. Now the decisive change in the small town came withthe railroad. When the life of the small town changed—was no longer based on a horse but was based on the railroad—the possibility of trade brands and a national market was created; material basis for a national market became existent. One factor in the change of the small town is the introduction of the trade brand. After the 1920's America had reached the point—there was an interruption by the depression—whereby it was sufficiently rich so that the goods of life could be spread widely. The goods of life were spread widely at a time—and after the second world war the spread of prosperity was much further. And with that there was new media of communication. This consumer emphasis is seen most strongly in a war of the trade brands. And because of the fact that we have television, we have television operated as it is, that has given those who do the advertising a growing control over American culture. Now there is a difference between a consumer emphasis, there is a difference between the treatment of leisure and consumption in stories and the manipulation of culture in order to sell goods, in order to practice what is now called, hidden persuasion. The bigness that was attacked in the 20's has survived. It survived in the consumption industries, and it has also survived to the point that the other tendencies, at the moment at least, seem defeated. The one tendency of the 20's we can notice is the one which was most attacked but has survived, and that is bigness and bigness in the consumer and service industries manipulating the mind of America. In the 20's was a protest against bigness, many of the leading writers of the time protested against bigness, they protested against the values by which many people lived, lived in a way that was unparalleled in the history of America. And with that, there was originality and creativity in both social and political thinking, and there was originality and creativity in the writing of the time. Now this is part of the history of the 1920's. These are some of the features as we can see them today. And I would emphasize, I would state this. I began by stating the question of America always growing up or becoming of age. It's a meaningless statement to make. But we can see in the 1920's and through, if my comments and analysis are correct, the process of a changing consciousness of America, a changing consciousness of America in relation to the changing social and economic and political conditions of the country. There is never a change only or solely in one field. Thee are changes in many fields. And the 20's is significant because, we can dateline the beginning of a new kind of emphasis and new developments in America. We can see that after 1918, in terms of the goods of life, in terms of the development of the people, America had become a sufficient success so that leisure was a mass problem and not a class problem. I mentioned Thorstein Veblen. Another of his books was *The Theory of the Leisure Class. The Theory of the Leisure Class* was an attack on the rich, and it presented the rich as an aristocracy. It presented the rich, or the people of leisure, as those who had developed a culture developed habits, of conspicuous consumption—a phrase still used but quite frequently—because they wanted to show that they had nothing to do.

Well, by the 1920's, many people had more leisure, had much time in which they had nothing to do. Today it is more pronounced and the conspicuous consumption became conforming consumption from the 20's to the 50's. Now, in ways like that we can see the beginning of these changes in American consciousness, in American conditions and in American life. Where they are going to end we do not know. But if we look back, if my analysis is correct, we can say that the 1920's was one of the germinating periods of change, of all-sided change in American life. If it is studied in that way, and if we recognize that there are many tendencies and influences at play, we will perhaps gain more insight than if we look up the 20's in stereotypes, as some of the literary and other critics are doing at the present time. And that is the substances of the remarks and analysis I wanted to offer this evening.

HEMINGWAY

Official Red Cross Bulletin / *kindly allowed to print* / *cold facts – that's why there* / *is no story –* F.14

REPORT OF THE DEPARTMENT
OF MILITARY AFFAIRS

January to July, 1918

[handwritten signatures] Fredk W Spiegel
Bill Horne

14, VIA SARDEGNA

ROME

Hemingway's copy of the *Report of the Department of Military Affairs* (Rome: American Red Cross, 1918). *McKeldin Library, University of Maryland.*

C.E. FRAZER CLARK, JR.

AMERICAN RED CROSS REPORTS ON THE WOUNDING OF LIEUTENANT ERNEST M. HEMINGWAY – 1918

The wounding of Lieut. E. M. Hemingway was officially reported in two 1918 publications of the American Red Cross, surviving copies of which appear scarcer than Poe's *Tamerlane*.

Hemingway, impatient for more action than was to be had after three weeks of driving ambulances for ARC Section Four behind the Italian front, worked a transfer which placed him, as he told an Oak Park classmate, out in front of a dugout in a nice trench 20 yards from the Piave River and 40 yards from the Austrian lines. It was here, on the banks of the Piave, around midnight, on or about 8 July 1918, that an Austrian minenwerfer round exploded, wounding Hemingway seriously in both legs. He was further wounded by machine-gun fire on the way to the aid station.

What may be the first published notice of Hemingway's wounding is recorded in the *Report of the Department of Military Affairs* (Rome: American Red Cross, 1918):

> The men serving these canteens not only distributed coffee, cigarettes and chocolate at the canteen bases, but also carried supplies into the front line trenches. During such a trip, E. M. Hemingway was wounded by the explosion of a shell which landed about three feet from him, killing a soldier who stood between him and the point of the explosion, and wounding others.

fective work during the months of June and July, and in
several cases were taken over by the canteen service as part
of the permanent system of front line canteens.

The men serving these canteens not only distributed coffee, cigarettes and chocolate at the canteen bases, but also
carried supplies into the front line trenches. During such
a trip, E. M. Hemingway was wounded by the explosion of
a shell which landed about three feet from him, killing a soldier who stood between him and the point of explosion, and
wounding others.

PERSONNEL. — Captain James Gamble was in May appointed Field Inspector of the service. Captain Utassy has
acted as Quartermaster from the beginning, except for the
period of his trip to America, during which time Captain
Bates acted in his place. The headquarters of this service
have been from the start located at Vicenza in conjunction
with those of the ambulance service.

Each canteen is in charge of an A. R. C. lieutenant,
and the work done by these officers is of a nature which
calls upon all the resources of the versatile and adaptable
American temperament. It is necessary that these officers
in order effectively to fulfill their duties should be men who
can readly establish cordial relations with Italian officers.
At the same time it is essential that they should know how
to impress soldiers of the ranks of the sincerity and friendliness of the message which they have been delegated to
transmit. The chief aim of this service is to make clear to
the Italian soldiers that the American people are grateful
to them for the services which they have rendered to the
cause of civilization during the long years which Italy has
been engaged in the war, and that in addition to sending
over troops to fight for the same cause, the Americans desire
in every tangible way possible to express their appreciation.
Consequently these lieutenants must be men who like and

— 14 —

Report of Lieutenant E.M. Hemingway's wounding in the *Report of the
Department of Military Affairs* (Rome: American Red Cross, 1918).
McKeldin Library, University of Maryland.

Hemingway sent a copy of this ARC report home on which he noted in typical Hemingway style, "Official Red Cross Bulletin Only allowed to print cold facts—that's why there is no story—P. 14." The Hemingway copy is in the McKeldin Library, University of Maryland. A second copy is located in the collection of Frederick W. Spiegel, who also served in ARC Section Four.

A second report of Hemingway's wounding appears in "American Red Cross Ambulance Section 4—'The Shock Unit' of the Italian Army," *The American Red Cross Central Division Bulletin* (7 December 1918), which quotes from Hemingway's own account of the wounding:

> The wounds from the trench mortar didn't hurt a bit, and the machine gun bullet just felt like a smack on the leg by an icy snow ball. I got up and got my wounded to the dug-out.
>
> It gives you an awfully satisfactory feeling to be wounded; it's getting beaten up in a good cause. There are no heroes in this war. We all offer our bodies and only a few are chosen. They are the lucky ones. I am proud and happy that mine was chosen, but it shouldn't give me any extra credit.

Hemingway tore the page with the Section Four story out of his copy of the ARC *Bulletin* and mailed it home. This page—subsequently annotated by Bill Horne, another survivor of Section Four—and a complete copy of the *Bulletin*, are in the McKeldin Library, University of Maryland. Another copy is also preserved by Frederick W. Spiegel.

After Hemingway returned to Oak Park, reports of his exploits and his wounding were published in *The Oak Parker* (1 February 1919) and the *Trapeze* (7 February and 21 March 1919).

American Red Cross Ambulance Section 4—"The Shock Unit" of the Italian Army

They range from college professors to boys just out of the high school. Most of them have been decorated by the Italians. Jerome Flaherty and Lawrence T. Barnett, of Glencoe, Illinois; Frederick V. Spiegel, of Kenilworth, Illinois; and Augustus W. Green, of Chicago are receiving the War Cross of Merit. Solomon J. Simmons, of Kenosha, Wisconsin; Scott Bone, Howell G. Jenkins, and Arthur Meyer, all of Chicago, are members of the section.

Jerome Flaherty and Lawrence Barnett, seventeen year old ambulance boys, were driving without lights through the rain their first night on duty, when they lost their way. They came on a soldier who told them to stop their engine because they were in No Man's Land within 600 feet of the Austrian trenches. In the dread of being captured by the Huns they waited to make their escape until Austrian star-shells lit up the road.

Frederick Spiegel worked forty-eight hours with only two hours sleep and for five days and nights with only about three hours sleep a night. Augustus Green went into the first battle of the Piave river and drove for four days without resting long enough even to take off his shoes.

Although A Lieutenant Ernest M. Hemingway, of Oak Park, Illinois, was wounded in 237 places, he carried a helpless comrade to safety before he collapsed. He is cited to receive the Silver Medal of Valor, the second highest award of the Italian command. He writes:

"The wounds from the trench mortar didn't hurt a bit, and the machine gun bullet just felt like a smack on the leg by an icy snow ball. I got up and got my wounded to the dug-out.

"It gives you an awfully satisfactory feeling to be wounded; it's getting beaten up in a good cause. There are no heroes in this war. We all offer our bodies and only a few are chosen. They are the lucky ones. I am proud and happy that mine was chosen, but it shouldn't give me any extra credit."

Lieutenant Hemingway, convalescing from 237 wounds, being driven around Milan by an Italian Officer.

The American Red Cross Central Division Bulletin (7 December 1918), annotated by Bill Horne. *McKeldin Library, University of Maryland.*

Page 12

THE OAK PARKER

February 1, 1919

Published every Saturday at 723 Lake
street, Oak Park, Ill., by
THE OAK PARKER COMPANY
Phones: Oak Park 7800, 7801, 7802

ALBERT E. BERRY.................President
M. A. J. BERRY..........Secretary-Treasurer

Entered as second class matter at the Oak Park,
Ill. Postoffice.

Subscription rate $2.00 per year, payable in
advance
Advertising rates upon application

FIRST LIEUTENANT HEMINGWAY

Comes Back Riddled With Bullets and Decorated With Two Medals

By Roselle Dean

When the war broke out Ernest M. Hemingway was wielding a pencil for the Kansas City Star. His future looked promising as a newspaper man, for Ernest had a style of diction that was all his own. When uniforms began to collect and circulate about the streets, the young scribe lost his interest in "scoops" and "spreads" and waxed moody and restless. The spirit of the war was in his veins! One day he tossed the pencil into the waste basket and started out to enlist. But here his patriotic spirit met with rebuff—for one of Ernest's bright brown eyes did not work as nimbly as it should in the estimation of the navy and Marine Corps recruiting inspectors. Even the British army could not overlook that eye—which to all appearances, is a perfectly good orb. But Ernest had the patriotic spirit and enthusiasm of nineteen years, and he made up his mind to "go over" at all costs. Then his opportunity came to get into the Italian ambulance service, and the young scribe sailed across—with the eye that had caused him so much trouble in enlisting—and had no doubt to its credit a record for breaking hearts. Last May he landed in the Trentino mountains of Italy and was in the big Austrian offensive along the Piave river. He moved later to Fossalta and became attached to an Italian infantry regiment there, remaining from the middle of June until he was wounded on the 8th of July. In the fight at Fossalta he was wounded three times when he went with a motor truck into the front lines to distribute cigarets and block chocolate to the soldiers. In No Man's Land, he was at the observation post when a big shell came in and burst, hitting him and killing two Italian soldiers at his side. This felled the young hero, deeply implanting shot in both knees. As soon as he was able to crawl, however, and still under fire, he picked up a wounded man and carried him on his back into the Italian trenches, despite the fact that he was knocked down twice by machine gun fire, which struck him in the left thigh and right foot. In all, Lieutenant Hemingway received thirty-two 45-caliber bullets in his limbs and hands, all of which have been removed, except one in the left limb which the young warrior is inclined to foster as a souvenir—if his surgeon-father does not deprive him of this novel keepsake.

In view of all the shot and shell which lodged itself in this soldier's body while

he plunged without fear into the most dangerous places, his commission, the silver medal of valor and the cross of war are honors none too great for him to bring back. The greatest thing of

FIRST LIEUTENANT HEMINGWAY
Returns from the Ambulance Service in Italy

all, perhaps not to him, for death could have had no terrors for one who persisted in facing it as he did, but to those who love him, was that he has lived to come back.

Lieutenant Hemingway scoffs at being referred to as "a hero." "I went because I wanted to go," he said, in his frank way. "I was big and strong, my country needed me, and I went and did whatever I was told—and anything I did outside of that was simply my duty." To interview this officer, something over six feet tall and handsome as an Apollo, was quite enervating, for, after having beguiled him into The Oak Parker office, he was not disposed to talk about himself. Only in a general phase of conversation were his views on the war gleaned. His valor, however, preceded him across seas—his medals and Italian newspapers tell the rest. On being pinned down, he did admit that encountering a bullet was like being hit with an icy snowball, the pain arriving some time later. Lieutenant Hemingway submitted to having twenty-eight bullets extracted without taking an anaesthetic. His only voluntary comment on the war is that it was "great sport" and he is ready to go "on the job" if it ever happens again.

No story is quite complete without a thread of romance, and we are inclined to believe that somewhere in sunny Italy there is a dark-eyed, olive-skinned beauty, whose heart beats for one—and one only—"Americano" soldier, who arrived in the U. S. on the Verdi about a week ago and is now domiciled with his parents, Mr. and Mrs. C. E. Hemingway, at 600 North Kenilworth avenue.

A soldier-grandfather, Anson T. Hemingway, at 400 North Oak Park avenue, who did his bit in the Civil War, also rises with the rest of us to salute "First Lieut. Ernest M. Hemingway, hero of the Italian war ambulance service."

FIRST PRESBYTERIAN NOTES

Dr. John M. Vander Muelen of the First Presbyterian church preached in Detroit last Sunday, occupying the pulpit of Dr. Joseph Vance, formerly pastor of the Hyde Park church of Chicago. In his absence the pulpit of the First Presbyterian church was filled morning and evening by Rev. John E. Kuizenga of Holland, Mich., a professor in the Western Theological seminary of the Reformed Church of America and a long-time friend of the Oak Park pastor.

Dr. Kuizenga is one of the strong men of the denomination and, unlike some other specialists in his profession, his work in the study and classroom has not diminished his power as a great preacher. His large audiences both morning and evening expressed their high appreciation of the man and his message.

Dr. Kuizenga selected as his theme for his evening serman "The Limitations of Life," based on Paul's words in "Remember my bonds." He said when Paul wrote these words he was chained to a Roman soldier, and this was his delicate apology for his signature to a letter which he had dictated to another person. Every life, he said, had its limitations either of birth, of race or of conditions. In the second place, God reckons with our limitations. At the end He will not ask, "How far did you get?" but "How far have you come?" Browning expresses this thought in the words, "All that I aspired to be, but failed to be, comforts me." In the third place, our limitations are our supreme opportunity. "This does not mean that we accept the doctrine of submissions as a sort of fatalism," said the preacher. "I know a girl who hated God because she was homely, and her mother had told her that she ought not to complain, for God had made her that way. But God overrules the limitations of life and makes even the afflictions and hard experiences to widen the spiritual horizon and minister to the freedom of the soul."

A solo by Mrs. Smith of the choir, beautifully sung, reinforced the appeal of the sermon.

Music at Second Presbyterian

Program of music to be given Sunday evening, February 2, at the Second Presbyterian Church by the quartet, composed of Mrs. Alfred Newman, soprano; Miss Anna C. Braun, contralto; Arthur Jones, tenor; Murray C. Eldredge, bass, and Miss Edna L. Whitmore, organist:

Prelude—Grand Offertoire in D	Batiste
Miss Whitmore	
The Strain Upraise	Buck
Quartet	
Watchman, What of the Night?	Sargent
Mr. Jones and Mr. Eldredge	
Oh, For a Closer Walk With God	Radcliff
Quartet	
The Voice in the Wilderness	Scott
Miss Braun	
Sanctus	Gounod
Postlude—March in B Flat	Silas
Miss Whitmore	

The Edgar Rice Burroughs home at 325 North Oak Park avenue has been leased to W. W. Fowler, 426 Clinton avenue. The lease was made by G. Whittier Gale & Co.

It Pays
Well
To Pay
Attention

THE TRAPE

VOLUME VIII. NO. 13   OAK PARK, ILL., FRIDAY, MARCH 21, 1919

Oak Park Wins Tra

HEMINGWAY SPEAKS TO HIGH SCHOOL

With Italian Ambulance Service of Red Cross—Later Commissioned in Italian Army

WOUNDED IN PUSH ON PIAVE

By Edwin Wells

Lieut. Ernest M. Hemingway '17, late of the Italian Ambulance Service of the American Red Cross and then of the Italian Army spoke of his experiences in Italy at assembly last Friday. Caroline Bagley a classmate of the speaker introduced him to an audience the greater part of which already knew him.

"Stein" as he has been nicknamed, had lost none of the manner of speech which made his Ring Lardner letters for the Trapeze of several years ago so interesting. He told of his experiences first in a quiet sector in the Lower Piave and last in the final big Italian drive.

The "Arditi"

He seemed especially interested in a division of the Italian Army called 'Arditi'. "These men" he said, "had been confined in the Italian penal institutions, having committed some slight mistake such as --well--murder or arson, and were released on the condition that they would serve in this division which was used by the government for shock troops.

Armed only with revolvers, hand grenades, and two bladed short swords, they attacked, frequently stripped to the waist. Their customary loss in an engagement was about two-thirds."

On the day of which Lieut. Hemingway was speaking, they came up in camions, the whole regiment singing a song which from any other body of men would have meant three months in jail. Hemingway sang the song for the audience in Italian and then translated it. Several hours after their initial engagement with the enemy, Lieutenant Hemingway saw a wounded captain being brought back to a field hospital in an ambulance.

He had been shot in the chest but had plugged the holes with cigarettes and gone on fighting. On his way to the hospital he amused himself by throwing hand grenades into the ditch just to see them go off.

Continued on Page 3

CROSS COUNTRY RUN SCHEDULED FOR APRIL 18

By Ormond Lyman

The date of the annual Cross Country Run has been set for Friday afternoon April 18th. This will give

ERNEST HEMINGWAY

DRAMA CLUB SHOW WILL BE GIVEN MAY 16

By Geraldine Barry

At the Drama Club meeting Tuesday afternoon, it was decided that the club would give its annual show on May 16. The play or plays to be given at this time have not yet been chosen.

There is to be a contest in the senior class for the best stunt to be given on Class Day. This will be conducted in the same manner as that for the class song.

Up to this time the class day stunt has been a short hastily constructed affair, and most of the afternoon has been taken up with the awarding of athletic numerals. This year a longer and more pretentious program will be given.

The girls and boys drama clubs have been united with Harold Wright president and Margaret Patch, treasurer.

At the try-outs, held on Thursday of last week, seven girls and eleven boys were chosen.

The girls are Miriam Arey, Virginia Scarritt, Marjorie Garvey, Romona Dalzell, Ethlyn Rounseville, Geraldine Barry and Erma Neil.

The boys were Steward Pettigrew, Harold Lewis, William Wallace, Gorton Ritchie, Lawton Tabor, Joseph Godfrey, Donald Patten, William Whitner, Lawrence Foster, Harold Ruggles and Jean Schureman.

GYM BOYS PROTEST AGAINST GOVT. TAX

OAK PARK TROUNCES BLOOM IN FAST HEAVYWEIGHT CONTEST---SCORE 22-6

By Frank Schreiber

With all the old-time pep and punch, Oak Park walloped the Bloom heavyweight basketball team in a fast game at the gym, last Saturday by a score of 22 to 6.

The team work was fast and at no time was the local team in danger. Barney and Sinden featured with their strong guarding, Barney hanging up two ringers. The drafted guard, Moore, kept up his end of the game and kept down all advances that came his way.

Hoff led the scoring with four ringers, while Popken hung up two baskets and four free throws.

Many Fouls Made

The game was marked by frequent infringement of the rules. Oak Park was charged with nine infringements and Bloom with thirteen. The game was not rough but scrappy and all of the cases of fouls were for misinterpretation and slight misjudgments.

In the second half two of the lightweights, Moore and Fellman, were substituted and each gave a good account of themselves. Blackmer played during the last period and caged a ringer with his old ease. Caruso and Swirels were put in the game but time was called before they got into action.

Bloom Team Slow

Bloom's team was slow. They failed to get into action altho the individual work of Toll had the best effect on their team play. Bloom presented a husky aggregation but were poor shots.

Tonight the team meets the La Grange squad. The team will have a chance at the championship, if they win this game, but if they lose they are out of the running for the

Continued on Page 3

Don't Miss These Games!

The Oak Park heavyweight and lightweight basketball teams have their last opportunity, this evening, to beat teams that have caused us defeats. The heavies lost to La Grange—the lights were defeated by Deerfield. Tonight, in a doubleheader in our gym, the heavies and lights play La Grange and Deerfield, respectively.

The Teams Need Your Support!

The teams deserve your support, since victories will mean a chance to win the championship.

Games Start At 7:45, Tonight

SENIOR APRIL FOOL DANCE

The senior April Fool Dance is to be given at the Colonial Club on

TEAMS

Athletes

FRANK C

By Jos

TABL

Oak Park .
Evanston ..
U. High ..
Deerfield
La Grange

Oak Park
U. High ..
La Grange
Evanston ..
Proviso ..

Oak Park's won two c school last Patten gymna the annual i events of the seniors ran u the nearest c juniors won v to its closest had most fol given as prize

Coffin an

Frank Coff scoring mach seniors with t ber of the wi total of 16½ **50-yard dash** 220 in 24 4-5 broad jumps feet 7 inches. up a total o honors in the for first in th in the high the three ju pound shot p

Heavy

Of the twe Park placed first place in juniors won fi in every event teams this ye best group o the school ha teams that h more big ho ends. Steger winners were

Fast R

The half-m affair. Kraft trailing Picka

FRANCIS E. SKIPP

METEMPSYCHOSIS IN THE STREAM, OR WHAT HAPPENS IN "BIMINI"?

Thomas Hudson, the hero of Ernest Hemingway's posthumously published novel, *Islands in the Stream*, is a well-to-do professional painter who has come to the Bahamian island of Bimini in the 1930's to live and to paint. He has left behind him three broken marriages, his three boys, and a world which reached from Paris to Mombasa. He regrets as bitterly the failure of his first marriage as he regrets contracting the second except for its consequences, the boys David and Andrew. He loves them and their older half-brother Tom with an affection so intense that he can make their absence bearable only by retreating into the isolation of his work. Work and the anodyne of order and routine, as they sometimes did for Nick Adams and Jake Barnes, control the anxieties which threaten to overwhelm him. Like Jake, Thomas Hudson does not care what it is all about. He has settled for learning how to live in it by narrowing his life, reducing his exposure, cutting his risks, holding tight. His only hostages to fate are his three boys. As he loses them, first David and Andrew, and then Tom, he retreats further and further within the confines of his nostalgia, into an ever narrower life, until at last in a channel along the Cuban coast, where the mangrove presses close on either hand, he finds his death. The three bullets whose trajectories he has come so far to intersect strike with symbolic force: one for each of the dead sons he loved so well, one for each of his broken marriages.

"Bimini," the first book of the three comprising *Islands In the Stream*, functions within the larger scheme to dramatize the affectionate, confident, and understanding relationship which exists between Thomas Hudson and his vacationing sons. Each boy is distinct and individual, and each on at least one occasion is given the center of the stage. But it is the slender, thirteen year old David who dominates "Bimini's" longest, most complex, and most significant episode, a day-long fishing trip in the Gulfstream where he hooks, fights, and loses a giant broadbill. The complexity of the episode lies in the subtle transformations which radiate symbols pointing to a redemptive sacrifice and suggesting an answer to a question pointedly left unanswered at the chapter's end.

The circumstances which combine to give the episode its striking signficance involve the presence on the island of Roger Davis, a close friend of Thomas Hudson's since their young years together in Paris. Davis is a writer whose talent has been tainted by his reliance on a commercially successful formula and a taste for the lurid. The honest novel he is capable of writing is locked inside him by guilt for his failure as a twelve-year-old to save from drowning his eleven-year-old brother, David. "I tried to go down after him," Roger says, "but I couldn't find him. It was too deep and it was really cold."

Overcoming his superstitious aversion to diving, an aversion arising out of his sense of guilt, Roger joins Thomas Hudson's boys on the reef along the edge of the Gulfstream for a morning's spearfishing. Of the three boys, David is most at home in the water, the most enthusiastic and coolly competent diver. Neither Roger in the water nor Thomas Hudson on the bridge of his sport fisherman nor Eddy, the Bimini-born cook in the galley below, have reckoned sufficiently on an unusually high tide. When David, too far out on the reef, shoots a fish, the blood attracts a big hammerhead invading the normally safe waters. Eddy kills the shark with a submachinegun burst from the boat, but Roger, swimming to David's assistance in what certainly would have been a futile attempt to rescue him, is oppressed by a sense of guilty failure once again. "Oh, hell," Eddy says to the remorseful Roger, "What do you want to drink?" Roger replies, "Have you got any hemlock?"

"Cut it out, Roger," Thomas Hudson says. "We were all responsible."

"Irresponsible," Roger replies.

As a consequence of this episode, Roger Davis comes to associate

David Hudson with the ·drowned David Davis, to feel his failure recapitulated and his guilt renewed.

At nine on the morning of the following day Thomas Hudson, Roger Davis, Eddy, and the three boys head through Bimini channel aboard the sport fisherman for a day's trolling on the edge of the Gulfstream between Bimini and the Isaacs, rocky cays to the northward. The day is sunny and calm, the water as blue as ink. The two baits running from the outriggers are "dipping and leaping in the curl of the waves the wake raised as it cut the calm." David and Andrew are in the fishing chairs, each with a rod. Just at noon David's bait is struck by a very large broadbill. With Thomas Hudson at the wheel, and Roger Davis, an experienced blue water fisherman beside the boy to coach him, the long fight begins. On Roger's instructions David tightens the drag on his reel to stop the whizzing line, hauls back on the rod and sets the hook. Overpowering the drag, the fish again begins to strip line from the reel, and David, uttering something between exclamation and prayer, says "devoutly"—the word is Hemingway's—"Oh, God, I think I've got it into him." As David works to reel in some of the line the fish has taken, the eldest brother, Tom, like a pious mariner vowing to the Virgin to reform his life and build a chapel if she will intercede for him in some extremity, says "I'll do anything if we can get him. Anything. I'll give up anything, I'll promise anything."

It is a really big fish, but after two hours David, though suffering, fights him uncomplainingly. Eddy puts a cap soaked in sea water on the boy's head to protect him from the sun which stands almost at the zenith. "The fish will get tired," says Thomas Hudson to reassure young Tom. "It's the fish that has the hook in his mouth." "But he's monstrous," young Tom replies. "And Dave's fastened to him just as much as he is to Dave." With young Tom's words, the ambiguous equation between the fisher and the fished-for (which Hemingway would develop fully in *The Old Man and the Sea*, one of the books of the manuscript which became *Islands In the Stream*) emerges for the first time. The entire episode is given vividly, lucidly, with Hemingway's characteristic respect for accuracy of detail. In a sentence whose movement helps convey "the sequence of fact and motion that made the emotion" Hemingway writes, "Then, astern of the boat and off to starboard the calm of the ocean broke open and the great fish rose out of it, rising, shining dark blue and silver, seeming to come endlessly out of the water, unbelievable as his length and bulk rose out of the sea into the air and seemed to hang there until he fell with a splash that drove the water up high and white."

But without compromising the realism of his surfaces, Hemingway carries forward the hints radiating from the earlier "prayers" of David and Tom to make the action suggest religious equivalents. "David's a saint and a martyr," young Tom says to his father, "I'm going to pray for him." And indeed, young Tom prays as he makes tall drinks of coconut water and gin for his father and for Eddy—Roger Davis declining in deference to his responsibility. Watching as David calls on some inner resource of strength Tom says to his father, "Look how sort of slab-sided he is. His chest and his back are all the same. He looks sort of like he was glued together. But he's got the longest arm muscles you could ever see. They're just as long on the back of his arms as on the front." With Tom's description of David there begins to emerge the image of a medieval wood sculpture of the Christus. The image is reinforced less than a page later when David, as the fish in its great strength begins again to strip line from the reel, "shut his eyes a moment, braced his feet against the wood, hung back against the rod, and rested." It is hardly necessary to see "rod" as the etymological equivalent for "rood" to see David against the cross.

After an interval of high suspense when the fish is nearly lost young Tom says, "Papa . . . I was looking at his feet when I made the drinks. They're bleeding." "He's chafed them against the wood," Thomas Hudson replies. The stigmata soon appear on his hands, too. "He's had blisters and now they're all open," young Tom says, and Eddy's Bahamian diction adds to the emerging symbol when he assures David, "Now listen, Davy. Your hands and feet don't mean a damn thing. They hurt and they look bad but they are all right . . . . But is your bloody head all right?"

"Fine," David replies, adding a little later, "He's the one with the hook in his goddam mouth. He isn't giving me a beating. I'm giving him a beating." His voice unsteady, cursing the fish to find an outlet for his pain, David says at last, "I don't care if he kills me, the big son of a bitch," and then as what he feels becomes suddenly clear to him he confesses, "Oh, hell, I don't hate him. I love him." Here, when the long struggle is nearly over, the crucified transcends his agony in love and forgiveness for the crucifier. Watching, Thomas Hudson "could see David's bloody hands and lacquered-looking oozing feet and he saw welts the harness had made across his back and the almost hopeless expression on his face as he turned his head at the last finish of a pull." Head, hands, feet, and side, and the agony in the face.

At this point it is not yet clear why David, in an exhuasting and painful struggle with a broadbill of a thousand pounds or more, should be shown as man crucified in his determination to draw from the sea—since we are now on the symbolic level—a mighty emblem of fertility, of life, of spirit, or of redemption, an emblem which, it already has been hinted, bears an ambiguous equivalency to the crucified fisherman himself. The thought, however, that Hemingway intends some significance to emerge from his suggestive imagery urges itself in the remainder of the episode and its sequel.

The fish, subdued at last and nearly at the surface, hangs by a thread of tissue, for the hook has been cutting through his bony mouth. Roger lifts him softly and gently by the leader. Then from lifting, he straightens, all strain gone, holding the slack leader in his two hands. Hemingway writes, "The great fish hung there in the depth of the water where he was like a huge purple bird and then settled slowly. They all watched him go down, getting smaller and smaller until he was out of sight." In the transparent waters of the Stream, in the cold depths of half a mile or more, the fish, as Roger Davis assures David later, begins to regain its strength.

The long agony over, Hemingway describes the descent from the cross as Thomas Hudson says to Andrew, "Take Davy's rod, Andy. Unhook it" (the rood, God's hooks), and then writes, "Roger lifted the boy out of the chair and carried him over to the bunk at the starboard side of the cockpit and laid him down in it. Roger's arms were around David and the boy lay flat on his face on the bunk." Pieta. The day of fishing is over. It is six o'clock in the evening. Nine hours have elapsed. A darkness is coming over the world as the boat heads back for Bimini.

Dejection seizes the apostles and holds them for a time. But as David is resurrected from his exhaustion Andrew sits on the bunk and says, "If you'd caught him you'd have probably been the most famous young boy in the world." David disclaims a desire for fame, but all the others declare they would have become famous simply through their connection with the achievement. For famous we can read sanctified. And the fish? "He'd be the most famous of all," Andrew said. "He'd be immortal."

Assured by Roger that the fish will be all right, David agrees to tell how he felt. " 'Well,' said Davis with his eyes shut. 'In the worst parts, when I was tiredest I couldn't tell which was him and which was me.' "

" 'I understand,' Roger said."

" 'Then I began to love him more than anything on earth.' "

" 'You mean really love him?' Andrew asked."

" 'Yeah. Really love him.' "

" 'Gee,' said Andrew. 'I can't understand that.' "

" 'I loved him so much when I saw him coming up that I couldn't stand it,' David said, his eyes still shut. 'All I wanted was to see him closer.' "

" 'I know,' Roger said."

As the chapter ends, David says, "Thank you very much, Mr. Davis, for what you said when I first lost him." "Thomas Hudson," Hemingway writes, "never knew what it was that Roger had said to him."

What had Roger said? Hemingway never tells us. A complicated succession of events, however, can be summarized in this fashion: Roger Davis, admiring David's lightly-worn courage, feeling his own failure of responsibility to the boy in the spear-fishing episode, has come to identify the boy with his own lost brother David. In the long fight with the great fish, Roger assumes responsibility for David Hudson's success and welfare, and like Thomas Hudson, sees the boy's struggle as a rite of passage. "There is a time boys have to do things if they are ever going to be men," says Hudson. "That's where Dave is now .... I know that if David catches this fish he'll have something inside him for all his life and it will make everything else easier."

But Roger Davis surely never said to David Hudson anything so banal as "Now you're a man, my son." Rather, he might have said, "This makes us brothers, Dave. I'm proud to claim you," and felt his old sin redeemed by David's struggle. For Roger understood how David Hudson-David Davis had come to feel himself identified through love with that life symbol, the broadbill. He understood how David Hudson (David Davis) drew up from those cold depths where he had swum for so many years David Davis (David Hudson). In the mystery of metempsychosis David Davis was resurrected in David Hudson—even though both still swam in the cold depths. The mystery came to pass only through the equivalent of David Hudson's crucifixion, a crucifixion which redeemed the guilty Roger. His guilt erased, Roger's creative powers presumably are freed. We feel this to be a reasonable certainty when we remember that before the spear-fishing episode and after telling Thomas Hudson the story of the drowning of David Davis Roger asks, "Do you truly think I could write a novel that would be any good?" to which Hudson replies, "You never will if you don't try. You told me a hell of a good novel tonight if you wanted to write it. Just start with the canoe—"

"And end it how?"

"Make it up after the canoe."

Roger in self-deprecation then gives a parody of the way his commercial talent would falsify the events.

"No," Thomas Hudson answers him. "You could just make the canoe and the cold lake and your kid brother—"

"David Davis, Eleven."

"And afterwards. And then make it up from there to the end."

"I don't like the end," Roger says.

Now, however, through the sacrifice made by David Hudson, Roger Davis is able to confront the materials of his life from which an honest fiction can be wrought. Before "Bimini" ends he leaves for the west with what Richard Cantwell might have called his "last and only love," to undertake his first honest piece of writing. If he can tell his story purely enough it will last forever, and David Davis, resurrected from those cold depths,—"he'd be immortal."

So impressive does Hemingway's achievement appear to me in this long episode that Roger Davis's leaving the novel at the end of "Bimini" seems an especially unfortunate consequence of the fact that *Islands In the Stream* was still unfinished when it was published as a posthumous work. "Bimini" stands, therefore, as a succession of episodes varying in quality from the superb to the embarrassing. They all develop the background and character of Thomas Hudson and concentrate upon showing that his ability to live affirmatively is dangerously dependent upon the survival of his sons in a violent world, preparing us to follow his retreat into ever narrowing paths as the boys are taken from him. The episode of the broadbill helps accomplish these things to be sure, but the agony of David Hudson and the redemption of Roger Davis raises it to a place apart. If that place is a little outside the novel as it has been given to us we might be moved toward charity in our judgment of the author, who, after all, never designated his manuscript a finished work of art.

University of Miami

HANS-JOACHIM KANN

ERNEST HEMINGWAY AND THE
ARTS—A NECESSARY ADDENDUM

Hemingway research may have reached its last frontier with the publication of Emily Stipes Watts's *Ernest Hemingway and the Arts* (Urbana: University of Illinois Press, 1971), but the admirable book cannot of necessity have fully "accomplished the only significant thing that . . .was left to be done with Hemingway" (Philip Young's remark on the dust jacket). Having edited *The Hemingway Manuscripts* (Pennsylvania State University Press, 1969, together with Charles W. Mann, Young should know best that much (still more than thirty pounds) of the Hemingway material (mediocre as it may be in its literary quality) has not yet been published—any new publication will therefore add new material in order to at least quantitatively reduce the validity of an otherwise almost exemplary book.

Thus, the eight hitherto-unpublished Nick Adams sketches in Ernest Hemingway, *The Nick Adams Stories* (New York, 1972, preface by Philip Young), can furnish a commonplace dialog excerpt on cathedrals:

> " . . .this kind of woods makes me feel awfully religious."
> "That's why they build cathedrals to be like this."
> "You've never seen a cathedral, have you?"
> "No. But I've read about them and I can imagine them . . . ." (p. 90)

and an important section on Cézanne:

> He could see the Cézannes. The portrait at Gertrude Stein's . . . . The two good ones at the Luxembourg, the ones he'd seen every day at the loan exhibit at Bernheim's. The soldiers undressing to swim, the house through the trees, one of the trees with a house beyond, not the lake one, the other lake one. The portrait of the boy. Cézanne could do people, too. But that was easier, he used what he got from the country to do the people with. Nick could do that, too. People were easy . . . .
> He knew just how Cézanne would paint this stretch of river. God, if he were only here to do it . . . .
> Nick, seeing how Cézanne would do the stretch of river and the swamp, stood up and stepped down into the stream. (pp. 239-240).

Still, even this important quotation cannot change Mrs. Watts's results but only supplement them (as will future publications of other Hemingway manuscripts).

But, besides some minor items,[1] Mrs. Watts has left out one body of material which is admittedly as hard to find as it is important: the catalog of Hemingway's private library in Cuba.[2]

In many respects the catalog of a private library cannot be an exact indication of its owner's interests because many titles may simply be presents from friends, admirers, or publishing companies; moreover, only an examination for pencil marks and marginal notes can substantiate estimations about what has been read, simply leafed through, or not read at all.

Since working in the Hemingway Museum is as yet out of question, the catalogue[3] is a considerable help though not entirely reliable; upon the author's request, however, Mrs. Mary Hemingway was kind enough to read through a list of 91 titles in order to establish, wherever possible, who had bought the respective books:

> Remembering as precisely as I can, I have checked your list and noted which of our books in paintings and artists (watercolors and drawings, too, of course) were acquired by Ernest or me. But they were all mixed in together in our library in Cuba and scattered around the house and our guest house and our bedrooms—more than 8,000 books—without any index or arrangement in any sort of order, the art neighboring U.S., British, French or Spanish fiction or biography or history. Where I have put question marks (??) I can't remember who bought the books or whether or not we actually had them. We were forever picking up books

when we were in the U.S. or Europe, and forever receiving them, autographed, in Cuba from their authors (Letter, 8/28/72).

Of the 91 titles (40 were added later), 22 were marked: 1 with "?? E. H.", 7 with "[E.H.]?", 7 with "M.H.", and 7 with "E.H."–the marks will be included in the bibliographical data below.

The titles cover the following areas: filming (Ernest Lindren, *The Art of Film; an Introduction to Film Appreciation* [New York, 1948]); photography (A. Hammond, *Help for Beginners* [Boston: American Photographic Publishing, 1938]); sculpture and handicraft[4] (6), architecture (9), and pictorial arts (114).

The books about paintings and painters can be subdivided into the following groups:

4 drawing techniques;
24 general;[5]
1 Russian art (Helen Rubison, *The Art of Russia* [New York, 1946]);
1 Chinese art (Arnold Silcock, *Introduction to Chinese Art and History* [New York, 1948]);
5 German art;
11 Italian art;
14 Dutch/Flemish/Belgian art;
14 American art;
17 French art;
23 Spanish art.

Very much has been written about Hemingway's writing techniques–very little about his knowledge of drawing and painting techniques; Mrs. Watts remarks very briefly: "He also learned specific technique: according to Strater, Hemingway 'learned the technical part of [painting] from Miro and me'" (p. 20). Mrs. Hemingway answered the author's question "Did he consult any of those books (especially the artist's handbook-type books) when writing *Islands in the Stream?*" quite definitely: "For his writing he never consulted the books, I believe I can state flatly. He had an artist's eye and retained a scene in his head, as in the description of the crew bathing in the storm in Iits [cf. Watts, pp. 164-165]. For that sort of thing he needed no instruction."

It is true that Hemingway had a most remarkable perception, but any author who is about to start a book with a painter for its hero is likely to at least initially fall back on some technical literature. It may thus not be mere chance that Hemingway owned four books on drawing techniques: Arthur Zardenberg, *Anyone Can Draw* (Cleveland, 1939 ["?"]), Adolf Dahn, *Water Color Painting* (New York, 1945), George P. Ennis, *Making a Water Colour* (London, 1943), and Ralph Mayer, *The Artist's Handbook of Materials and Techniques* (New York, 1945). It is not unlikely that Hemingway bought these books himself (none of them are marked as Mrs. Hemingway's—who married Hemingway in March 1946) after he had started working on the first part (1941) and the last part (1944) of what in 1970 appeared as *Islands in the Stream*.

The list of general titles—besides showing a considerable amount of art reading matter available—also suggests that Hemingway had visited more museums (Museum of Natural History, Canadian National Exhibition in Toronto—this seems not to have been connected with his journalistic tasks) than the 11 Mrs. Watts has enumerated (p. 234), also that his visits may have been more frequent than indicated by the 36 quotations supplied by Mrs. Watts. Nesides museums, art galleries should not be forgotten, such as for instance the Galerie Flechtheim in Berlin (cf. the following paragraphs) or the "loan exhibit at Bernheim's" (*The Nick Adams Stories*, pp. 239-240).

In Mrs. Watt's book, German pictorial art is hardly mentioned at all—the only exception is the Swiss surrealist Paul Klee, whose picture (mentioned pp. 85, 109; reproduced p. 91) "Monument in Arbeit" (1929) Hemingway had bought and had described in *Iits* (Mrs. Watts deals with or mentions Klee on pp. 21, 82-92, 94-95, 98, 106-9, 132, 138, 141, 178, 223).

These seem to be extensive mentions but a few more details can be added. Hemingway found Klee's picture during one of his stays in Berlin:[6] "he loved to look at it and he remembered how corrupt it had seemed when he first bought it in Berlin . . . . He knew no more about it now than when he first saw it in Flechtheim's Gallery in the house by the river that wonderful cold fall in Berlin" (*Islands in the Stream*, London, 1970, pp. 208-9). Hemingway had bought not only the picture, he also brought back an exhibition catalog (*Ausstellung 1929* [Berlin: Galerie Alfred Flechtheim, 1929]) and allowed the Flechtheim[7] Gallery to publish the first chapter of *A Farewell to Arms* in English as well as to reproduce a photograph of Hemingway by Helen Breaker and the Klee painting in *Omnibus: Almanach auf das jahr 1931* (Berlin & Düsseldorf: Verlag der Galerie Flechtheim, 1931, pp. 73-74). Later on, the Hemingways owned G. di San

Lazzaro, *Klee: A Study of His Life and Works*, tr. Stuart Hood (New York, 1957).

A book that Hemingway most probably bought in Berlin as well is a volume about a German sculptoress: *Reneé Sintenis (Berlin, 1930)*. Another book that Hemingway may have acquired at this time is Julius Meier-Gräfe, *The Spanish Journey*, tr. J. Holroy-Reace (New York, n.d.)—Hemingway's scathing criticism[8] of Meier-Gräfe's representation of Spanish painters in *Death in the Afternoon* (1932)—not made use of Mrs. Watts—is obviously based on this translation. Hemingway possessed three more books on German art and artists: Gabriel R. *Peinture Allemande, XIV-XVIme siècle* (Paris, n.d.), George Grosz, *A Little Yes and a Big No; The Autobiography of George Grosz*, tr. Lola Sachs Dorin (New York, 1946), and a *Wilhelm Busch Album* (Verlag von Bafferman, n.d.). His general uninterest in most German art was certainly not counteracted when, in October 1927, a German woman "usurped the dinner conservation [in Sinclair Lewis' and Hemingway's presence] with a long monologue on the emptiness of all non-German painting through the time of Cézanne" (Baker, *ibid.*, p. 188).

Mrs. Watts's remark that "the Italian painters, as a group . . .are least influential in Hemingway's work" (p. 23) can be balanced by the evidence of the library: Tankred Borenius, *Later Italian Paintings from Titain to Tiepolo* (London, 1946), Hans Tietze, *Tintoretto, the Paintings and Drawings* (London, 1948), Tankred Borenius, *Italian Paintings up to Leonardo and Raphael* (London, 1946), Dimitrov Merej Rowaki, *The Romance of Leonardo da Vinci*, tr. Bernhard Gilbert Guernay (New York, 1928), Bernard Berenson, *The Italian Painters of the Renaissance* (London, 1948 ["M.H."]), Bernard Berenson, *Italian Pictures of the Renaissance* (Oxford, 1932), Jean Dominique Rey, *Fra Angelico* (New York, 1954), Jean Dominique Rey, *Giotto, Frescoes in the Upper Church, Assisi* (New York, c. 1954), Guiseppo Piocco, *Mantagna* (Milano, n.d.), *Giotto: la capella degli Serovegni* (Milano, 1946), and John Pope-Hennessy, *Sienese Quattrocento Painting* (Oxford, 1947).

Van Gogh and Brueghel dominate[9] the Dutch/Flemish/Belgian part of the Hemingway's library: Michael Edouard, *Pierre Brueghel, le vieux (vers 1525-1569)* (Paris, n.d.), Gustav Gluck, *Peter Brueghel, le vieux* (Paris, 1933), *Die Gemälde Peter Brueghels, des älteren (Wien, 1941)*, Jean de Heucken, *Vincent van Gogh, un portrait* (Bruxelles, n.d.), Frank Elgar, *Van Gogh* (Paris, 1949 ["?"]), Frank Elgar, *Van Gogh; a Study of His Life and Work* (New York, 1958,

"M.H."), *Van Gogh, Paintings and Drawings* (Chicago, 1949-50), Charles Estienne, *Van Gogh* (n.p., 1953), Paul Furens, *Van Gogh* (Paris, c. 1948), Paul Fiereme, *Peinture flamande, des origines à 1550* (Paris, n.d.), Leo Van Pukvielde, *Les Enquisses de Rubens* (Bale, 1948), Josef Muls, *Rubens* (Paris, 1955), F. Feis, *James Ensor* (Geneva, 1947), and Leo Van Puyvelde, *Hubert and Jan Van Eyck* (New York, 1956).

Within the framework of Hemingway's writing it is certainly true that, overtly, "there is little indication that Hemingway *used* or was influenced by the paintings of any American artist" (p. 22). But the dry remark that "In his creative works, Hemingway only briefly mentions his friend Peirce and . . .a painting by Thomas Eakins. He also, at one time, indicated admiration for Winslow Homer and for . . .C.W. Russell" (pp. 21-22[10]) can be illustrated by further details.

Peirce had accompanied Hemingway to Spain and Key West in 1927 (cf. Hanneman, G 426), sketched Hemingway in 1928 for a Malcolm Cowley article (H 101), furnished a *Saturday Review of Literature* review with a drawing in 1929 (H 124), painted the cover painting of Hemingway (H 336) for *Time* in 1937, designed the dust jacket (B 23) for Jerome Bahr's *All Good Americans* (New York, 1937, preface by Hemingway), and supplied a 1939 Swedish review with a portrait (H 396). Hemingway, on the other hand, owned Margit Varga, *Waldo Peirce* (New York, 1944) and Waldo Peirce, *New York, American Artist Group* (1945 ["E.H."]).

Mrs. Hemingway had bought *Winslow Homer, a Retrospective Exhibition* (New York: Metropolitan Museum of Art, c. 1958 ["M.H."]), but P. Watson, *Winslow Homer* (New York, c. 1942) may have been bought by Hemingway himself (possibly around the time of the first drafts of *Iits*, cf. Watts, pp. 101-103). For John Groth, *Studio: Europe* (New York, 1945), Hemingway had written an introduction.

More general books about the American art scene are Grace Ragano, *Contemporary American Painting. The Encyclopedia Britannica Collection* (New York, 1945), *Art in America*, XLVI, no. 3 (Fall 1958), Jean Lipman, *American Primitive Painting* (London, 1942), Frederic H. Douglas, *Indian Art of the United States* (New York: Museum of Modern Art, n.d.), *The New Nation America* (New York: Metropolitan Museum of Art, n.d.), *Colonial America: 1607-1776* (New York: Metropolitan Museum of Art, n.d.), Fiske Kimball, *Great Paintings in America* (New York, 1948), James Thomas

Flexner, *American Painting: First Flower of Our Wilderness* (Boston, 1947).

Of important French painters, Mrs. Watts can mention only Cézanne, Degas, and Gauguin; we find them in the library again: John Rewald, *Paul Cézanne,* tr. M. H. Subman (London, n.d.), John Rewald, *Edgar Degas* (Paris, n.d.), Jean Mene, *Gauguin* (Paris, 1918 ["?"]). The following artists, however, are represented only in the library: Roch Grey, *Henry Rousseau* (Paris, 1942), Daniel C. Rich, *Henri Rousseau* (New York, 1942), Jean Cocteau, *The Journals of Jean Cocteau* (Paris, n.d. ["E.H."]), Francis Jourdain, *Utrillo* (Paris, 1949 ["?"]), Robert Coughlan, *The Wine of Genius, a Life of Maurice Utrillo* (New York, 1951), *Matisse: seize peintures: 1939-1943* (Paris, 1943), Francis Jourdain, *Pierre Bonnard* (Genève, n.d.), *Bonnard, seize peintures: 1939-1943* (Paris, 1943), *Claude Monet, huit reproductions* (Switzerland, 1947), Paul Valery, *Daumier, XIXme siècle* (Genève, n.d.), Gilles de la Tourette, *Lautrec, XIXme siècle* (Genève, n.d.), Francis Posca, *Coubert, XIXme siècle* (Geneve, n.d.).

The number of books on French art is rounded off to two general treatments: Maurice Raynal, *Histoire de la peinture moderne de Baudelaire à Bonnard* (Genève, 1949 ["?? E.H."]) and George Besson, *la peinture francaise au XIXme siècle* (Paris, 1949).

Mrs. Watts is able to make extensive use of references to Spanish artists: the following list of books can thus do little more than supplement her findings. The Hemingways had: André Malraux, *Dessin de Goya au Musée du Prado* (Genève, 1947 ["E.H."]), Jean Adhimar, *Les Caprices de Goya* (Paris, n.d.), *Prado Gallery; Souvenir Guide* (Madrid, 1953), P. Gassier, *Goya* (n.p., 1955), Eugenio D'Orz, *La Vie de Goya* (Paris, 1929), *Goya, neuf reproductions* (Switzerland, 1947), James Thrall Soby, *Joan Miro* (New York, 1959 ["?"]), Clement Greenburg, *Jean Miro* (New York, 1948 ["?"]—it contains Hemingway's Miro article), Picasso, *Forty Years of His Art* (New York: Museum of Modern Art, 1939), Alfred H. Rarr, *Picasso, Fifty Years of His Art* (New York: Museum of Modern Art, 1946 ["M.H."]), J. Sabartes, Picasso, *an Intimate Portrait,* tr. Angel Flores (New York, 1948), Pablo Picasso, *L'oeuvre gravé de Picasso* (Lausanne, 1955), *Paintings and Drawings of Picasso, with a Critical Survey* (New York, 1946), Tristan Tzara, *Picasso et les chemins de la connaissance par Tristan* (Genève, n.d.), *Picasso Party* (n.p., 1960), Maurice Legendre, *El Greco* (New York, c. 1947), Eduardo Ordonez, *El Greco y Yo* (Madrid, 1955), James Thrall Soby, *Juan Gris* (New

York: Museum of Modern Art, 1958 ["M.H."]), *Velasquez, huit reproductions* (Switzerland, 1947), Luis Quintanilla, *All the Brave* (New York, 1939 ["E.H."]—the book contains three prefaces by Hemingway[11]).

The only really new items are the already mentioned book about Spanish art by Julius Meier-Gräfe and James Thrall Soby, *Salvador Dali* (New York, 1941[12]).

Finally, the catalog contains books about Spanish, French, English, Italian, and German architecture: Manuel Ayala Lopez, *La Cathedrale de Burgos* (Burgos, 1951), Martin Hulimann, *La France; architecture et paysages* (Paris, c. 1947), Allan Temko, *Notre-Dame of Paris* (London, 1956), Henry Adams, *Mont Saint Michel and Chartres* (Boston, 1933 ["E.H."]), Pierre-Marie Querville, *Blois, son chateau, ses musées − ses monuments* (n.p., 1952), Y. Delaporte, *Les Trois Notre-Dames de la Cathedrale de Chartres* (Chartres, 1953), C. B. Nicholson, *England's Greater Churches* (London, 1946), Joseph Fattorusso, *Florence, the Churches, the Palaces, the Treasures of Art* (Florence, 1957), and Gerhard Hauptmann, Kurt Hielscher, *Deutschland: Baukunst and Landschaft* (Berlin, 1927)—this list may serve as an addition to Mrs. Watt's short chapter "Architecture" (pp. 199-207).

Even though a mere catalog cannot always supply definite information, the collected evidence may add outlines and color to our Hemingway image—especially on the levels of "Hemingway and art books in general," "Hemingway and the artist's handbook," "Hemingway and museums/galleries," "Hemingway and individual artists," "Hemingway and German, Italian, Dutch, Belgian, French, American, and Spanish art," and "Hemingway and architecture."

But in spite of all details we should never forget that creative work is different from research, that an artist selects instead of compiling: "E. perused the books for pleasure. Not as a student. You remember he wrote or spoke of trying to write as Cézanne painted country. That was in the early days in Paris when he first encountered Cézanne's structured landscapes and enjoyed them. A pleasure of the eye, I should imagine" (Mary Hemingway).

Pleasure, however, can be the first step toward creation just as can study—thus it is never idle to investigate an artist's life in his surroundings.

---

[1] Cf. author's review in *Kritikon Litterarum*, I (1972). 243-5. Mrs. Watts also overlooked an early essay (James Thrall Soby, "Hemingway and Painting,"

Saturday Review, XXXVII. [4 Dec. 1954, 60-61]) and Robert Harling's account "A Journey to Hemingway," *London Sunday Times* (19 Dec. 1954), p. 10–besides the paintings by Klee and Miro, Harling mentioned a Dutch hunting scene in Hemingway's study; he also called Hemingway an expert in Cuban, American, and European art.

[2] *Catalogo de la biblioteca del Museo Hemingway* (Habana, 1966). For descriptions of Hemingway's Cuban home (and, occasionally, its library) see Audre Hanneman, *Ernest Hemingway: A Comprehensive Bibliography* (Princeton University Press, 1967), G56, 186, and 210; H 57, 584, 930, 1025, 1177, 1181, 1318, 1442, 1445, 1468, 1536, 1547, 1554, and 1587; also Elisabeth Stiel-Beuerle, "In Hemingways Finca auf Kuba," *Frankfurter Allgemeine Zeitung*, 29 July 1967 (with a picture of part of the library). For references to Hemingway's house in Key West, Florida (and its fewer than 100 books) see Hanneman, *ibid.*, H280 and 1500; also the author's *Übersetzungsprobleme in den deutschen Übersetzungen von drei anglo-amerikanischen Kurzgeschichten* (München, 1968). Mainzer Amerikanistische Beiträge, X, p. 6, n. 27.

[3] It took the author a complicated correspondence and almost two years to acquire a microfilm copy supplied by the Biblioteca José Marti, Habana.

[4] George C. Vaillant, *Masterpieces of Primitive Sculpture* (New York, Museum of Natural History, 1946); George C. Vaillant, *Artists and Craftsmen in Ancient Central America* (New York, 1949); Frederic H. Douglas, *Indian Art of the United States* (New York, The Museum of Modern Art, 1941); *Renée Sintenis* (Berlin, 1930); Jo Davidson, *An Exhibition of Sculpture* (New York, n.d.); *India's Gods and Kings* (New York, The Metropolitan Museum of Art, n.d.).

[5] *Masterpieces; the Home Collection of Great Art, I* (Chicago, 1950); San A. Lewison, *Painters and Personality: A Collector's View of Modern Art* (New York, 1948); Thomas Craven, *Modern Art, the Men, the Movements, the Meaning* (New York, 1934, "?"); *The Frick Collection–Paintings* (New York, 1949); Olga Strettova, *Baroque Portraits* (Artia, n.d.), listed twice: portifolio including art news manual (New York, 1959); *Moscow, Musée de l'art occidental moderne* (Moscow, n.d.); Leo Stein, *Appreciation: Painting, Poetry, and Prose* (New York, 1947); Osbert Lancaster, *Classical Landscapes with Figures* (Boston, 1949 ["M.H."]); Herman J. Wechsler, ed. *The Pocketbook of Old Masters, Containing 64 Reproductions of Paintings* (New York, 1949); Thomas Craven, *Men of Art* (New York, 1931 ["E.H."]); Thomas Bodkin, *An Approach to Painting* (London, 1945); Albert C. Barnes, *The Art of Painting* (New York, 1937 ["M.H."]); Thomas Craven, *Famous Artists and Their Models* (New York, 1949); L. J. Bulliet, *Art Masterpieces in a Century of Progress, Fine Arts Exhibition at the Art Institute of Chicago* (Chicago, 1933); *Canadian National Exhibition. Catalogue of Paintings and Sculpture by British, Swedish, and Canadian Artists and International Graphic Art* (Toronto, 1923); *Animals that Never Were* (New York, The Metropolitan Museum of Art, n.d.); Chandler R. Post, *A History of Painting* (Cambridge, M., 1950); Gérard Bauer, *Dessins de maitres (XVe-XVIIIe siècle* (Paris, n.d.); Freres Farias, *Antiquaries. Paintings and Sculptures by Old Masters* (Paris, n.d.); A. F. Hochwait, *The Modern Painter* (n.p., 1923); Jean Leyhaaris, *Impressionism* (n.p., 1955).

[6] He had been in Berlin three times: 1927 (a few days), 1929 (a few days), and

1931 (two days); cf. Carlos Baker, *Ernest Hemingway: A Life Story* (New York, 1969), pp. 188, 205, and the author's "Ernest Hemingway's Knowledge of German," *Jahrbuch für Amerikastudien*, XV (1970), p. 224. The picture must have been bought, when, "in mid-November . . . Hemingway followed the bike racers to Berlin" (p. 205).

[7] " 'He was a very able picture-dealer,' wrote Ernest," Baker, p. 134.

[8] Cf. the author's "Ernest Hemingway and German Culture," *Neusprachliche Mitteilungen*, XXVIII (1975), 16-20.

[9] This may balance out Mrs. Watts's findings—on the basis of the written evidence she mentions Brueghel 15 times but Van Gogh only twice (Hemingway nowhere mentioned either Van Eyck or Ensor).

[10] Mrs. Watts mentions Peirce on pp. 21, 24, and 178; Eakins on pp. 21, 178, and 179-80; W. Homer on pp. 22, 101-3, 106, and 190; Russell on p. 22—but see also the more extensive list of references on pp. 228-233.

[11] Hemingway had written a preface for a 1938 Quintanilla catalog, too; cf. Hanneman, B 28 and C 278. Quintanilla had drawn portraits/caricatures of Hemingway for *Time*, XX (26 Sept. 1932), 47; *Bookman*, LXXV (Oct. 1932), 622; *Town & Country*, LXXXXVII (15 Oct. 1932), 50; *Time*, XXIX (5 April 1937), 21.

[12] Hemingway possessed two books by Soby; Mary Hemingway bought a third one—it may have been more than just chance that Soby was the first critic to deal with "Hemingway and painting" (cf. note 1).

BERNARD F. RODGERS, JR.

The Nick Adams Stories:
FICTION OR FACT?

The *Nick Adams Stories* provides one more example of the biographical emphasis which has dominated, and to a certain extent, distorted Hemingway scholarship.[1] Though reviews of the book have justifiably pointed out the inferiority of the previously unpublished selections, the assumptions which underlie the arrangement of the stories have so far gone unchallenged.

Philip Young first conceived of *The Nick Adams Stories* twenty-five years ago before the publication of his influential *Ernest Hemingway* (1952).[2] By 1948 Hemingway had published fifteen Nick Adams stories in three of his collections, but since they had been presented in "jumbled sequence," Young felt that their full impact and importance had not been perceived. He proposed that Scribners publish all the stories in one volume and arrange them in the chronological order of Nick's advancing age. Though his father rejected the idea in 1948, Charles Scribner, Jr. accepted it in 1967.[3]

The question here is whether Philip Young's arrangement of the stories in this book is "in the chronological order of Nick's advancing age." I would answer that it is not, if we look to the stories, and not Hemingway's biography, for guidance.

If Young had collected the stories in 1948 their arrangement would have been quite different from that of *The Nick Adams*

Stories. In *Ernest Hemingway* Young described "The End of Something" and "The Three-Day Blow" as companion stories of Nick's pre-war adolescence. "The End of Something" was about "... the end of a sort of love affair that an adolescent Nick had with a girl named Marjorie." "The Three-Day Blow," which describes actions that occur almost immediately after those of the previous story, was "... a many-sided story ... a skillful representation of the conversation of adolescent boys ... ," which documented Nick's introduction to drunkenness.[4] Both stories would have been placed after the stories of Nick's childhood ("Indian Camp," "The Doctor and the Doctor's Wife," and "Ten Indians") and before the war stories ("Nick sat against the wall ... ," "Now I Lay Me," "A Way You'll Never Be," and "In Another Country").

Most critics have adopted the same chronology, though I have found no complete explication of the two stories which justifies this ordering.[5] Hemingway's own arrangement of the stories in *In Our Time* suggests that he saw them in a similar order. Both Edmund Wilson and Clinton S. Burhans, Jr. have written analyses of *In Our Time* which recognize the internal unity of that book and the chronological progression which Hemingway intended for the Nick Adams stories within it.[6]

In *The Nick Adams Stories*, however, "The End of Something" and "The Three-Day Blow" are both presented as *post*-war stories. Young's explanation is that:

> ... there is no *really* good way of arranging it. The two stories ... are based on experiences Ernest had—and people he knew—in that *post*-war summer, during half of which he was still a teen-ager. He is seeing himself as Nick in all these, and Nick comes across as immature because despite the war Ernest still was. I elected to stick with Marcelline who tells us that at 21 her brother acted more like 16 ...[7]

In other words, in spite of disclaimers in both the Preface to *The Nick Adams Stories* and his original introduction to the book which was published in *Novel*, Young has equated Nick and Hemingway in his arrangement of the stories. Thus "The End of Something" and "The Three-Day Blow" are categorized as post-war stories because the events which they are based on in Hemingway's life occurred in Michigan during the summer and fall of 1919. But is the identification of Nick with his creator, and his chronology with Hemingway's, supported by the two stories themselves and the stories which

precede and follow them in Young's arrangement? If we accept
Young's view of the stories as chapters in a kind of novel we must
demand that the protagonist of "The End of Something" and "The
Three-Day Blow" be a veteran who has lived through the experiences
described in the war stories and that there be nothing in the stories
which will date their action earlier than 1919. Since "The Three-Day
Blow" occurs immediately after "The End of Something," if we can
date the later story we have also dated the earlier one.

A re-reading of the two stories leaves a general impression worth
noting. The stories describe, we feel as we read them, the first pains
of youthful love and its romanticized loss which each of us can
identify with. In our innocence we too felt our first love would be
eternal. It ended and we felt, as Nick does, that "everything was gone
to hell inside," and we didn't quite know why. We too tried to
forget, to put it all out of our mind—perhaps by our first
drunkeness—and to talk of other things. We too saw ourselves as deep
philosophers after the experience. But this all happened—and this is
why the experience was so indelible—the *first* time our innocent
illusions were shattered; and we feel that it is all happening to Nick
for the first time in these stories. But can we find the sources in the
story which evoke this feeling?

In the context of our discussion it is also important to note any
specific references in the story which might date them as pre-war
experiences. There is a reference in "The Three-Day Blow" which
does just that. In their discussion of the day's newspaper reports
about the close of the baseball season, Nick and Bill mention that the
Cardinals lost a double-header to the Giants coached by "McGraw"
(p. 207). Since John J. McGraw managed the Giants from 1902 until
1932, this reference alone does not help too much in dating the
action. However, the boys also mention a player McGraw had
recently acquired—Heinie Zim. Heinie Zim (Henry Zimmerman,
1887-1969) was acquired by McGraw during *the latter half of the
1916* season from the Chicago Cubs. Hemingway's use of an actual
ballplayer's name and his specific reference to the player's recent
acquisition certainly suggest an effort on his part to date the story
for his readers as occurring before Nick's war experiences.[8]

The war stories are also important because they describe experiences which Nick should already have had before the action of
"The Three-Day Blow" if we are to accept the chronology of *The
Nick Adams Stories*. If Nick had undergone the wounds, both
physical and psychological, which occur in these stories could he

experience the sense of painfully lost innocence we feel in these two stories? *Could* the Nick Adams of "The Three-Day Blow" have lived through the war experiences recounted in the stories about his life—not Hemingway's?

The first war experience which Nick has is the wounding described in "Nick sat against the wall . . . . " This wounding, as Philip Young has shown, is one of the central experiences in Nick's life. In "Cross-Country Snow" and "Big Two-Hearted River," the stories Hemingway placed after the wounding in each of his collections, the effects of the wounding are evident. In "Cross-Country Snow" Nick cannot Telemark because of his bad leg (p. 250). In "Big Two-Hearted River" the psychological wound of the veteran Nick is subtly presented. There is no reference in either of the stories under discussion to any kind of wound or its after-effects. Yet Young places both stories *before* "Big Two-Hearted River" and the new story "Summer People" which begins with Nick putting his arm down into a spring and thinking " . . . I wish I could put all of myself in there. I bet that would fix me" (p. 217).

Nick's nightmares and insomnia—after-effects of his wounding—are the center of "Now I Lay Me" and become almost automatic in any reference to sleep made by the Hemingway hero. But in "The Three-Day Blow" Nick refers to the loft of the cabin as a place where he occasionally sleeps with Bill and Bill's father without any suggestion of these traumatic elements.

"A Way You'll Never Be" has Nick tell Para that "I was stinking in every attack" (p. 159), yet most of the humor in "The Three-Day Blow" clearly is caused by the attempts of two inexperienced drinkers to act as though they have everything under control. From Bill's opening imitation of an adult host's nonchalant "Have a drink?" the story progresses to attempts at adult discussions of literature, baseball, life, and love—all conducted as the boys grow progressively more drunk. After Bill's opening remark, Nick "*reached* [my italics] the whisky bottle from the shelf above the fireplace" as though it were placed there so that the boys could not reach it (p. 206). They then discuss the quality of the Irish whisky in an imitation of overheard adult connversation:

> "It's got a swell, smoky taste," Nick said, and looked at the fire through the glass.
> "That's the peat," Bill said.
> "You can't get peat into liquor," Nick said.

"That doesn't make any difference," Bill said.
"You ever seen any peat?" Nick asked.
"No," said Bill.
"Neither have I," Nick said. (p. 206)

Nick's concern for showing how practical he can be while drinking seems to suggest a necessity for proving that he can hold his liquor which is not in character with the soldier in "A Way You'll Never Be," but smacks of adolescent competition: "Even if his father had never touched a drop Bill was not going to get him drunk before he himself was drunk" (p. 211). And the repeated "Let's get drunk," spoken by both boys, is not the statement of an experienced drinker.

Finally, the Hemingway hero, as delineated in the post-war stories of Nick Adams and the novels which followed, prides himself on being able to hold his liquor—the initiated are never "messy" in their drinking or in anything else. It is quite clear from both the dialogue and the author's use of understatement and ironic commentary that Nick is a "messy" drunk—a forgivable fault only because he has not yet learned the importance of self-control which the mature hero realizes. Notice the irony directed at Nick's "practicality":

Nick came in with the log through the kitchen and in passing knocked a pan off the kitchen table. He laid the log down and picked up the pan. It had contained dried apricots, soaking in water. He carefully picked up all the apricots off the floor, some of them had gone under the stove, and put them back in the pan. He dipped some more water onto them from the pail by the table. He felt quite proud of himself. He had been thoroughly practical (p. 211).

"That's a swell log," Nick said.
"I'd been saving it for the bad weather," Bill said. "A log like that will burn all night."
"There'll be coals left to start the fire in the morning," Nick said.
"That's right," Bill agreed. They were conducting the discussion on a high plane (p. 211).

The discussion of literature which the boys engage in also contributes to our impression of them as inexperienced pre-war adolescents. Punctuated by critical judgements which range from "It ain't a bad book, Wemedge" to "It's a swell book" and "That's a real book," the discussion of Walpole and Chesterton concludes that Chesterton " ... must be about the best guy there is," because "Chesterton's a classic" (pp. 208-9). Could the Nick Adams who had seen the horrors and brutality of war so graphically presented at the beginning of "A Way You'll Never Be" seriously find *The Forest Lovers* and *Fortitude* "real books"? Could the same Nick Adams who had gone through the war stories, and whom we have heard speak in them, actually have a vocabulary limited to "Boy!" "swell," "great," "That's a swell book," " . . . he's a better guy"? Isn't it more likely that the plot of these novels would appeal to adolescents who have not yet seen the world of the war stories? And that the dialogue would be spoken by such adolescents and not by war veterans?

"Big Two-Hearted River" and the fragment "On Writing" which was once a part of it are also important to compare to "The Three-Day Blow." Could the Nick Adams who avoids thought at all cost in "Big Two-Hearted River" indulge in the adolescent philosophizing of the latter story?

> "There's plenty more, but Dad only likes me to drink what's open."
> "Sure," said Nick.
> "He says opening bottles is what makes drunkards," Bill explained.
> "That's right," said Nick. He was impressed . . . . He had always thought it was solitary drinking that made drunkards (p. 210).

> "He [Nick's father] says he's missed a lot himself," Nick confessed.
> "Well, Dad's had a tough time," Bill said.
> "It all evens up," Nick said.
> They sat looking into the fire and thinking of this profound truth (p. 211).

Certainly a veteran Nick Adams who had seen death and corruption could not believe that "Nothing was finished. Nothing was ever lost" (p. 215).

It is not surprising that Hemingway cut the section titled "On Writing" in *The Nick Adams Stories* from "Big Two-Hearted River" during his revisions. It is a fragment confused in point of view and intention which probably would have destroyed "Big Two-Hearted River." However, the fact that it was originally a part of Hemingway's conception of that story is worth noting here. It includes references to the early writings of "Nick" and to friends from both Michigan and Paris. Of course, here Nick *is* actually Hemingway, which is probably one of the reasons Hemingway did not publish the section. It does present Hemingway's view of "The Three-Day Blow," however, and in doing so reinforces our argument for dating the action of that story earlier than that of "Big Two-Hearted River." While fishing—that is, on the same fishing trip described in "Big Two-Hearted River"—Nick thinks of the past:

> All the books. He and Bill had fun with the books in the old days. They all started with a fake premise. Like fox hunting . . . .
> Most about fishing he and Bill had discovered together. They worked on the farm and fished and took long trips in the woods from June to October (pp. 233-34).

The books that he is thinking back on and the fall fishing he is describing are those of the "Three-Day Blow." If an original part of "Big Two-Hearted River" refers to the action of "The Three-Day Blow" as having occurred in the past, how can we accept the chronology of *The Nick Adams Stories?*

All of the evidence advanced here, as well as our impressions of the stories, suggests that it is not satisfactory to say that Nick is an adolescent in these stories because Ernest was. The Nick Adams who appears in "The End of Something" and "The Three-Day Blow" is a *pre*-war adolescent. Philip Young was right in 1952, before the spate of biographical material culminating in Carlos Baker's *Ernest Hemingway: A Life Story* filled in all the gaps in Hemingway's life and allowed critics to identify him with his fictional creation—even when the parallels are not supported in the stories themselves. There is a *"really* good way" to arrange the stories: approach them as fiction not fact.

University of Chicago

---

[1] New York: Scribner's, 1972. Hereafter all references to the stories in this edition will be included parenthetically in the text. In spite of Philip Young's apparent dissatisfaction with the inclusion of the "fragments" in this edition—a decision made by the publisher—he has said, "Beyond the trivial Preface, the only things I am indeed responsible for in this book are the selection and ordering of the 'real stories'—matters that are not as simple as they may appear." " 'Big World Out There': *The Nick Adams Stories,"* (*Novel,* VI [Fall 1972], 6). Since the ordering of the stories is the issue here, I will refer to the book as "Young's edition."

[2] New York: Rinehart, 1952.

[3] See Young, " 'Big World Out There': *The Nick Adams Stories,"* which discusses the genesis of the book and comments on each of the stories and his arrangement of them in this article which was originally intended as an introduction to *The Nick Adams Stories.*

[4] *Ernest Hemingway,* pp. 5-6 and *passim.*

[5] However, Horst Kruse, "Ernest Hemingway's 'The End of Something,' " *Studies in Short Fiction,* IV (Winter, 1967), does discuss Nick's age in that story and

concludes that he is between sixteen and eighteen which would make the story pre-war experience. His analysis of this story is thorough and most convincing in arguing that "EoS" is an artistic whole which does not require "Three-Day Blow" to complete its meaning.

[6] Wilson's article is included in John K. M. McCaffery, ed., *Ernest Hemingway: The Man and His Work* (Cleveland and New York: World, 1950), pp. 236-257; Clinton S. Burhans, Jr.'s discussion of "The Complex Unity of *In Our Time*," *Modern Fiction Studies*, XIV (Autumn 1968), 313-328, also includes references to Hemingway's correspondence with Wilson about *In Our Time* in which he emphasized the importance of the arrangement. The Nick Adams stories in *In Our Time* appear in the following order: "Indian Camp," "The Doctor and the Doctor's Wife," "The End of Something," "The Three-Day Blow," "The Battler," "Nick sat against the wall . . .," "Cross-Country Snow," and "Big Two-Hearted River."

[7] Philip Young to Bernard F. Rodgers, Jr., 20 October 1972.

[8] Zimmerman later gained notoriety for his error in the decisive game of the World Series of 1917. Bill and Nick refer to him as a "bonehead" which is what his error in the Series was called ("bonehead play"); but 1917 still pre-dates Nick's war experience.

STEPHEN L. TANNER

Hemingway: The Function of Nostalgia

Wright Morris once made the statement: "The 'subject' of Wolfe, Hemingway, and Faulkner, however various the backgrounds, however contrasting the styles, pushed to its extremity, is nostalgia."[1] In the case of Hemingway, there is much truth in this observation. Hemingway's biography clearly reveals his marked susceptibility to nostalgia, and this susceptibility determined in large measure the subject and nature of his writing. Even as a young writer he was beginning, in Carlos Baker's words, "to make fictional capital of the remembrance of things past."[2] But nostalgia is important to the study of Hemingway not simply as it relates to his subject matter, but also in the way it functions as an artistic device for developing characterization, vivifying settings, and producing dramatic rhythm and intensity.

I use the term "nostalgia" advisedly because the meaning of this word is rather ambiguous. In the past it simply meant homesickness, but now, according to *Webster's Third International Dictionary*, it means "A wistful or excessively sentimental sometimes abnormal yearning for return to or return of some real or romanticized period or irrecoverable condition or setting in the past." But even this broad definition is not completely satisfactory, probably because of the subtlety and evanescence of the feelings to which the term nostalgia

163

is applied. In the essay quoted above, Mr. Morris says: "The power and sources of nostalgia lie beyond the scalpel. Nostalgia sings in the blood, and with age it grows thicker, and when all other things fail it joins men in a singular brotherhood. Wherever they live in the present, or hope to live in the future, it is in the past that you will truly find them. In the past one is safely out of time but not out of mind."[3] Nostalgia is not associated with any particular era or any particular civilization or culture. It is ancient and modern, rural and urban. It is found in primitive societies as well as in advanced. It is a phenomenon fundamental to the human creature. Beardsly Ruml, in "Some Notes on Nostalgia," has asserted that "A recognition of the fundamental and pervasive influence of the nostalgic, under whatever names, will enable us to interpret human behavior with a new realism. This re-interpretation of human behavior will make it possible for us to rewrite the drama of sin and self and sex."[4] As I use the term "nostalgia," I will be referring primarily to a person's emotional response to memories of places and events which are, for him, associated with pleasure or satisfaction of some sort, keeping in mind that such emotional response is basic to the human psychology. Ernest Hemingway seemed to realize that an understanding of the nostalgic "will enable us to interpret human behavior with a new realism," and he did make use of the nostalgic in creating his version of "the drama of sin and self and sex."

Nostalgia is often associated with sentimentality, and sentiment seems foreign to the popular image of Hemingway and the Hemingway hero. But the Hemingway hero is not, as many people have thought, a tough, insensitive brute obsessed by an appetite for blood-sports, drink, and women. He is, on the contrary, deeply sensitive and suffers profoundly from the shocks of experience. Hemingway, himself, was not the hard-boiled tough guy that many would have us believe. Instead, he was, as Michael F. Maloney has remarked, "a poet with fine awareness of the manifold impressions of sight and sound and smell and taste, a poet for whom the Michigan hemlock forests of his boyhood are forever at the tips of his senses."[5] Sean O'Faolain claims that Hemingway's "realism" is merely "the carapace or shell that protects, grips, holds from overspilling a nature fundamentally emotional and tender."[6] Anyone who has read Hemingway's work carefully should be well aware that his nature was fundamentally emotional and sensitive and not without sentimentality, though he might have tried to conceal it.

Hemingway led an extremely active life. It was packed with

shooting, big-game hunting, fishing, fighting, traveling, and about as much physical punishment in war, road, and air accidents as the human body can take. He enjoyed activity and adventure and it seems natural that such enjoyment would not be confined to the time of experience, but would last in his memory so that particularly good or exciting times would be reviewed with feelings of nostalgia. Repeatedly in his writing he stressed the importance of remembering. He did not have very much to say about the future, but it is obvious how important the past was to him. In the account of his interview with Hemingway, George Plimpton provides a detailed description of Hemingway's work room. The room indicates on inspection, he says, "an owner who is basically neat but cannot bear to throw anything away—especially if sentimental value is attached." One book case has an odd assortment of momentos—broken toys, insignificant knick-knacks—a collection the quality of which is "that of the odds and ends which turn up in a shoebox at the back of a small boy's closet." It is evident to Mr. Plimpton, though, that these tokens have value, a value growing out of their association with a special person, place, or event in the past. "It cheers me to look at them," Hemingway says.[7] The past had great meaning for Hemingway and he was strongly affected by nostalgia. Malcolm Cowley said of him: "Ernesto never learned that you can't go back. He always tried to go back."[8]

Hemingway was not only particularly susceptible to nostalgia, but was aware of that susceptibility and in certain ways catered to it. Evidence from both his life and his writing indicates that he thought the value of memories is something to consider in deciding one's actions in the present. This means that one might do something not only for the immediate pleasure or excitement involved, or perhaps despite the immediate pain and fear involved, in order to enjoy the pleasure that comes in remembering he has done it. In *Death in the Afternoon* he tells of the young men who participate in the *capeas*, or town-square bullfights. These young men are amateurs who seek experience with the bulls purely for sport, for the immediate excitement, and "for the retrospective pleasure, of having shown their contempt for death on a hot day in their own town square. There is absolutely nothing for them to gain except the inner satisfaction of having been in the ring with a bull; itself a thing that any one who has done it will always remember."[9] Hemingway is speaking here from experience, for as a young man in the early 1920's he had participated in the running of the bulls and had been bumped around with the rest of the crowd of daring amateur *toreros*.

Undoubtedly he enjoyed a "retrospective pleasure" and "inner satisfaction" from having done this because it is the kind of action which produced the sort of memories he valued most.

Green Hills of Africa provides many examples of the importance nostalgia had for Hemingway. Whenever a sportsman relates a hunting experience, it is seldom untinged by nostalgia, and this is true with Hemingway as he narrates his experiences in Tanganyika. Carlos Baker says "The form of the book has in fact been conditioned throughout by Hemingway's 'emotionated' recollection of the best and worst parts of the safari."[10] Hemingway fell in love with Africa immediately, perhaps because it provided such good hunting, or maybe because it reminded him so much of Spain. "I loved this country," he says of Africa, "and I felt at home and where a man feels at home, outside of where he's born, is where he's meant to go."[11] Africa seemed to have a special nostalgic significance for him: before the hunt is half over he says, "All I wanted to do now was get back to Africa. We had not left it yet, but when I would wake in the might I would lie, listening, homesick for it already" (p. 72). His own strong emotional attachment to Africa is reflected years later in the nostalgic reminiscences of the characters in The Old Man and the Sea (1952) and "Get a Seeing-Eyed Dog" (1957). Hemingway himself, of course, returned to Africa a number of times, and kept himself surrounded by his African game trophies and skins right up to his last years.

There are a number of examples in Green Hills of Africa of Hemingway's notion that one's present actions can be evaluated in terms of how one will look back on them in memory. Hemingway derived great pleasure and excitement from hunting big game; in fact, he repeats nine times within the first seventy-two pages that he is doing what he likes most and is having a wonderful time. But in addition to this immediate enjoyment, he is aware that his trip will provide many pleasant memories to enjoy in the future. In his narration of stalking a lion in deep grass with only M'Cola his native tracker along with him, Hemingway says, "I knew that if I could kill one alone, without Pop [the white hunter] along, I would feel good about it for a long time" (p. 141). After he has made an exceptionally good shot and killed a rhino, his wife says, "You're pretty pleased with it yourself," and he replies, "Don't worry about how I feel about it. I can wake up and think about that any night" (p. 80). In both of these examples there is a concern for how he can look back on what he has done; in other words, part of the value of each experience lies in what kind of memory it will make. When Hemingway is feeling discouraged because his kudo were not quite as large as the one of his friend Karl, Pop says to him, "You can always remember how you shot them. That's what you really get out of it" (p. 293). Hemingway's sense of constructing in the present a past worth remembering is a rather unique characteristic. It is as though his mind were a camera and he were collecting snapshots to fill an album which would provide hours of nostalgic enjoyment in the future. He would like to watch the sable on the hillside "and see them long enough so they belonged to me forever" (p. 282). After he has shot a kudu and examined the beautiful animal lying on the ground, he does not want to watch the natives skin it because he would like to remember it as he found it (p. 235). As the hunting party passes through a little village where one of the group had been stalked by a lion while hunting kudu, he suggests they drink some special German beer "in order that we might remember the place better and appreciate it more" (p. 159).

Hemingway found pleasure in closely observing and remembering not for their own sake alone, but also because they were the wellspring of his writing. He had carefully trained himself always to be aware of places, people, happenings, and his own feelings, to observe them carefully and remember them in detail. He advised his brother Leicester, an aspiring young writer, to do the same: "And remember, keep observing all the time. This is college for a writer."[12] "Try to remember everything about everything."[13] Although Hemingway tried to remember everything about everything, in his writing he was very selective in the impressions he used. He felt that if you had observed closely and remembered, then you knew your subject well enough that you could afford to be selective. In *Death in the Afternoon* he asserts: "If a writer of prose knows enough about what he is writing about he may omit things that he knows and the reader, if the writer is writing truly enough, will have a feeling of those things as strongly as though the writer had stated them. The dignity of movement of an iceberg is due to only one-eighth of it being above water" (p. 192). Part of Hemingway's concern for remembering, then, comes from his desire to write and to know his subject well enough that he can write with a special quality, but another part of that concern derives simply from the nostalgic enjoyment that comes from remembering. It is very possible that the basis of his motivation to write and the satisfaction he got from writing was this special tendency to retain and cherish memories of past experience.

Hemingway's main themes were violence and death, and the question immediately arises: What could these themes possibly have to do with nostalgia? It is in regard to this question that I differ with the mainstream of Hemingway criticism. It is generally believed that, for Hemingway, writing was "an exhausting ceremony of exorcism," as Malcolm Cowley puts it.[14] Hemingway himself can be quoted to support this view. For example, Robert Jordan in *For Whom the Bell Tolls* says that he can get rid of an unpleasant experience "by writing about it. Once you write it down it is all gone." Some critics have said that Hemingway wrote out his experience of being wounded as a kind of therapy which would help him get rid of emotional scars. The theory seems to be that Hemingway came out of the First World War with painful memories of which he wanted to rid himself by setting them all down. But if this theory is true, why were those memories not gone after he had written about them? Take, for example, his wounding. He did not rid himself of that memory by writing about it; on the contrary, he wrote about it again and again and over a long period of years. I do not think he really wanted to lose such a memory—he valued it and it was an important part of his writing. He cherished the experience of his wounding with a strange kind of nostalgia.

Hemingway was always concerned with being professional—knowing the right gun and ammunition, the right fishing gear, the correct military strategy—to the ridiculous extreme of reaching for a bottle of Valpolicella "accurately and well" in *Across the River and Into the Trees*. His wounding was important to him because, as he says in *Death in the Afternoon*, he wanted to write truly about violence and death. He valued his own wounding as he did all of his war experience because it helped to qualify him as a kind of "professional." He said that other writers in writing about death closed their eyes at the last instant (pp. 2-3). He did not want to do this, and, I am sure, felt that his wounding and other war experiences qualified him to write accurately about the moment of violent death. In *Green Hills of Africa* he asserted that an experience of war is a great advantage to a writer, being "one of the major subjects and certainly one of the hardest to write truly of and those writers who had not seen it were always very jealous and tried to make it seem unimportant, or abnormal, or a disease as a subject, while, really, it was just something quite irreplaceable that they had missed" (pp. 48-49). Our bodies do not remember pain, and our psychic processes obliterate, or at least attempt to obliterate, those parts of memories which are painful. This means that as we remember experiences which were very unpleasant at the time they happened, we tend to remember only the less painful parts. In this way we might become nostalgic about events that have been important to us even though there was nothing particularly pleasurable about them when they transpired. This is certainly the case with Hemingway and many of his experiences. There is no doubt that his wounding was horribly painful and was an extremely traumatic experience, but at the same time, he took a certain pride in it. According to Carlos Baker, "His experience in being blown up, in rescuing a wounded companion, in courageously enduring the pain of his wounds, had enlarged his confidence." He was pleased at the acclaim he received in the Chicago newspapers and wanted all his friends at home to know the full details of his wounding and his behavior. "He enjoyed the brotherly admiration of his comrades-in-arms, and gloried in his consciousness of having behaved well throughout his ordeal by fire and the long recuperation."[15] When he returned home he gave a speech at his high school in which he recounted his wounding "and held up for inspection his incredibly torn and blood-stained uniform breeches."[16] This hardly seems the thing he would do if he were really so intent on "exorcising" the memory of his wounding. The point is that although Hemingway often drew upon experiences we might consider most unpleasant, these experiences were important to him and he valued them because they helped him to accomplish what he desired in his writing. Such experiences had nostalgic significance for him, and it is important to realize this when examining how he converted them into fiction. Nostalgia, therefore, is at the very center of the process by which Hemingway created art from his own experience and does indeed have much to do with his main themes of violence and death.

In addition to the way it affects Hemingway's subject matter, nostalgia also functions in his writing as an artistic device, as an important part of his narrative technique. A few rather random examples will make this clear.

Hemingway's consistent test for authenticity in an art object was the involuntary subjective response of the perceiver. In his writing he often used nostalgia as a means of evoking this kind of response. He communicated unexpressed emotions by making the reader identify himself with the objectively-described settings and actions and reactions of his characters. Nostalgia, a basic and persuasive human emotion, became a vehicle by which he elicited the subjective response he desired from his reader. "All good books are alike," he remarked in *Death in the Afternoon*, "they are truer than if they had really happened and after you are finished reading one you will feel that all that happened to you and afterwards it all belongs to you: the good and the bad, the ecstasy, the remorse and sorrow, the people and the places and how the weather was" (p. 191). His writing is pervaded by a strong sense of place. He had a love of landscape which is revealed in his descriptions—for example, the Irati River country in *The Sun Also Rises*, the high valleys and streams of *For Whom the Bell Tolls*, or the game country of Tanganyika in *Green Hills of Africa*. Yet seldom in these descriptions does the uniquenesses of the places receive special emphasis. In discussing the description of the Irati River country, Carlos Baker says: "One recognizes easily the generic type of the clean and orderly grove, where weeds and brush do not flourish because of the shade, and the grass gets only enough light to rise to carpet level. Undoubtedly, as in the neo-classical esthetic, the intent is to provide a generic frame within which the reader is at liberty to insert his own uniquenesses— as many or as few as his imagination may supply."[17] Much of Hemingway's description is actually designed to utilize the reader's own nostalgic images. When Hemingway is successful in doing this, what appears to be very objective writing becomes charged with emotion and takes on a subjective significance for the reader.

Hemingway aspired to a permanent quality in art and prophesied in *Green Hills of Africa* that it could be achieved if the artist "is serious enough and has luck" and can get beyond a three-dimensional imitation of actuality into a "fourth or fifth dimension." There has been much speculation about what he meant by a fourth or fifth dimension and whether he himself achieved it. One of the most insightful treatments of these questions is F. I. Carpenter's "Hemingway's Fifth Dimension" in which Mr. Carpenter points out that often in Hemingway's work:

A brief, immediate experience, observed realistically, is described first as it occurred "in our time"; the protagonist is intensely moved, but remains confused, so that the meaning of it seems nothing or "nada." But this immediate experience recalls individual memories of other, similar experiences .... And these "mediate" experiences are suggested by "flashbacks," or by conversations .... And these fragmentary remembrances of similar experiences, by relating the individual to other people, places and times, suggest new meanings and forms. Finally this new awareness of the patterns and meanings implicit in the immediate, individual experience intensifies it, and gives it a new "dimension" not apparent at the time it actually happened.[18]

Regardless of whether or not the nostalgic flashbacks and conversations which appear so often in Hemingway's work constitute the fifth dimension in question, as Mr. Carpenter suggests, it is certain that Hemingway learned to use a peculiar overlay of the past upon the present in order to intensify character and dramatic situation. He always strove for economy, and this method of interweaving the past into the present made it possible for him to give meaningful depth to the present condition of his characters with what appears to be a few casual brushstrokes. Keiichi Harada, in discussing the alternation of dream-memory and actual experience in *The Old Man and the Sea*, remarks that "The experiences of the past are not meaningless facts but are often 'recaptured' by the self through the discriminating and organizing process of the mind in order to establish one's self-identity. Associations and remembrances do not take place at random but are directed toward such an end."[19]

This special overlay of the past upon the present is particularly evident in the novels which treat a short span of time such as *The Old Man and the Sea* and *For Whom the Bell Tolls*. Santiago's brief recollection of his arm-wrestle with the Negro in Casablanca, for example, adds much to an understanding of the old man in his present struggle with the great fish. The time, setting, and personae of *For Whom the Bell Tolls* are rather limited, but Hemingway transcended these limitations and achieved an amplitude and complexity which he had not previously attempted. Because of the fictional requirement that a lifetime be compressed into three days, he made a fuller dramatic use of the memory flashback and of the inner monologue in this novel than in any other. S. F. Sanderson describes the technique in this way: "By dipping into the thought-stream of the hero as he contemplates his present task and the events which have brought him to it, by making Pilar and other members of the guerrilla band relate their accounts of earlier episodes in the war, and by taking us inside the thoughts and memories of various characters, he enlarges its scope to almost epic proportions."[20] Of course, all the memory flashbacks in this book are not nostalgic, but the element of nostalgia is present in many of them, and when it is, it is there for a purpose: to make time past work in a special way in time present.

A somewhat similar technique of using nostalgic flashbacks appears in *Green Hills of Africa*. While Hemingway is hunting for rhino, he sits down to rest under a tree where his thoughts turn to his early years in Paris and he begins to remember places and happenings. These nostalgic flashbacks come from time to time in the course of the narrative, usually as Hemingway is resting during a strenuous hunt, and on the surface appear to have no connection at all with the action of the present. But, in addition to clarifying and expanding our understanding of the hunter's present condition and state of mind, they obviously serve to vary the tempo of the narrative, for they often come just before a sudden rush of action. This device of establishing a tempo for the narrative by alternating reminiscence with reality is used to a greater extent in *The Old Man and the Sea*. The old man's long combat with the fish consists of periods of nostalgic calm (i.e., the dreams of lions on the African beach) alternating with periods of abrupt violent action, giving the story a kind of pulse beat.

Nostalgia often serves, in Hemingway's writing, as the key to what a man is. It seems to constitute what we call the self, for in terms of Hemingway's naturalism a man is what he has experienced, and nostalgia seems to be the process by which the most meaningful of those experiences are selected to be actively remembered. In order for a man to be in control of himself, he must be in control of his memories. If he cannot put his memories into some kind of order, or if he is dishonest about them, his life becomes confusing and depressing. Sometimes pleasurable reminiscences can soothe, comfort, and encourage, and perhaps aid in achieving emotional stability in times of crisis, but they should never become merely an avenue of escape from reality.

Nick Adams' return in "Big Two-Hearted River" to the "good place" which is associated with happy times in the past and his deliberate nostalgic recollections of trout fishing in "Now I Lay Me" suggest the way nostalgia functions to promote emotional stability in times of stress—how it functions in Hemingway's concept of "grace under pressure." The enticement provided in *The Fifth Column* by Dorothy (whose name might have been "Nostalgia" Hemingway tells us in his preface), the solace provided by the flask of absinthe in *For Whom the Bell Tolls* (which serves as a kind of objective correlative for nostalgia[21]), and the reassuring comfort provided in *The Old Man and the Sea* by the old man's recollection of his victory over the great Negro from Cienfuegos in the hand game at Casablanca—all these illustrate the way Hemingway employed nostalgia in order to create conflict within a character and thereby heighten dramatic intensity. Although nostalgia can have a stabilizing and comforting effect at the proper time, there is no place for it when one must face reality in a desperate situation and comport himself as a man.

Wright Morris contrasts the nostalgia of Hemingway with that of Scott Fitzgerald, saying that nostalgia is abundant in the writings of both men, but Fitzgerald takes it seriously and Hemingway does not. Hemingway's nostalgia, says Morris, "is carefully de-mothed before he wears it"—he can control it and, at times, laugh at it, but Fitzgerald, whom Morris calls the esthete of nostalgia, admits to its crippling effects.[22] This notion is borne out by the number of Hemingway characters who must struggle to keep sweet memories in check.

A Moveable Feast, Hemingway's collection of reminiscences of Paris in the twenties, has as an epigraph this statement which Hemingway made to A. E. Hotchner in 1950: "If you are lucky enough to have lived in Paris as a young man, then wherever you go for the rest of your life, it stays with you, for Paris is a moveable feast."[23] Apparently, Hemingway was fond of the phrase "a moveable feast" about that time because it appears twice in *Across the River and Into the Trees* which was published that same year.[24] In one of the places it appears in that novel it is part of this sentence: "Happiness, as you know, is a movable [sic] feast." When we combine this statement with "Paris is a moveable feast," we see that what Hemingway was getting at was that pleasant memories provide a kind of feast, or, in other words, nostalgia is a moveable feast. This feast provided Hemingway with much nourishment as a creative artist. Nostalgia influenced him in his choice of subjects, it influenced him in the treatment of those subjects, and it even functioned as part of his narrative method.

University of Idaho

---

[1] *The Territory Ahead* (New York: Harcourt, Brace & World, 1958), rpt. *F. Scott Fitzgerald: A Collection of Critical Essays*, (Englewood Cliffs, N.J.: Prentice Hall, 1963), p. 25.

[2] "Introduction: Citizen of the World," *Hemingway and His Critics* ed. Carlos Baker (New York: Hill and Wang, 1961), p. 9.

[3] Morris, p. 26.

[4] *Saturday Review*, XXIX (22 June 1946), 7.

[5] "Ernest Hemingway: The Missing Third Dimension," *Fifty Years of the American Novel*, ed. H. C. Gardiner (New York: Scribners, 1951), rpt. in

Hemingway and His Critics, p. 181.

[6] "A Clean Well-Lighted Place," *Short Stories: A Study in Pleasure,* ed. Sean O'Faolain (Boston: Little, Brown, 1961), rpt. *Hemingway: A Collection of Critical Essays,* ed. Robert P. Weeks (Englewood Cliffs, N.J.: Prentice-Hall, 1962), p. 113.

[7] "An Interview with Ernest Hemingway," *The Paris Review,* XVIII (Spring, 1958), rpt. *Hemingway and His Critics,* p. 21.

[8] From a tape-recorded interview with Mr. Cowley included in a ninety-minute radio program on Hemingway produced by the Canadian Broadcasting Corporation. Available on LP recordings through CBC Publications, Toronto, Canada.

[9] *Death in the Afternoon* (New York: Scribners, 1932), pp. 23-24.

[10] *Hemingway: The Writer as Artist* (Princeton: Princeton University Press, 1956), p. 171.

[11] *Green Hills of Africa* (New York: Scribners, 1935), pp. 283-84.

[12] Leicester Hemingway, *My Brother, Ernest Hemingway* (Cleveland: World, 1963), p. 178.

[13] *Ibid.,* p. 156.

[14] "Nightmare and Ritual in Hemingway," *The Portable Hemingway,* ed. Malcolm Cowley (New York: Viking Press, 1945), rpt. Weeks, *Hemingway,* p. 43.

[15] *Ernest Hemingway: A Life Story* (New York: Scribners, 1969), pp. 48, 49.

[16] *Ibid.,* p. 58.

[17] *Hemingway: The Writer as Artist,* p. 51.

[18] *American Literature and the Dream* (New York: Philosophical Library, 1955), rpt. *Hemingway and His Critics,* p. 196.

[19] "The Marlin and the Shark: A Note on *The Old Man and the Sea,*" Journal Number 4 of the College of Literature, Aoyama Gakuin University, Tokyo, rpt. *Hemingway and His Critics,* p. 271.

[20] *Ernest Hemingway* (New York: Grove Press, 1961), p. 92.

[21] "All the things he had enjoyed and forgotten" came back to Robert Jordan when he tasted the absinthe—*For Whom the Bell Tolls* (New York: Scribners, 1940), p. 51.

[22] Morris, pp. 28-29.

[23] A. E. Hotchner, *Papa Hemingway* (New York: Random House, 1966), p. 57.

[24] *Across the River and into the Trees* (New York: Scribners, 1950), pp. 48, 273.

PHILLIP R. YANNELLA

NOTES ON THE
MANUSCRIPT, DATE, AND SOURCES
OF HEMINGWAY'S "BANAL STORY"

The manuscript of Ernest Hemingway's "Banal Story" presents some interesting problems while it suggests much about the actual sources of the story, its date of composition, and its full meaning. The manuscript, together with several other significant Hemingway items, is now located in the Rare Book Room of the University of Wisconsin—Milwaukee, having been acquired as part of the Library's *Little Review* collection.[1] Its four-and-one-half pages are in good condition and permit an exact reconstruction of the original. This is important, for the manuscript was changed in three places by one of the editors of the *Review*. The story as it has come down to us is not the story as Hemingway wrote it; and though restoring the text to the original does not make it a superior Hemingway work, it does at least set the record straight.

The three changes occur close to the beginning and relate to the same occurrence. In the first paragraph, between the sentence reading, "Inside the electric stove seemed to give no heat and rising from his writing table he sat down upon the stove," and the sentence reading, "How good it felt,"[2] the following occurs: "He farted silently into the warm depths of the electric stove." Between paragraph two and paragraph three, a sentence has been deleted: "He farted unvoluntarily." The same sentence occurs again after the

175

paragraph reading, "Our deepest convictions—will Science upset them? Our civilization—is it inferior to older orders of things (p. 215).

These deletions were not made arbitrarily by either Margaret Anderson or Jane Heap. In a letter to Jane Heap accompanying the manuscript, the changes were suggested by the author himself, in case the Post Office authorities would not allow the word "fart." No doubt the editors were a bit gun-shy at this point—they had of course experienced difficulties with the Post Office before—and had no intention of making this rather slight short story a test case on the limitations of freedom and the government's right to censor. So the changes were made. Why the sentences were not restored by the author in subsequent printings is a matter of conjecture.[3] My own guess is that the original was forgotten by Hemingway; the only true copy was in the hands on the *Little Review* editors. Furthermore, it could be argued that "Banal Story" is not unsuccessful in its published version and that there was no great need to restore the three sentences.

However, the original version is superior, if only because it underscores the connection between banality and anality. The character's responses to the pages of Henry Goddard Leach's *The Forum: A Magazine of Discussion* are, in their way, poignant and appropriate. They are not only proper but necessary.

The manuscript of "Banal Story" was sent to Jane Heap from the Hotel Taube, Schruns, Austria, and though the year is not included in the dateline, which reads simply January 30, there is no doubt that this was 1925. A remark in the accompanying letter, to the effect that Danny Frush had indeed been knocked out in the second round by the French featherweight Edouard Muscart (the correct spelling; Hemingway misspelled it as Mascart in both the letter and the story) dates it exactly. The fight, for the featherweight championship of Europe, took place in Paris on the night of 27 January 1925. This indicates that Hemingway was writing the story, or putting the finishing touches to it, between 28 January and 30 January.

The remarks on the death of the bullfighter Maera near the end of the story, are also helpful to dating it. Maera had died in Sevilla, in the barrio of Triana, approximately a month before, on 11 December 1924.

But most conclusive—and most suggestive for critical purposes—is the fact that many of the details of the story, many of the rhetorical pomposities and stock phrases of lowbrow romance and yellow journalism are drawn directly from the pages of the January 1925 issue of *The Forum*. This magazine, edited in New York, was in its day one of the prime organs for the dissemination of what passed as concerned intelligence. In the years of Harding's Presidency it appealed to what it termed a great "silent majority." It offered articles on such topics as the youth movement, civilization and its prospects, the future of science; and it printed poems, usually by ladies with three names, dealing with the wonders of nature, and short stories and serialized novels about the trials and tribulations of virtuous young persons.

The manifesto of *The Forum* for the.year 1925 became one of the phrases taken up in "Banal Story"; " 'Send your mind adventuring!' is the invitation of *The Forum* for the new year, the fortieth of its life as a magazine,"[4] is parodied by Hemingway in, "Are Modern paintings—and poetry—Art. Yes and No. Take Picasso. Have tramps codes of conduct? Send your mind adventuring" (p. 216). The sentence in the story, "Our civilization—is it inferior to older orders of things," (p. 215) draws on the subject of a new *Forum* series discussing the topic, "What is Civilization?" In the first entry, introducing India's answer to the question, Leach writes, "In this age of vast material progress, too many of us are prone to limit our definition of civilization by the very prejudices born of our own particular type of culture." He goes on to add, with great banality, that all civilizations have had something to give to the "brilliant kaleidoscope of history."[5]

The type of romance printed by *The Forum* is well exemplified by the serialized novel *Soundings*, by Arthur Hamilton Gibbs. Hemingway perfectly catches the essence of the novel in his paragraph reading, "And what of our daughters who must make their own Soundings? Nancy Hawthorne is obliged to make her own Soundings in the sea of life. Bravely and sensibly she faces the problems which come to every girl of eighteen." (p. 215) The actual sense of this incredible potboiler is suggested by the summary which precedes the January entry:

Nancy Hawthorne, a charming young English girl, has been spending a year of freedom in Paris,—living the life of a bachelor girl, sharing a studio with her wealthy American friend, Cornelia Evans. During the year Cornelia's brother, Lloyd, and his room-mate at Oxford, Bob Whittaker, have come over to Paris to spend a fortnight with the girls. Nancy Hawthorne has felt herself attracted to Bob. But she is not sure of herself. Her single previous contact with sex has been only an incident; a boy, "Curly", in the little village of Brimble, England, where she has lived with her artist father (her mother died giving birth to her), kissed her one night, but she felt no reciprocal emotion.[6]

And so forth. The rest is just as hackneyed, just as predictable. It was precisely the sort of thing made to offend a writer trying to produce serious fiction.

What I have recounted is not spectacular. But there are some implications that need to be cited. First of all, it should be clear that, contrary to what Carlos Baker indicates in his biography, Hemingway's writing was not in a state of "eclipse" while he was at Schruns in late 1924 and early 1925; at least the eclipse was not total.[7] Second, because of Hemingway's obvious reliance on another text for many of the details of the story—and it should be noted that I have mentioned only the more significant of these—I think it is clearly evident that even before the writing of *The Torrents of Spring* he was showing an interest in the uses of pastiche and parody. Third, a knowledge of the sources of the story helps to clarify its point, that is, the alternatives to fake art and fake reality.

The Forum, in its emphasis on what Leach persistently refers to as "the romance of the unusual," represents only one aspect of the phoniness which bothers the character in the story. Most of the things he alludes to are dubious in value, spurious in substance. At the end, however, when the character turns his attention to the death of Maera, it is plain that what is at issue is the distinction between reality and romance, good art and bad art. The lithographs bought by Maera's fans are poor images of the bullfighter's art: the fans "lost the picture they had of him in their memories by looking at the lithographs" (pp. 216-7). The bullfighters who join the funeral cortege are also suspect; their respect is exceeded by their relief at the death.[8] The only solididy of substance and grace of execution present in the story is represented by Maera. His accomplishments are not developed, though; nor does Hemingway enforce the point sharply. The ending, in fact, is anticlimatic, underwritten. Of course, this is exactly what Hemingway wanted, as an apt contrast to the "romance of the unusual." The real is a matter of unadorned facticity: "And meanwhile, stretched flat on a bed in a darkened room in his house in Triana, Manual Garcia Maera lay with a tube in each lung, drowning with the pneumonia" (p. 361).

Temple University

[1] I should like to thank the Director of the Library for permission to examine the manuscripts and to quote from them. Most notable among the other Hemingway items is a two-page letter to Jane Heap, written shortly after he had finished the first draft of *Fiesta* (*The Sun Also Rises*). In the letter Hemingway discussed at some length the novel's lack of autobiographical elements and its "funniness."

[2] *Men Without Women* (New York: Scribner's, 1927), p. 214. Further references will appear in the text.

[3] Hemingway did revise the story after its first printing in *The Little Review*. Phrases dealing with the character's reading in a "booklet" were not part of the original.

[4] "An Introduction by the Editor," *The Forum*, LXXIII (January 1925).

[5] *Ibid.*, 1.

[6] *Ibid.*, 116.

[7] Carlos Baker, *Ernest Hemingway: A Life Story* (New York: Scribner's, 1969), p. 139.

[8] The original was changed by Hemingway from "Bull fighters were very relieved he was dead, because he did always in the ring the things they could only do sometimes and made them seem cheap and vulgar." The last clause was dropped.

Benjamin Glazer's adaptation of *The Fifth Column* ran for 87 performances at the Alvin Theatre in New York, March-May 1940. Top right: Franchot Tone.

WAYNE KVAM

HEMINGWAY'S
"BANAL STORY"

"Banal Story" first appeared in *The Little Review*, the Spring-Summer issue of 1926,[1] and after slight changes and additions it was reprinted in *Men Without Women*, published by Scribners in 1927.[2] Perhaps because of its brevity and lack of plot, the story has attracted little attention among Hemingway's critics. Those few who have discussed "Banal Story" have failed to penetrate its surface. Joseph Defalco, for example, states that Maera, as an archetypal Christ figure, is the focal point of the story: "The world will not accept true heroes for long, and when heroes die the danger to convention goes with them. In 'Banal Story' . . . the focus points to the addiction of people to unimportant tabloid romances while a singular event is taking place: the death of a hero."[3] According to Nicholas Joost, "Banal Story" is not a story, but a sketch which depicts "the banality and sterility of American life, as typified by the stories, editorials, and advertisements of *The Forum* . . . . Hemingway contrasts American life to life in Spain, as typified by his great Spanish culture-hero Manuel Garcia, the matador known professionally as Maera."[4] In his recent biography of Hemingway, Carlos Baker passes over the story, labeling it simply a "final tribute to the matador Maera."[5]

It is my contention that "Banal Story" is more than a tribute, a sketch, or a satirical attack on *The Forum*; rather, it is a carefully constructed parable that embodies an aesthetic theory, the same theory that Hemingway was to express in various forms throughout his career. A knowledge of the original version of the story and the subsequent alterations, which were made sometime between 1926 and the publication date of *Men Without Women* in 1927, aid one in piecing the apparently divergent parts together. (1) In paragraph three of the second version (214.15), "mused" was changed to "read," thereby removing the narration from a free-flowing stream of consciousness and linking it concretely with *The Forum*, a prominent American magazine of the 1920's. (2) The introductory sentence of paragraph six (215.2) was changed from "His thoughts raced on" to "He read on"; thus the preceding statement—"I must read them"—is to be understood as a brief pause in the actual reading rather than an interruption in a thought process. (3) The next significant change occurs after paragraph eleven (215.25), where "It was a splendid booklet" is added. This informs us that "he" is still reading from *The Forum*. The irony in this statement becomes evident at the end of the story. (4) A final addition occurs at the end of paragraph eighteen (216.17). The statement "He laid down the booklet" separates *The Forum* material from the subject of Maera's death which follows.

The above alterations and additions clarify the two major divisions of the story. The first consists of paragraphs 1-2, 9, and 19 (beginning, middle and end); and the second, paragraphs 3-8, and 10-18. Paragraphs one and two introduce the "He" of the story (either Hemingway writing about himself or a fictional consciousness serving as a Hemingway spokesman) and offer a definition of life, followed by a definition of Romance. Paragraph nine links the beginning and ending of the story, the definitions of life and Romance with the account of death. Intervening are paragraphs 3-8 and 10-18, which illustrate the responses of the Hemingway writer, "he," to the editorial policy and contents of *The Forum* magazine. These two divisions establish the main conflict in the story—that between the true and false responses to life and death.

As is the case with Hemingway's topical satire in *The Torrents of Spring* and *The Sun Also Rises* (also written in the mid-1920's), the satire in "Banal Story" loses much of its impact if considered apart from its historical context. To a new generation of readers unfamiliar with *The Forum* of the 1920's, the middle section of the story must indeed appear puzzling. According to the autobiography of Henry G.

Leach, who assumed the editorship of *The Forum* in 1923, "In five years from 1923 to 1928, the circulation of *The Forum* increased from 2,000 to 102,000, which was in those days deemed satisfactory for an 'intellectual periodical.' " Carl Sandburg, Leach proudly recalled, "was so generous as to call *The Forum* 'the barometer of American intelligence.' " Known as the "magazine of controversy" in the 1920's, *The Forum* directed its appeal to what editor Leach felt was the thinking minority in the American populace. The major portion of each monthly issue was devoted to philosophical debates on the most controversial topics of the decade: prohibition, science vs. religion, the race question, sexual freedom, revolutionary trends in the arts, the population explosion, immigration, and the war debt. "Our editorial policy," Leach stated, "was to keep the magazine objective and recognize that there are sometimes more than two sides to any problem. There is seldom a 'yes or no' and often a 'both-and' in public issues, and we usually presented more than just two facets of a contemporary issue. My personal formula for *The Forum* was that it should 'encourage technological habits of thinking. ' "[6]

Although *The Forum* of the 1920's could be considered progressive, at least from an intellectual standpoint, its literary standards were decidedly conservative. In judging fiction for publication, "*The Forum* demanded," according to Leach, "the three unities of plot, characterization, and style prescribed for the short-story of Poe and Hawthorne." In addition, Leach required that each issue contain "some humor and some religion."[7] Since *The Forum* debates, advertised as "high adventures of the mind," were seldom written in a humorous vein, it was the fiction which was often intended to supply a lighter side to the magazine. It is this combination of intellectual pomposity and critical naiveté in *The Forum's* editorial policy that Hemingway is parodying in paragraphs three and four of "Banal Story."

To stimulate interest in the controversies sponsored by *The Forum*, Leach frequently posed a series of rhetorical questions in his editorial introductions. The following excerpt from the introduction to the March, 1925, issue is a typical example:

> What constitutes a good poem? Is it merely a matter of opinion, of individual taste? Or are there standards which must be adhered to? By whom were they established? ... To-day poetry is being written which does not adhere to the standards of the past: is it, then, to be banned? Or if we accept free rhythms and an absence of those conventions which

formerly constituted good poetry, do we thereby repudiate the old
standards as obsolete and unnecessary?[8]

The questions in the middle section of "Banal Story" parody this
stylistic mannerism, and nearly all of them have specific sources in
the monthly issues of *The Forum* published during 1925.

Corresponding to paragraph six in "Banal Story," for example, are
the following questions from Leach's introductions: (1) May, 1925:
"*The Forum* professes to discuss in the coming years not only the
mechanical means proposed to check war, but the substitutes that
must be discovered for war if it is to be eliminated as a perennial
purger of the human race .... If the Japanese are not to be
decimated by war, where will they find a place under the sun?"[9] (2)
September, 1925: "How shall war be abolished? *Can* war be
abolished? Ever? in our time? How can wars be made safer,—not for
the individual, obviously,—but for mankind?"[10]

The problem of shifting populations on an overcrowded globe,
alluded to in paragraph seven of "Banal Story" by the question "Or
will we all have to move to Canada?" was a familiar subject in *The
Forum*. In the introduction to the May issue of 1925 Leach asked,
"Can the waste places of central Australia and the Canadian arctic
and the wet jungles of the Amazon be inhabited?" and "Will
scientific agriculture and diet and housing make more room?"[11] The
first sentence of paragraph eight ("Our deepest convictions—will
Science upset them?") refers to another major concern of *Forum*
contributors during 1925.[12] In introducing a series of articles under
the heading "Evolution and Daily Living" in the February issue,
Leach wrote, "Science has of late been going the way of the agnostic
and mechanist, forgetful of the mind, let alone the soul .... Some
theologians, on the other hand, have made an equally sorry mess of it
by blindfolding their eyes to science. The time has come for a
reconciliation ...."[13] Two months later (April, 1925), Leach
stated, "In bringing together the views of future-minded scientists
and religious thinkers, *The Forum* is trying to plumb the depths of a
spiritual reawakening that may help to fuse into effective meaning
the chaotic mass of facts with which modern research has over-
whelmed us."[14]

The second sentence of paragraph eight in "Banal Story" echoes
Leach's introduction to a series of anthropology studies under the
general heading "What is Civilization?" which *The Forum* initiated in
January, 1925: "The Editor is setting out upon the impossible

adventure of discovering civilization. He has been told that twentieth century America, for all its radio and its bull markets, is not the be-all, nor the end-all of human life. Is it possible that men have already known better ways of living in the past and that we their descendants have recklessly obliterated the highroads they have built to happiness?"[15]

Hemingway was not only parodying Leach's stylistic mannerisms and the technological habits of thought which he sought to promote, but also the format which *The Forum* debates followed. Leach outlined this format in his introduction to the April, 1925, issue:

> *The Forum* believes that the best way of dispelling the ignorance and the bias that obscure these tremendous issues is to present in juxtaposition, the interpretations,—no matter how divergent—of writers who have devoted to them the most earnest consideration. Steel and flint are hard and useful *per se*, but only when they come into sharp impact do they strike off the incendiary spark of truth.[16]

The parody of this formula in "Banal Story" is two-fold. As we have already noted, the structure of the story itself follows *The Forum* pattern. Divergent interpretations (those of the Hemingway writer as opposed to those of *The Forum*) of "tremendous issues" (life and death) are juxtaposed. More specifically, Hemingway is reducing the formula to the level of the absurd in such examples as the following. In paragraph ten of "Banal Story" he borrows the title of a *Forum* article, "Big Men—Or Cultured?"[17] and proposes to answer the question according to Leach's formula of juxtaposing opposites: "Take Joyce. Take President Coolidge." The remainder of the paragraph follows the same pattern. The author of the article "Big Men—Or Cultured?" was a Yale student voicing a protest against the spirit of "be a big man or bust," which he felt had invaded the Yale campus. Hemingway asks, "What star must our college students aim at?" and answers with another set of opposites. Doctor Henry Van Dyke, whom *The Forum* advertised as "philosopher, poet, essayist, spiritual teacher, and master teller of tales,"[18] is placed between two prominent American prize fighters of the 1920's, Jack Britton and Young Stribling.

The rhetorical question which introduces paragraph eleven refers to Arthur Hamilton Gibbs' novel *Soundings*, serialized in *The Forum* from October of 1924 through April of 1925. Nancy Hawthorne, the heroine, is an eighteen-year-old English girl whose mother died at her birth, and whose father attempts to raise her alone in the small village of Brimble. One night Curly, a village boy, kisses Nancy and she becomes restless, bringing "both father and daughter to the tardy realization that she is grown up."[19] As a result, Nancy's father decides to send her off to the Continent alone, to make the "Soundings" of life for herself. The novel, as one might suspect, is mawkishly sentimental. Nancy's hero is a major in the United States Army, who after "strafing the Huns" returns to her to live happily ever after, and the virtuous, strong-minded girl is rewarded with marriage and children. *Soundings* is an example of the fiction which *The Forum* advertised as "bits of real life." Holding the heroine Nancy Hawthorne up as a model for young girls to follow, is as false, Hemingway is saying, as substituting "some humor and some religion" for a realistic depiction of death and tragedy. The next statement, "It was a splendid booklet," then, is to be understood as sarcasm on the part of the writer as he pages through *The Forum*. The paragraph which follows is a return to the parody of editor Leach's formula for problem solving, illustrated in paragraph ten.

The attack on *The Forum's* editorial policy continues in paragraph fourteen. "Think of these things in 1925," rather than "feel" or "experience" these things, corresponds to Leach's promise of the "high adventure of the mind."[20] The question, "Was there a risqué page in Puritan history?" possibly relates to an article "In the Wicked Old Puritan Days," published in *The Forum* American Series in April of 1926.[21] The question, "Were there two sides to Pocahontas?" is another playful treatment of *The Forum* debates. "Did she have a fourth dimension?" a question added after the first printing of the story, could refer to Leach's introductory statement in the August, 1925, issue. Here the editor wrote "that civilization is a multiplication of so many factors that it will be differently defined by every mind that attempts an analysis. It belongs to the 'fourth dimension' terms that baffle the average understanding."[22]

The sources for paragraph fifteen of "Banal Story" ("Are modern paintings—and poetry—Art? Yes and No. Take Picasso.") can also be found in specific issues of *The Forum*. In June, 1925, Leach wrote, "Music has long claimed the right to be abstract as well as to imitate nature; but can painting and sculpture also break away altogether from illustrating things as they are, and claim to be pure art?"[23] Following, was a debate entitled "Is Cubism Pure Art?" Walter Pack contributed the first article, "Picasso's Achievement,"[24] and Alfred Churchill countered with "Picasso's Failure."[25] The topic was introduced again at the end of the July, 1925, issue when Leach reprinted letters from the readers under the title, "Pure Art? Or 'Pure Nonsense'?"[26]

The first sentence of paragraph sixteen—"Have tramps codes of conduct?"—likely refers to the article "Tramps and Hoboes," by Towne Nylander, published in *The Forum* in August of 1925.[27] "Send your mind adventuring," the next sentence of the paragraph, was one of Leach's favorite mottoes. In the December issue of 1924, for example, Leach wrote, "Send your mind adventuring! is the invitation of the December *Forum* . . . ." Introducing an article by Vilhjalmur Stefansson, he added, "Stefansson carries the mind adventuring to the Orient by short cuts through the air across the Arctic ice. And the adventure of the mind is continued in other articles . . . ."[28] In the following issue, January, 1925 Leach announced: "Send your mind adventuring! is the invitation of *The Forum* for the new year, the fortieth of its life as a magazine."[29]

The two concluding paragraphs of *The Forum* section of the story imitate Leach's manner of editorial advertising and are intended to be read ironically. Paragraph seventeen parallels the introduction of a new serial to appear in *The Forum* of May, 1925: "Readers of *The Forum* have learned to expect a serial of wit and charm, rich in situations, brilliant in character development, challenging in thought."[30] Paragraph eighteen echoes Leach's statement in the December, 1924, issue: "Other journals may follow other high adventures,—sex, success, travel—but for *The Forum* we modestly announce the high adventure of the mind."[31]

Serving as a deliberate contrast to the responses to life offered by editor Leach and *The Forum* are the writer's responses to life and death, arranged at the beginning, the middle, and the end of "Banal Story." With this contrast in mind, we can follow the shift in tone which occurs in the middle section. In the first two paragraphs the writer is responding to the immediate, the commonplace and physical; therefore, he is emphatic ("How good it felt!") and colloquial ("Mascart had knocked Danny Frush cuckoo"). Turning to *The Forum* in paragraph three, Hemingway imitates the formal diction, the logical, abstract approach to experience, and the Socratic method of debate which *The Forum* prided itself upon.

Life that concerns the Hemingway writer is demonstrated in paragraph one. Life, "he" proclaims after rising from his writing-table, consists of that which one perceives with one's senses, whether it be in the *tasting* and *smelling* of an orange, *seeing* the snow turn to rain, or *feeling* the heat of the stove on one's bottom. The writer's definition of life also includes romance, but this is not "the Romance of the unusual," which *The Forum* promises will intoxicate the minds of its readers, but it is the romance of everyday struggle encountered by people of all countries and all educational levels. Not limited to the writer's immediate environment, it is the romance that one might find recorded in the daily newspaper: a boxing match "Far away in Paris," a heavy snow-fall "Far off in Mesopotamia," or a cricket match "Across the world in distant Australia."

In paragraph nine, the writer's mind suddenly jumps from the pages of *The Forum* as he hears in his imagination the sound of the axes of gum-choppers in "the far-off dripping jungles of Yucatan." Why does Hemingway allow for this particular shift? There are at least three sources in *The Forum* of August, 1925. Leach explained that "The cover design of *The Forum*, in use for eight months, was drawn by Alfred C. Bossom from old Mayan Indian motifs." The August issue contained an explanation of the design by Herbert J. Spinden.[32] This same issue featured an introductory poem "To the Mayas" by H. Phelps Clawson,[33] and an essay entitled "The Answer of Ancient America," which dealt with the Mayan civilization in the Yucatan.[34]

Unlike the scholars represented in *The Forum*, the Hemingway writer approaches the Indians of the Yucatan on the level of the immediate and the physical. The sensual experience of sound reminds us of his response to life in paragraph one, while the adjective "far-off" links the action of the gum-choppers with the sense of struggle that characterizes his definition of Romance in paragraph two. At the same time, the introductory "And meanwhile" of paragraph nine links this thought with the one introduced by the parallel "And meanwhile" in the final paragraph of the story. In this paragraph, the account of Maera's death completes the writer's response to life. As Hemingway was to write in *Death in the Afternoon*, "all stories if continued far enough end in death; and he is no true story-teller who would keep that from you."[35] This is something which *The Forum* writers with their "warm homespun, American tales, bits of real life . . . all with a healthy undercurrent of humor," have omitted.

The writer's response to death has none of the jealousy of Maera's fellow-bullfighters, who envied his skill and were secretly relieved at his death. As *Death in the Afternoon* was to make clear, the writer, or Hemingway in this case, was a great admirer of Maera for what he was as a bullfighter and as a man. He was aware of Maera's prolonged suffering and his tortuous battle with death, neither of which could be recorded in a special newspaper supplement.[36] The funeral mourners who sit out of the rain and lose "the picture they had of him [Maera] in their memories" by looking at colored pictures, are similar to *The Forum* writers, who substitute colored pictures of life for reality.

The Hemingway writer, however, does not allow the picture in his mind to be distorted; his task is to capture what a photograph cannot. Hemingway expresses a similar idea at the conclusion of *Green Hills of Africa*. After the safari, P.O.M. complains that she can no longer remember Mr. J.P.'s face: " 'I think about him and think about him and I can't see him. It's terrible. He isn't the way he looks in a photograph. In a little while I won't be able to remember him at all. Already I can't see him.' " Hemingway in turn responds, " 'I can remember him. . . . I'll write you a piece sometime and put him in.' "[37]

The one sentence of paragraph nine, then, carries a heavier burden in "Banal Story" than its length might suggest. Placed in the middle of the story, it serves to link beginning and end, the writer's reaction to life with his reaction to death. It also illustrates how the response of Hemingway's writer, occupied with what he can see, hear, feel, taste, and smell, differs from the intellectual abstractions in the pages of *The Forum*. The writer's definition of life in "Banal Story" is similar to the guerilla El Sordo's definition in *For Whom the Bell Tolls*: "living was a field of grain blowing in the wind on the side of a hill. Living was a hawk in the sky. Living was an earthen jar of water in the dust of the threshing with the grain flailed out and the chaff blowing. Living was a horse between your legs and a carbine under one leg and a hill and a valley and a stream with trees along it, and the far side of the valley and the hills beyond."[38] Talking about life in purely abstract terminology, as did *The Forum*, is "talking horseshit." As Hemingway explained to the Old Lady in *Death in the Afternoon*: "we apply the term now to describe unsoundness in an abstract conversation or, indeed, any over-metaphysical tendency in speech."[39]

According to Hemingway's aesthetic, the ability to deal directly with physical sensations in writing is what separates the good artist from the poor. To re-create Navarra, for example, one would have to "make clouds come fast in shadows moving over wheat and the small, careful stepping horses; the smell of olive oil; the feel of leather; rope-soled shoes; the loops of twisted garlics; earthen pots;

saddle bags carried across the shoulder; wine skins; the pitchforks made of natural wood (the tines were branches); the early morning smells; the cold mountain nights and long hot days of summer, with always trees and shade under the trees . . . ."[40] The same holds true for the painter. The reason Hemingway prefers Goya to El Greco and Velasquez, as he writes in *Death in the Afternoon,* is that "Goya did not believe in costume, but he did believe in blacks and grays, in dust and in light, in high places rising from plains, in the country around Madrid, in movement, in his own cojones, in painting, in etching, and in what he had seen, felt, touched, handled, smelled, enjoyed, drunk, mounted, suffered, spewed-up, lain-with, suspected, observed, loved, hated, lusted, feared, detested, admired, loathed, and destroyed. Naturally no painter has been able to paint all that but he tried."[41]

In *The Apprenticeship of Ernest Hemingway* Charles Fenton records a statement which Hemingway made to a circle of friends in Chicago in 1921. Discussing the responsibilities of the writer, he stated, "'You've got to see it, feel it, smell it, hear it.'"[42] It is this dictum, developed in the form of a parable with a deceptively ironic title, that is at the core of "Banal Story."

Kent State University

---

[1] Ernest Hemingway, "Banal Story," *The Little Review,* 12, No. 1 (Spring-Summer 1926), 22-23.

[2] Hemingway, "Banal Story," *Men Without Women* (New York: Scribners, 1927), pp. 214-217.

[3] Joseph Defalco, *The Hero in Hemingway's Short Stories* (Pittsburgh: University of Pittsburg Press, 1963), p. 95.

[4] Nicholas Joost, *Ernest Hemingway and the Little Magazines* (Barre, Mass.: Barre Publishers, 1968), pp. 150-151.

[5] Carlos Baker, *Ernest Hemingway: A Life Story* (New York: Scribners, 1969), p. 184.

[6] Henry G. Leach, *My Last Seventy Years* (New York: Bookman Associates, 1956), pp. 175-177.

[7] *Ibid.,* p. 180.

[8] Leach, "An Introduction by the Editor," *The Forum,* 73 (March 1925). The Editor's introduction usually appeared on the inside of the unnumbered cover page for each issue.

[9] *The Forum,* 73 (May 1925).

[10] *The Forum,* 74 (September 1925), n. pag. Henry P. Fairchild's "The Land-Hunger Urge to War," the first article in the series "War or Peace?" also appeared in this issue.

[11] *The Forum,* 73 (May 1925). Canada and Canadians were favorite topics of

the editor's, as the following statement from his autobiography illustrates: "Canada, dear Canada! My Canadian friends occupy a place in my affections beside the Scandinavian. The average Canadian is clear-headed, direct, objective, practical, and helpful." Turning to economic development, Leach added, "The Canadian dollar has a way of becoming more valuable than even the American dollar. Canada is today the Promised Land." *My Last Seventy Years*, p. 136.

[12] See, for example, J. B. S. Haldane, "Biology Moulding the Future," *The Forum*, 73 (March 1925), 331-341; H. F. Osborn, "Credo of a Naturalist," *The Forum*, 73 (April 1925), 486; Francis Crookshank, "The Threefold Origin of Man," *The Forum*, 73 (May 1925), 690-697; Osborn, "The Earth Speaks to Bryan," *The Forum*, 73 (June 1925), 796-803; William J. Bryan, "Mr. Bryan Speaks to Darwin," *The Forum*, 74 (August 1925), 322-324; E. E. Free, "The Origin of Life," *The Forum*, 74 (October 1925), 552-560.

[13] *The Forum*, 73 (February 1925).

[14] *The Forum*, 73 (April 1925).

[15] *The Forum*, 73 (January 1925).

[16] *The Forum*, 73 (April 1925).

[17] Laird S. Goldsborough, "Big Men—Or Cultured?" *The Forum*, 73 (February, 1925), 209-214.

[18] *The Forum*, 74 (October 1925), xiii.

[19] Arthur H. Gibbs, "Soundings," *The Forum*, 72 (December 1924), 838.

[20] *The Forum*, 72 (December, 1924).

[21] Roy Dibble, "In the Wicked Old Puritan Days," *The Forum*, 75 (April 1926), 518-524.

[22] *The Forum*, 74 (August 1925).

[23] *The Forum*, 73 (June 1925).

[24] "Picasso's Achievement," *The Forum*, 73 (June 1925), 760-775.

[25] Picasso's Failure," *The Forum*, 73 (June 1925), 776-783.

[26] "Pure Art? Or 'Pure Nonsense'?" *The Forum*, 74 (July 1925), 146.

[27] "Tramps and Hoboes," *The Forum*, 74 (August 1925), 227-237.

[28] *The Forum*, 72 (December 1924).

[29] *The Forum*, 73 (January 1925).

[30] *The Forum*, 73 (May 1925).

[31] *The Forum*, 72 (December 1924).

[32] *The Forum*, 74 (August 1925).

[33] "To the Mayas," *The Forum*, 74 (August 1925), 161.

[34] Herbert Spinden, "The Answer of Ancient America," *The Forum*, 74 (August 1925), 162-171.

[35] Hemingway, *Death in the Afternoon* (New York: Scribners, 1932), p. 122.

[36] *Ibid*., pp. 77-83.

[37] Hemingway, *Green Hills of Africa* (New York: Scribners, 1935), p. 295.

[38] Hemingway, *For Whom the Bell Tolls* (New York: Scribners, 1940), pp. 312-313.

[39] Hemingway, *Death in the Afternoon*, p. 95.

[40] *Ibid*., p. 275.

[41] *Ibid*., p. 205.

[42] Charles Fenton, *The Apprenticeship of Ernest Hemingway* (1954; rpt. New York: Mentor, 1961), p. 88.

FRANK M. LAURENCE

5000 Grand:
The Plagiarism Suit
Against Hemingway

In September 1937, John Igual De Montijo, a Mexican-American, registered for copyright a four-act drama entitled "The Rebel: or The Birth of a Revolution," based on his experiences as a partisan of Francesco I. Madero, the revolutionary who overthrew the government of Porfirio Diaz and was himself elected President of Mexico in 1911. In November 1939 De Montijo copyrighted a screenplay, *Viva Madero!*, which was, closely adapted from the stage play.[1]

Madero does not appear in either version, nor does any historical figure. The hero is a splendid young man named Julian Teran, who at the beginning of the play becomes betrothed to his beautiful sweetheart from childhood, Carmen. He will be taking Carmen to live at the hacienda of the wealthy landowner Del Real where Julian is newly employed. That worries Carmen's father, Don Pancho, for he believes Del Real to be a bad character, a supporter of the Diaz regime. Don Pancho even suspects that Del Real has been responsible for murders in the district, having ordered the death of anyone trying to lay claim to a new mine, then having stolen the claim for the government. (Later it will be discovered that Del Real murdered Julian's own father, a mining engineer, fifteen years before. Julian has always disbelieved the report of an accident and suspected foul play, since his father was shot in the back.)

193

Del Real himself does not realize that Julian is the son of a man he murdered. He arranges a fiesta for the marriage of Julian and Carmen, and promotes Julian to foreman, because he is much admired by all the peons. Nor does Del Real know that Carmen is the daughter of people he has suspected of giving aid to the revolutionary bandit Zapata. The morning after Carmen's wedding, Del Real's henchman, Gutierrez, and soldiers of Diaz ride to their home to kill him. Don Pancho returns to witness the murder of his wife. He kills nine of the soldiers, but, while he reloads his rifle, is himself slain.

With the report of their death Del Real also learns that Julian is their son-in-law, and he fears Julian's revenge. And it will be God's revenge too, for God knows that he is a wicked man who goes to church on Sunday to watch the girls and plot their seduction. To get rid of Julian, Del Real plans to accuse him of revolutionary activities, have him arrested, let the soldiers shoot him as if he tried to "escape" from their custody. And then Del Real will have Carmen, who is now the object of all his lust.

Julian has not until now been a revolutionary, but he receives a message from a respected friend asking him to become a leader in the revolution being planned by Francisco I. Madero, "a good and honest man like you." Julian's patriotic spirit is aroused by the idealism of the movement. Then another messenger tells Julian that his parents-in-law have been murdered. Julian returns home to tell Carmen and learns that in his absence Del Real has attempted to seduce and assault his wife.

Julian is no coward; he will challenge Del Real and Gutierrez. In the morning, with all the peons as witnesses, he goes to the yard and calls out to his enemies: "Here I am you dirty dogs! .... come on out and fight like men!" Shots ring out; Julian staggers and falls. But he is only faking; he has not been hit. When Del Real and Gutierrez come out to see his body, he shoots them dead.

Julian leads Del Real's peons into the mountains to fight for Madero's cause. He wins great victories, and his ranks rapidly grow larger as captured federalist soldiers come over to his side and pledge allegiance to Madero. To Julian's great joy Carmen gives birth to a son. But for their sake he sends Carmen and the child to safety in Mexico City, as he prepares for a great battle against the army of Diaz: to be his first victory as General Teran—"the Napoleon of Mexico."

The plays were utterly without literary merit. The characters are stereotypes, the situations conventionally melodramatic. The dialogue is stilted, trite, and sometimes shows a comic lack of command of English cliché, as in Gutierrez's fearful description of Julian's marksmanship, "He always hits the spot!" Long passages of the play are only so much political cant. The plays were neither stage worthy nor screen worthy, and they were neither published nor produced. And yet, according to John Igual De Montijo, these plays were the direct source for Ernest Hemingway's novel *For Whom the Bell Tolls*. On 27 May 1941, in the District Court of the United States for the Southern District of California, De Montijo brought civil suit against Hemingway and his publisher, Charles Scribner's Sons, charging plagiarism, deprivation of his "international literary credit and reputation," deprivation of "the exclusive rights, privileges, and profits" to which he was entitled as author—in compensation for which De Montijo asked a total of five million dollars in damages.[2]

Editors at Scribners hardly knew what to make of the outrageous charge when a summons was duely presented at the publisher's offices a few days later. In a letter to Hemingway, who was in Cuba, Maxwell Perkins speculated that it was "racketeer business."[3] Hemingway's lawyer, Maurice Speiser, had been advised by the attorney representing Scribners in Los Angeles (Homer Mitchell, for the firm of O'Melveny and Meyers) that De Montijo was "mentally unbalanced."[4] Evidence of a certain paranoia was the fact that De Montijo was concurrently sueing Paramount for having plagiarized the film *Northwest Mounted Police* from "The Rebel" and "Viva Madero," just as he had previously—unsuccessfully—sued Twentieth Century-Fox for having plagiarized *Viva Cisco Kid* and *Cisco Kid and the Lady*. There were other possible explanations for De Montijo's action. Perhaps he was seeking publicity. Perhaps he was receiving very bad counsel from his attorney, P. Talbot Hannigan.

When Maxwell Perkins read the scripts in question he could not really imagine how De Montijo had a case. It seemed that the only point of resemblance was that at the end of the De Montijo's plays and Hemingway's novel all the characters were in the mountains involved with guerilla warfare.[5] But in court depositions, De Montijo in effect admitted that the plagiarism was not obvious, because material pirated from his play had been "cunningly and shrewdly combined" with Hemingway's own material, some of it allegedly from Hemingway's experience, some of it borrowed from Hemingway's own earlier book, *Death in the Afternoon*. Various incidents had been invented by Hemingway merely to distract from the plagiarism. Robert Jordan's blowing up the bridge, for example, was part of this "smoke screen," the prosecution argued. The operation of blowing the bridge was really a trivial incident in the book: "No one would wade through four hundred and seventy-one pages of any book to find out about the blowing up of a bridge." To cover his theft, Hemingway had contrived to adopt the style of Shakespearean language, as in the use of "thy" and "thou" in lines of dialogue. Furthermore, "Ernest Hemingway, in order to better conceal the piracy, injected into and intermingled with the plaintiff's said literary compositions the vile, lewd, and lascivious language, descriptions, and irrelevant incidents, and gave to plaintiff's said literary compositions a filthy shroud of immorality, perversion, profanity, and obscenity." In spite of this obfuscation, in the "real story and interest" of Hemingway's novel were to be found "the plaintiff's characters, characterization, incidents, story, locale, and properties that have been lifted from the plaintiff's work into the defendent's book." To prove this, De Montijo and his attorney would present to the court during the course of the proceedings hundreds of pages detailed comparative analysis of the plays and the novel.

The comparison showed instance after instance of parallel dialogue. Robert Jordan had a way of addressing Maria as, "My rabbit"; similarly, Julian Teran addressed Carmen as "My Little Virgin." Robert talks to Maria about going to Madrid and how they will buy clothes there: "good ones and thou wilt be beautiful in them." When he attempts to seduce Carmen, Del Real promises her he will take her to Paris: "You will dress like a Queen!" The morning of the assault on the bridge Jordan leaves Maria to stay with the horses. "I would rather be with thee," she tells him. Jordan tells her no. Similarly, Julian tells Carmen she must stay behind when he has military matters to attend. The many other examples were of the same substantiality.

The plaintiff's comparison of character was more ingenious, though sometimes it misrepresented the play and very often misrepresented the novel. Julian Teran and Robert Jordan came from similar family backgrounds, having fathers who died of gunshot wounds (a reference to Jordan's father's suicide). Julian Teran and Robert Jordan were both men who would "go beyond duty to punish the crooks who enslave the honest innocent people." Both were men "who kill but never murder, fast on the draw, sure shots." Both had loved many women but had had only one "real love." Both men, the plaintiff argued, aspired to be Generals in their respective revolutionary armies.

Carmen and Maria were both only daughters of parents who loved them dearly (for the purposes of the prosecution's argument, Pablo and Pilar are Maria's foster parents). Carmen's parents were murdered, as were Maria's (her real parents). Both were "virgins at heart," though Maria had had things "done to her" against her will. Carmen married Julian and bore him a son. Maria became Jordan's common-law wife and was pregnant by him, hoping to bear a son—so the plaintiff argued. At the end of the play Carmen is sent to Mexico City for her safety; and allegedly Maria was sent to Madrid, for her "confinement." These were the major similarities, and there were a multitude of minor similarities. Both girls, for example, liked their lover's hair. De Montijo offered the same kind of comparison for pairs of minor characters.

According to De Montijo and his attorney many of the major episodes were directly derived from situations in the play. Chapter 27 of *For Whom the Bell Tolls*, for example (El Sordo's fight on the hilltop) was based on De Montijo's scene of the gun fight between Don Pancho and the soldiers. In the play script, he sees his wife killed. From behind the rock where he is hiding Don Pancho shouts, "Kill me too! .... you bandit sons of ?%&(+!" (in the screenplay he has the same line, but in Spanish). The shooting is over very quickly, with bodies all over the stage and screen. In his dying words, Don Pancho calls on his son-in-law to avenge his death. The scene is no more complicated than that, yet in court deposition it took six columns of legal-size paper to describe Don Pancho's thoughts as he hid behind that rock, as in the following passage:

> He was not afraid of dying but he was angry at being trapped on this hill. But whether a person has fear or not, one's death is difficult to accept, and Pancho had accepted it, because there was no sweetness in life for him.

The passage simply paraphrased the novel. Hemingway wrote of El Sordo:

> He was not at all afraid of dying but he was angry at being trapped on this hill which was only utilizable as a place to die. Whether one has fear of it or not, one's death is difficult to accept. Sordo had accepted it but there was no sweetness in its acceptance (p. 312).

To believe De Montijo would mean that Hemingway had even stolen his title from material shortly later in this scene. Don Pancho, behind his rock, remembers the church in the village, as if the bell were tolling for the happiness of his daughter and the death of his wife.

Such evidence of plagiarism would not seem convincing in the slightest except to someone totally unfamiliar with the plays and the novels. It is difficult to imagine that a jury, which would surely be instructed to read both works, would not see that the plaintiff's summaries were egregious distortions. But before a jury would be convened, a judge had to be persuaded that the plaintiff had substantial enough evidence to warrant a trial. And in a plagiarism case it is necessary for the plaintiff to show that the defendant had access to the plagiarized work. In other words, De Montijo had no hope of getting a trial, let alone a conviction, unless he could persuade the presiding judge that Hemingway knew "The Rebel" or "Viva Madero!" before he wrote *For Whom the Bell Tolls*.

The circumstances by which Hemingway knew his play De Montijo described in notarized testimony submitted to the court. On 16 February 1939, at the De Mille Manor apartment house in Los Angeles, a meeting was arranged for De Montijo to read his play to Virginia and Eddie Kaye, who were representatives of Sue Carol & Associates, a literary and theatrical agency, and other persons, among them representatives of Twentieth-Century Fox and two Mexican film companies.[6] There was another person there whom De Montijo did not know, but he was a writer, and the others called him "Ernie." He was there during the reading, and afterwards one of the other people asked him what he thought of this play, "The Rebel." Quoting De Montijo:

> Ernie say, "I think it is a wonderful play. You know, in a book it will be terrific," he say. And then he say, "You know what I like is the style. It is the style .... I don't believe that even in the whole United States is writers who writes the way this man writes."

Shortly afterwards, this man Ernie left, and it was not until two years afterwards, De Montijo said, that he learned his identity. It was during the law suit against Twentieth Century-Fox, when it was going badly. He walked out of his lawyer's office "kind of hot and boiled," and saw a *Life* magazine on the stand, and to cool off he bought the *Life* magazine, and there was Hemingway's picture inside. (This would have been the issue of 24 February 1941.) "Then I say, why this is the man who was with me in the apartment with those people."

De Montijo had no corroboration for his story. On June 27, 1941, Hemingway gave sworn statement before the American vice-counsel in Havana saying that he did not know and had never met John Igual

De Montijo, that he had never seen "The Rebel" or "Viva Madero" and that its contents had never been related to him, that he had never been to such a meeting as described by De Montijo, and that on the date in question he was living at the Sevilla Biltmore Hotel, in Havana. Presumably Hemingway's statement of itself was nearly enough to ruin De Montijo's case. Defense counsel asked for a summary judgment so there would not have to be a trial. That determination would be slow in coming since the plaintiff's depositions were complex and tedious. On February 16, the defendent's motion for summary judgment was granted, and the case, as is said, was thrown out of court. De Montijo appealed; his appeal was denied. Judge H. A. Holly, U. S. District Judge, dismissed the case finally on 21 May 1942.

The whole matter was not much of an inconvenience for Hemingway. No action was required of him except to give testimony before the American vice-counsel. What he experienced of aggravation was more with Scribners for having deducted $1000 from his royalties as his share of the legal fees.[7] That was the price you paid for being as famous as the Cisco Kid.

Mississippi University for Women

---

[1] The registration number of the Copyright Office of The Library of Congress for "The Rebel: or The Birth of a Revolution" is D unpub. 52845. The registration number for "Viva Madero!" is D unpub. 66413.

[2] All the court papers pertaining to the case, from which this and subsequent quotations are taken, are filed at the Federal Records Building in Bell, California.

[3] Maxwell Perkins to Ernest Hemingway, 9 June 1941. I wish to thank Professor Carlos Baker for allowing me to see correspondence pertaining to the case.

[4] Homer Mitchell to Maurice Speiser, June 1941.

[5] Maxwell Perkins to Maurice Speiser, 14 July 1941.

[6] Virginia and Eddie Kaye, as well as Sue Carol & Associates, were also named as defendants in De Montijo's suit against Hemingway and Scribners.

[7] Carlos Baker, *Ernest Hemingway: A Life Story* (New York: Scribners, 1969), p. 366.

RICHARD E. BRAUN

ECHOES FROM THE SEA:
A HEMINGWAY RUBRIC

That Hemingway derives situations from antique texts is well known. Having noticed, for instance, the use he made of the Tristan romance in *In Our Time*,[1] one is prepared to see the catalogue of yachts in Chapter 24 of *To Have and Have Not* as parody of Homer's famed prototype—the catalogue of the Greek fleet and heroes in Book Two of the *Iliad*—which had long since been mocked by Ovid in his catalogue of dogs in the eighth book of the *Metamorphoses*. The impression is strengthened by an unrelated sequence. Hemingway names an adulteress *Hélène* Bradley, making Richard Gordon her Paris of the day. Just as Oenone, the true love of Homer's Paris, did, so does Helen Gordon, Richard's wife, leave him to his doom. Once noticed, this parody suggests that more classicism may be in the novel than its "unclassic" form indicates.

Beside the Homeric parody, an historic parallel alerts readers to the possibility that in *To Have and Have Not* Hemingway is concerned with the relevance of the symbols and value systems of the past. The chief character is called Harry Morgan; he owns a boat, which he uses to smuggle liquor and Chinese immigrants; he is married to a woman who has bleached her hair "just like gold"; his adventures take place in the Straits of Florida; his enemies are Cubans. All this may remind one that there was, in the later

201

seventeenth century, an English pirate, Henry Morgan, who, after gathering a vast fortune in Spanish gold on the seas between Haiti and Panama, was knighted. But Harry Morgan's cargoes of golden rum and human gold bring him no security; and at the prime age at which Sir Henry was appointed Lieutenant Governor of Jamaica, Harry is shot dead. All this may remind readers that the 1930's is not an heroic decade, but it also shows the concern with connecting past and present which constitutes a fair part of classicism.

The title *To Have and Have Not* can be paraphrased in two ways: some have what others lack; and the same people both have and have not—either the losses of some become others' or no one's gain, or people lack what they appear to have. I doubt that enough attention has been paid to the second of these. The broader division—between the wealthy yachtsmen and the deprived veterans, the Washington bureaucrat and the bootleggers, the Chinese immigrants and their exploiters—is obvious enough. The theme of loss, of having then having not, is equally pervasive. One feature of this theme is its frequent association with that of prostitution—a state where one, in having, yet hath not.

Richard Gordon, already figuratively, as Carlos Baker points out, a "kept man"—a proletarian novelist in leisure-class society—becomes literally Helene Bradley's whore, and directly, as has been noted, loses his true wife, Helen.[2] Professor Mac Walsey who, since the death of his wife has lost himself in alcoholism, hopes in turn to marry Mrs. Gordon and to begin for both a personal recuperation. When the Gordons break up (Chapter 21), one of the charges Helen brings against Richard is that he has made her remain barren, even forced her once to undergo an abortion—to have then have not. They have had a marriage and had none; not only was it sterile, it was also unsanctified by religion, of which Helen says: "I had one once and I'm going to have one again. And you won't be there to take it away. Like you've taken away everything else." People, like property, may change hands, for better or worse. While this break goes on, the local bank is being robbed by Cuban revolutionaries.

The same theme of loss and prostitution is found in the catalogue of yachts. Henry Carpenter has lost most of his inherited income; now she has and has him not; for he, unconscious with alcohol, lies Hollywood director," mistress of "a professional son-in-law of the very rich," is careful to sleep with her face off the pillow, remembering "how terribly bad it is for the face." She will lose her looks, but hopes to postpone the loss. She knows that when she loses her looks, or sooner, she will lose her lover to another woman. Even now she has and has him not; for he, unconscious with alcohol, lies flat in the next bunk and she is left, this night, to her own resources. The once oversexed, now impotent grain broker has become rich by ruining many men; everyone's loss is someone's gain. Now, to forget that the Treasury Department is investigating him, he drinks knowing that to drink will soon kill him, that he will lose even what he now has. Meanwhile, around Harry Morgan's borrowed boat, "small fish" and "sucker fish" feed on men's blood (Chapter 20).

In the cabin, beside the dead and dying lies money stolen from the bank. Harry Morgan has suffered the loss of his deep-sea tackle, and later, trying to keep solvent, lost his arm and his boat. He recovered the boat and lost it again. "All I've got is my *cojones* to peddle," he concluded. Lying wounded, he thinks of his wife Marie: "She's too old to peddle her hips now." A week after his death (Chapter 26), Marie Morgan, reflecting that she has lost her looks, thinks: "I'd have to hire a man to do it now." She has three daughters, but does not care about them; in the same way, she now has but has not the very precious memory of Harry's face, a homely face. Recalling how her dark hair was bleached gold for Harry, she concludes: "Everything inside of you is gone." Harry too (Chapter 14) had had no companionship with his daughters: "Those damn girls. That's all that old woman and I could get with what we've got. Do you suppose the boys in her went before I knew her?" Thinking those thoughts, he had parted with Marie, as it happened, forever. Helen Gordon could have envied this couple their daughters as they could have envied her her husband's money.

At times, the themes of loss and use are condensed into grotesque comedy worthy of Juvenal. The red-haired veteran (Chapter 22) who says "I don't have to hand it out. I can take it, see?" is also the man who tells about the "old guys with long beards" and who has lost his wife and doesn't even remember what country she is in. Again (Chapter 25), Mrs. Albert Tracy learns she has lost her husband, and promptly loses her upper plate in the sea where Albert's body is presumed to rest. "We'll dive it up in the morning," the skipper of the Coast Guard cutter tells her referring to the plate, "We'll get it all right."

It seems to me highly reasonable that the title *To Have and Have Not* should be an incitement to constant awareness of the themes of possession, use, and loss. No one owns but briefly. Property changes hands. People change. Each simultaneously has and, in self-sale, has not. Certainly, the antithesis of the haves and have-nots of the Depression is ever-present and indispensible; but it is ironical. For, all the people of the novel, regardless of class or circumstances, are subject to the same, continual changes of gain and loss.[3] To call this a proletarian novel, then, is a further irony.

Now, I have proposed that *To Have and Have Not* is in fact a work of classicism in that it illuminates, with stories of the American thirties, some judgments of value handed down in ancient literature. I have already noted Homeric parody in chapter 24; this is a device of classic satire. Readers familiar with Samuel Johnson's Juvenalian "Vanity of Human Wishes" will quickly see in this novel a similar systematic refutation of the supposed benefits of talent, courage, wealth, beauty, and longevity. Some indeed will feel that Hemingway is closer to Juvenal than to Johnson.[4]

The ancient passage, however, which I consider to be most strikingly relevant, is rather less accessible than Juvenal or Homer. It is to be found in Flavius Philostratus' *Life of Apollonius of Tyana*. Philostratus was a pagan traditionalist of the third century A. D. Apollonius was a first century philosopher and mystic who had acted—during and for long after the ministry of Jesus—as a revivalist on behalf of the Greco-Roman religion. The *Life* contains an Apology of Apollonius, in which the philosopher defends himself on charges of treason and witchcraft before the emperor Domitian.[5] At the end of the speech, these words are found:

> For the prosperity of men runs in a circle, and the span of happiness, my prince, lasts for a single day. My property belongs to another and his to another, and his again to a third; and each in having hath not. Think of this, my prince, and put a stop to your decrees of exile, stay the shedding of blood, and have recourse to philosophy in your wishes and plans; for true philosophy feels no pangs. And in doing so wipe away men's tears; for at present echoes reach us from the sea of a thousand sighs, and they are redoubled from the continents, where each laments over his peculiar sorrows.[6]

The ruinous intellectuals, the unemployed and hopeless workers, the exiled veterans of the Keys and Dry Tortugas, and the Cuban revolutionaries, as well as the agents of the American and Cuban governments, had their counterparts under the Terror of Domitian's reign. Apollonius' echoes of sighs from the sea are more drastic historical equivalents of the complaint of the "tall man" in Chapter 22 that: "Mr. Hoover ran us out of Anticosti flats and Mr. Roosevelt has shipped us down here to get rid of us." The decrees of exile and shedding of blood are, perhaps, even more easily comparable to the conditions in Cuba which Emilio describes in chapter 18. But most important is the sequence ending "and each in having hath not." This seems to specify the actual rubric which *To Have and Have Not,* in both its social and spiritual aspects, illustrates. I propose that the passage is worth investigation as a possible source of Hemingway's title[7] and as a potentially profitable point from which to view the figurative and reasoned basis of the whole novel.[8]

University of Alberta

---

[1] After establishing a mock-romantic scenic setting in "The End of Something" (New York: Scribners, 1930, p. 36), Hemingway introduces direct ironic allusion to a popular treatment of the Tristan legend in "The Three Day Blow," pp. 49-50.

[2] *Hemingway, the Writer as Artist* (Princeton: Princeton University Press, 1952), p. 212.

[3] For a further meaning, based on a suggestion by Ruskin, see Baker, pp. 215-6. Baker rightly wishes to allow the "possession" theme of the title to include personal qualities of the characters.

[4] For example, the outspoken account of the grain broker's physical condition—Juvenal, Satire X, 204-9—which Johnson omits in his imitation.

[5] VIII, 7; Teubner, 326. Note that Juvenal was a younger contemporary of Apollonius, and seems to have been much affected by the events of the reign of Domitian.

[6] Translation by F. C. Conybeare, in the Loeb Classical Library *Philostratus* (London and New York, 1912), II, 355. For a quite different rendering of the passage, *cf.* J. S. Phillimore, *Philostratus in Honour of Apollonius of Tyana* (Oxford, 1912), II, 236. The only other English version, by Berwick, was a rare book by the turn of the century.

[7] Ezra Pound, for one, could have brought Philostratus to the attention of Hemingway. Pound was noticeably influenced, during much of his career, by the work of G. R. S. Mead, whom he had met through Yeats at least as early as 1913. Mead published a study, *Apollonius of Tyana, the Philosopher-Reformer of the First Century A. D.,* in 1901. See Noel Stock, *Poet in Exile: Ezra Pound* (Manchester: Manchester University Press, 1964), pp. 20-1. It may also be significant that Apollonius was used as a character by Charles Grandison Finney in his celebrated short novel *The Circus of Dr. Lao* (New York: Scribners, 1935).

[8] The value of such an analogue is shown, for example, by Jerome L. Mazzaro in "George Peele and *A Farewell to Arms*: A Thematic Tie?", *Modern Language Notes*, LXXV (February 1960), 118-9.

206

Stephen Longstreet: Hem Paris '26—Place Contrescarpe.

WILLIAM F. NOLAN

THE MAN
BEHIND THE MASKS:
HEMINGWAY AS A
FICTIONAL CHARACTER

Considering his larger-than-life career as international novelist, big-game hunter, boulevardier, bullfight aficionado, Gulf Stream fisherman, wing shot, war correspondent, and husband to four wives it is not surprising that Ernest Hemingway has been appropriated as a fictional character in a variety of novels. Seven of these form an offshoot section of my Hemingway collection. In each novel the character's disguise is a thin one, and the fictional portraits are, for the most part, unflattering. Taking them in chronological order:

In *Glass Mountain* by Joseph Warren Beach (Philadelphia: Macrae Smith, 1930) the Hemingway character is named "Max Harder," and we encounter him (on p. 12) as a famous artist "the leader of a school of painting that goes in for a somewhat exaggerated virility . . ."; (and on p. 13) "I liked him well enough, though one soon tires of his type of conscious, flannel-shirted open-throated maleness. He is a big hearty pleasant-spoken fellow, frank and straightforward and full of the zest for life. A bit simple, to be sure."

The novel is loosely based on Hemingway's first marriage to Hadley (here dubbed "Norma") who loves him for his (p. 19) "hearty, though shamefaced, interest in literature . . . he never went fishing without the poems of Villon in his pocket. . . . He had by heart whole pages of Rabelais." He tells her (p. 30) that he has "to

207

go to Paris and show them how to paint." They have a child, called "the Rumpus" (Hemingway's first son, John, was nicknamed "Bumby") and eventually Max is lured away by "Grace" (the fictional version of Pauline Pfeiffer), described (p. 14) as "a college classmate of Norma's, her dearest and most trusted friend." Happily, Norma finds another husband.

Hemingway appears in *Chosen Country* by John Dos Passos (Boston: Houghton Mifflin, 1951) as "George Elbert Warner." We first encounter him as a boy toting a shotgun, who hates to fish with girls. "Georgie" is described (by another character on p. 59) as ". . . a lout . . . [with] unbrushed hair in black spikes on his forehead like an Indian's and [with] grime round the open neck of his blue shirt."

He grows a moustache, goes to war, wins a medal and comes home to work as a sports writer. His first bylined piece is described (on p. 279) as "a terse little account of a beaten prizefighter . . . ."

It is said of him (on p. 263) "The boy's got the brains. He learned more in the war, book learning too, than the average feller'll learn in four years of college."

He fades out of the action by mid-book, but before this we get one more glimpse of his talent for terse prose. "Got anything new for me to read . . .?" asks a female admirer (on p. 288).

"You don't want to read about a baseball player that broke his finger."

But she does. He hands her two pages "watching her face out of tense brown eyes." He tells her that "If there's one extra word I want to know it. . . . A man's got to learn not to write all over the page."

When Hemingway's younger brother, Leicester, wrote his first novel it was inevitable that one of the characters would be modeled after Ernest. In *The Sound of the Trumpet* (New York: Holt, 1953) Hemingway appears as war correspondent "Rando Granham," older brother to "Dan Granham" (Leicester Hemingway). In this novel of World War II, they meet in Paris, at the Ritz, where Dan asks Rando (on p. 86) how he managed to "wangle a spot like this?" Rando tells him, "Hell, we liberated the joint. Took a patrol through the basement and cleaned out some Krauts."

Rando contracts pneumonia and is laid up in his hotel room. Joking with him, (p. 134) Dan calls him "The indestructible Granhamstein." (Shades of Hemingstein!) He also calls him (p. 143) "Good old Stein." He later describes Rando (p. 144) as "bundled in his big fleece-lined flying jacket, he looked as big as a live Grizzly

..." and (on p. 145) mentions "a place in Illinois where they had both been born .... it was the biggest village outside Chicago ...." According to Dan, Rando walked "with a slight limp. It was from his luck in the other war. He had been banged around plenty in that one ...."

Advice on how to handle war experiences (p. 167) includes this from Rando to Dan: " ... use the whole war, Just make it like it was. Make it so real they'll know it. You can always change names ...."

In his book *My Brother, Ernest Hemingway* (New York: World, 1962) Leicester recalled that Hemingway "had been infuriated with a single line concerning a certain character in my novel" (p. 275). Although he did not specify which line Ernest objected to, it is safe to assume it is contained in a section of Dan Granham's thoughts about his older brother (p. 168 of the novel): "I've seen him the great admirer of other people, but when they did something he didn't approve of, he'd turn vindictive. More than that. Malevolent .... acting as though such people no longer existed. You've seen it with other wives and with old friends who saved his bacon in other wars .... Maybe he's the high priest of a new religion whose motto is, 'Muck 'em all', ... Don't be bitter, he told himself. You know there's nobody more loyal than Rando—to Rando. Why should you escape your turn, if you've seen him give it to others? Being in the same family is no protection. You're just a handier target."

After this section Rando drops out of the narrative, telling Dan that he "would head back for the States."

Dos Passos again used Hemingway as "George Elbert Warner" in a follow-up volume to *Chosen Country*. In the second novel, *The Great Days* (New York: Sagamore Press, 1958), Warner is a successful writer living in Key West "in a white frame house with an upstairs galley" (p. 12). They all go tarpon fishing, then retire to a restaurant to drink and talk—and (on p. 16) "George ... told about rumrunners through the Keys and Cuban fishermen smuggling chinks."

Warner turns up later (p. 114) as "a headliner among war correspondents ... a huge thickbarreled man ... exaggerated by the musette bags and spyglasses and automatics in holsters that dangled from him in all directions." And (p. 117): "For all his fluster and bluster George Elbert had an extraordinary nose for scenting out first rate people." One of them, in the book, is his wife "Maria," of whom Warner says (p. 119): " ... if I should manage to get myself bumped off . . . you know I couldn't care less . . . you and Grace be nice to Maria."

Later in the narrative, in Germany, the narrator (who is now also working as a correspondent) observes (p. 233): "I had managed to stay friends with him all these years by refusing to take his ill temper seriously: to be perfectly honest this time I thought he was worried for fear my story would get a better play than his did."

Turns out that Warner is angry over the idea that the narrator is going to return to the U.S. and (p. 236) "write a lot of goddam propaganda for the isolationists and the Fascists and the America firsters . . . . You take it from me . . . . You'll wake up one of these mornings and find yourself a back number."

To which the narrator adds: "From that day to this there has been no more friendship between us."

End of friendship. Yet, in memory, Warner appears one final time in the novel (pp. 290-291) as the narrator is "thinking of Paris, a rose antediluvian Paris where the streets always smelt of strawberries when young Georgy Warner used to bring his stories round to his hotel for him to revise . . . how they used to sit together over beers at cheap cafes reading Chronicles and Kings to improve their narrative style; and Georgy's hanger on who had a system that was going to make them all rich at the horseraces . . . . We always had a good time . . . when we were together."

In *The Land of Rumbelow* by Carlos Baker (New York: Scribners, 1963) Hemingway is an off-stage character, the legendary writer "Nicholas Kemp." In this novel by Hemingway's future biographer, Kemp is to be the subject of a book by college man "Dan Sherwood" author of a study on Keats (just as Hemingway was the subject of a book by Princeton's Baker, author of a study on Shelley). Thinking of Kemp (on p. 15), Dan refers to him as "the best of the novelists." Later he thinks of "The good bitter Kemp, like a draught of wormwood" (p. 60).

Chapter Five (p. 62) opens with a review of Kemp's accomplishments, and the author speaks of his subject's "tragic vision . . . dark and bloody fiction by which Kemp had established and consolidated an international reputation . . . . Luckily, the books were few . . . four major novels . . . the collected short stories . . . those early sketches . . ." Later (p. 64) he mentions "the evidently autobiographical stories of his Idaho boyhood . . . [in which] the theme of remorse ran through them so darkly that the Freudians had a field day when the book appeared . . . ."

The section on Kemp ends (p. 66) with a description of the novelist "holed up like a hibernating bear in his northern wilderness, drinking whatever wormwood it was which had made him the Dostoievsky of his age, and earned him a wide company of fanatical admirers. Including, Dan thought, myself."

A large section of the sixth chapter of Baker's novel is devoted to a biographical portrait of Kemp, including the fact that he'd been born in 1897 in Boise, Idaho, was in conflict with his father, had run off to war to lose an arm at Belleau Wood in 1918. Finally (on p. 80) the Baker character, Sherwood, asks himself: " . . . why are you so reluctant to probe into the biography of this writer named Kemp? You know that sooner or later you must . . . uncover the hidden motivations, the cowardly acts, the cruelties done or endured."

At another juncture, Sherwood reflects on just what made Kemp a great writer (p. 157): "And what is this greatness? It is the badge we issue to those who have tackled some of the more profound problems of behavior or belief . . . . Books like Kemp's are scars healed over: the traceable record of all the wounds, asked-for or accidental, self-inflicted or God-inflicted, that Kemp sustained in his time. Relief maps of his scar tissue."

On February 4, 1950 (novel time) Kemp writes a letter to Sherwood, attempting to stop Dan's biography, saying in part (p. 197): "The vultures will doubtless gather when I die. While I live, I can still give fair warning. I will tolerate none of this . . . . Leave me alone, Mr. Sherwood. If you should be foolish enough to persist, I will have to fight you."

It would be interesting to compare this fictional missive from Kemp with the early letters Hemingway wrote to Carlos Baker in the same vein when Baker was working on the rough draft of *Hemingway: The Writer as Artist* (Princeton: Princeton University Press, 1952).

Chapter Twenty-three begins with another long letter from Kemp to Dan Sherwood, dated May 21, 1950—covering eight pages of close-set type in the novel (275-282)—in which Kemp refers bitterly to "the tribe of wolves that call themselves critics." He recounts his problems with another young writer intent on doing a book on him. "I gain the impression that whether or not I agree to help will in some way determine whether he gets his promotion, whether . . . he and his wife . . . continue to get enough to eat. So I am put in the position of the ogre who denies them a livelihood."

Probably, this passage refers, in fictional terms, to the problems

Hemingway was having with Philip Young, then writing a book for Rinehart. Kemp agrees to allow Sherwood to go ahead on the book if the biographical elements are removed (as they were removed from Baker's first book). Dan writes it, sends it in to his publisher, only to discover (on p. 342) that a new Kemp work has just been finished, "a novella" which Sherwood reads in manuscript and which is described (p. 343) as a "naturalistic fable . . . . The whole tale, read like a parable [about a character who] would not accept defeat." Hastily, Sherwood adds a final chapter to his book dealing with this story (just as Baker added material dealing with Hemingway's then-just-completed *The Old Man and the Sea*) and his work is done. Kemp, says Sherwood, "got sick of the dark" (p. 348). With this novella, Kemp (and Hemingway) had come into the light.

In *Standing On a Drum* (New York: Putnam, 1968) Irwin R. Blacker transforms the full Hemingway myth into soap-opera fiction with his inflated saga of "Wade Tyree," described in the jacket blurb as "Rough, charming, irresistible and often hateful . . . a flamboyant man from Ohio . . . world-famous . . . obsessed with Women, War and Writing."

The book opens with Tyree's suicide, with Blacker declaring (p. 12): "He had fought his battles . . . . His eyes went up to the sky again, and he sought a star through the haze. God owed him at least one final star. The eyes set deep in his rutted face flashed in senseless anger . . . ."

Then (p. 14): "The shot rang through the house and the woman upstairs sat upright in her bed. Beyond was the window . . . where the wind washing the darkness revealed a single star."

The remainder of the book (all 377 pages of it) doggedly follows Wade as he carves his legend as a soap-opera hunter, lover, fighter, drinker, writer, from Ohio to California. It's an exhausting trip.

In *The Last Flapper* by George Zuckerman (Boston: Little, Brown, 1969) the Scott Fitzgeralds (as "Davis and Rannah O'Don-nell") get the same extended melodramatic treatment, with Heming-way threaded through the narrative as "Harry Ingram" (becoming, after O'Donnell's death, Rannah's lover). At the close of the book Zuckerman tells us about Harry's violent death in "his Montana hunting lodge."

"At six o'clock in the morning, September 1, 1961, he left his bed to keep the daily appointment with his typewriter. At twelve minutes past eight that morning Paula Ingram heard a rifle shot. She swore to the coroner that her husband had left no suicide note.

There was, however, a blank page in the typewriter. It was a blankness Harry Ingram could no longer endure. In death, free of the madness that late in life had dwarfed him, he is an American giant."

There will be more novels, more books involving big, bluff men named Max Harder and George Elbert Warner and Rando Granham and Nicholas Kemp and Wade Tyree and Harry Ingram.

Behind the facts of Ernest Miller Hemingway, the fictionalizing is not yet done.

JAMES GRAY WATSON

"A Sound Basis of Union"
Structural and Thematic Balance
in "The Short Happy Life of
Francis Macomber"

It has become a commonplace in criticism of Ernest Hemingway's fine story, "The Short Happy Life of Francis Macomber," to begin at the end of the story with a discussion of whether or not Margot Macomber purposely shoots her husband. As Robert B. Holland points out,[1] the argument to date is weighted heavily in favor of the Mrs. Macomber-as-murderess point of view; he identifies no less than ten prominent Hemingway critics who align themselves against her. Although the interpretations of the rest of the story vary from one to another of these critics, all agree whole-heartedly on Margot's guilt. Carlos Baker is typical. He sees in the second day's shooting and its outcome a "contest for the possession of a soul" ending in "murder"[2] and finds in Margot the prime representative of the destructive influence on men of women and money. Margot, he says, is "Easily the most unscrupulous of Hemingway's fictional females."[3] Holland, on the other hand, insists on accepting the word of the omniscient narrator, that "Mrs. Macomber, in the car, had shot *at the buffalo* with the 6.5 Mannlicher as it seemed about to gore Macomber and had hit her husband about two inches up and a little to one side of the base of his skull" (p. 135, italics mine).[4] Faced with this evidence from the author, Holland logically insists, the reader must discount the testimony of the all too fallible guide, Robert Wilson, who declares Mrs. Macomber a murderess. Holland reminds us that "It was Hemingway's virtue to report with exactitude what he saw, to render the thing as it was in all possible clarity."[5] Nonetheless, against the combined opinion of some of the most distinguished Hemingway scholars, only three voices have been raised. Holland, Virgil Hutton, and Warren Beck are willing to credit the word of the omniscient narrator.

Both Hutton and Beck approach the problem of Margot's guilt or innocence by discrediting her accuser, Robert Wilson. Hutton finds in the story an "unrelenting satire of Wilson"[6] and sees Margot's shot as a "fatal attempt to save her husband."[7] Beck too is unsympathetic to Wilson, finding him at best a seriously limited and curiously indecisive observer of the Macombers. He develops a convincing case for Margot's having attempted to save her husband's life "with that excess of recognition and penitence and hope in which love can renew itself."[8] While these arguments lead to similar conclusions, the former is far too hard on Wilson and the latter too generous to Margot. The guide is not merely an insensitive British imperialist with a "clownish red face"[9] that Hutton would have him, and Margot is something less than Beck's "enamelled but not altogether shallow or selfish human being" bravely striving for "a spontaneous and sustained intimacy"[10] with Macomber. She is, after all, an adulteress who, far from being pleased with her husband's emergent manhood, is frightened by it and refuses even to wish him luck as he moves into the bush after the wounded buffalo. While every reader is obliged to accept the word of the omniscient narrator and thereby reject the accusation that Margot is a deliberate murderess, he must not do so at the expense of the rest of the story. Baker's Margot-as-bitch reading and Phillip Young's famous Wilson-as-code-hero hypothesis cannot be entirely dismissed despite the fact that they culminate in a common misreading. The problem is one of perspective and balance—a problem, incidentally, with which the story is mightily concerned. Both the narrative and imagaic structure of the story suggest an internal balance which neither critical camp, dwelling on the apparently ambiguous ending, has sufficiently credited. I propose that a sustained reading of "The Short Happy Life of Francis Macomber" can be achieved by beginning not at the end but at the center of the narrative, where the ominiscient narrator describes the relationship between Francis and Margot Macomber prior to their Africal safari.

As has often been noted, the events of the story are about equally divided between the two days of hunting. The first day is summed up in the paragraph at the middle of the story beginning, "That was the story of the lion" (p. 120); the second day begins three paragraphs later at "about three o'clock in the morning" (p. 121). But between the close of the first day and the beginning of the second, at the precise center of the action, is a two-paragraph scene which balances Francis's nature against Margot's and concludes with an assessment of their mutual relationship from the point of view of an American society column. Francis is a gentleman sportsman who is certain that his wife will not leave him, despite his sexual inadequacy, because of his wealth and high position: "His wife had been a great beauty and she was still a great beauty in Africa, but she was not a great enough beauty any more at home to be able to leave him and better herself and she knew it and he knew it" (p. 120). For her part Margot is certain that Macomber will not leave her, despite her faded beauty and occasional affairs, because he is not better with women: "If he had been better with women she would probably have started to worry about him getting another new, beautiful wife; but she knew too much about him to worry about him either" (pp. 120-121). Each then has found in the other that physical quality by which they maintain their own self-images. The scene concludes: "They had a sound basis of union. Margot was too beautiful for Macomber to divorce her and Macomber had too much money for Margot ever to leave him" (p. 121). Logically, the scene belongs exclusively to neither the first nor the second day but is, rather, an interlude between the two concerned with a time and events prior to both. Nonetheless, it is the thematic center upon which the two days of the hunt are carefully balanced. The emphasis here is on security derived of mutual dependence, and the ironically "sound basis of union" is the central point in a remarkable narrative strategy that draws its force and complex unity from recurrent violations of the unique terms of the Macombers' marriage agreement. These violations lead inexorably to Margot's fatal shot not at Francis but "at the buffalo."

Both Francis, by his cowardice, and Margot, by her infidelity, break the marriage agreement and thereby threaten the identity of the other. Francis "spoils" Margot's trip, and Margot breaks her "promise" to him (p. 122). In order to re-establish their identities, each in turn is drawn toward the company of Robert Wilson, in whose "standards" they find security. Thus when Francis runs from the lion on the first day and shows himself "very publicly, to be a coward" (p. 103), he destroys the carefully nurtured image of masculine fitness upon which Margot's vanity as a faded beauty depends. She reaffirms her femininity to herself and regains security by turning to "the beautiful red-faced Mr. Robert Wilson" (p. 120), whose sexual standards are familiarly her own. However, her union with Wilson on the morning of the second day is as shattering to Francis as was his cowardice to her on the first. He is sexually innocent, knowing about sex only vicariously in "books, many books, too many books" (p. 120), and Margot's defection leaves him without the beautiful wife necessary to his self-image of manhood. Although Macomber knows that Margot "would not leave him ever now" (p. 120), he is equally certain that sexually "she was through with him" (p. 120), and his "nice" tolerance becomes "sinister" (p. 121). He discovers that, "of all the many men that he had hated, he hated Robert Wilson the most" (p. 122). Driven by hatred, and in the familiar surroundings of a motor car race, Macomber forgets his fear, is able to shoot well in the face of danger, and earns acceptance according to Wilson's hunting standards.

As Wilson himself makes clear, however, the ritual of the hunt constitutes a higher imperative in his scheme of things than that of sexual love.

> He, Robert Wilson, carried a double size cot on safari to accommodate any windfalls he might receive. He had hunted for a certain clientele, the international, fast, sporting set, where the women did not feel they were getting their money's worth unless they had shared that cot with the white hunter. He despised them when he was away from them although he liked some of them well enough at the time, but he made his living by them; and their standards were his standards as long as they were hiring him.
>
> They were his standards in all except the shooting. He had his own standards about the killing and they could live up to them or get someone else to hunt them (p. 125).

Because the hunting standards are separate from and take precedence over the standards of the double size cot, Francis displaces Margot in Wilson's community. To Wilson, Francis's bravery means "the end of cuckoldry" (p. 132), and he shares with him the "thing he had lived by" (p. 131), the quotation from Shakespeare. Margot is forced to recognize her displacement when Francis tells her, "If you don't know what we're talking about why not keep out of it?" (p. 133), and her contempt becomes "not secure" (p. 133). Isolated from both Wilson and her husband, Margot seeks security by attempting to meet the higher imperative of the hunt. When she shoots with the "manly" Mannlicher "at the buffalo," she is quite literally bidding to rejoin the society of her hunter-lovers by shooting well, and her primary motive is neither to murder her husband nor to save him but to save herself. In this it is not her motive but her method which is flawed. The cardinal rule of the hunt is, "You don't shoot them [animals] from cars" (p. 113). Moreover, it is a rule that Margot knows well, for she says when she thinks that it has been violated, "I didn't know you were allowed to shoot them from cars" (p. 128). As the evidence of the story clearly shows, then, her attempt to save herself fails not because she is a bitch, or even a woman, but because she violates the first principle of the society which she is trying to join. She fires "at the buffalo" while standing "in the car." Francis, of course, is lost to her because he is killed, and Robert Wilson rejects her as a murderess.

This reading places "The Short Happy Life of Francis Macomber" solidly within the tradition of those Hemingway stories which Joseph DeFalco calls "the marriage group"[11] and ties it thematically more closely than has previously been seen to its companion piece, "The Snows of Kilimanjaro." DeFalso claims, however, that in these two stories "the isolation of an individual because of marital difficulties is not the central purpose of the story."[12] Yet the basic circumstance in each of the stories is precisely the isolation resulting from a faulty marriage agreement. In this regard, the relationship between Harry and Helen is particularly instructive because it emphasizes the importance Hemingway attached to Francis and Margot's "sound basis of union." After several isolating tragedies, Helen has built a "new life" on Harry's physical vitality, and Harry has come to depend on her wealth to hide his spiritual weakness: "The steps by which she had acquired him and the way in which she had finally fallen in love with him were all part of a regular progression in which she had built herself a new life and he had traded away what remained of his old life" (p. 161).[13] Although Harry dies, the honesty of his final self-appraisal entitles him to ascend in spirit to "the House of God" near the summit of Mt. Kilimanjaro, while Helen is left alone with only her dream of "the house on Long Island" (p. 176). Hemingway's investigation of the theme of isolation and the accompanying search for security brought him to much the same conclusion in his second African story. Margot needs her husband as much as Helen needs Harry, yet she is as incapable of joining him with Wilson as Helen is of joining Harry with the pilot, old Compie. Furthermore, As Margot brings Macomber death literally, Helen symbolically represents death to Harry when, like the hyena's, her face comes "between him and the fire" (p. 173). It is, perhaps, not merely coincidental that Helen's final expression of grief, the words "Harry! Please, Oh Harry!" (p. 176), is much the same as Margot's last speech to Wilson, "Oh, please stop it . . . . Please, please stop it" (p. 136). Both women are giving vent to the anguished recognition that they have failed to save themselves, and Wilson's ironic accusation that Margot is a murderess is a no less agonizing reminder to her of her alienation from the safety of masculine society than is the hyena's growling laugh which wakes Helen.

If, as I suspect, the informing principle of these stories is the dangerously tenuous security of agreements based on mutual weakness, an answer is implied to those critics who have dismissed Wilson's standards as shallow and hypocritical. Hemingway was not setting forth as the be-all and end-all for man Francis Feeble's view of life when he had Robert Wilson cite Shakespeare's *Henry IV, Part II:* "By my troth, I care not; a man can die but once; we owe God a death and let it go which way it will he that dies this year is quit for the next" (p. 131). Rather, he was suggesting it as a more satisfactory code to live by in Africa, where the challenges do indeed involve life and death, than the one which the Macombers bring with them from America. Absolute infallibility and fearlessness are not, as Hemingway knew, traits of sane men, and Wilson is neither infallible nor fearless. In fact, he makes a point of qualifying the Shakespearean quotation when he distinguishes it from merely "fashionable" bravado, warning Francis, "Mind you, you'll be scared too, plenty of times" (p. 132). Wilson is a successful hunter and an independent man, and this is precisely what Francis Macomber becomes in the course of his "short happy life" and what Margot fails to become. Although she expresses the opinion that both men are "talking rot" (p. 132), she knows too well that her husband has displaced her with Wilson, and "her contempt was not secure. She was very afraid of something" (p. 133). She and Francis have thus undergone a perfectly balanced reversal of roles: her situation as outcast at the end of the second day is analogous to Francis's at the end of the first, and as he achieved the independence and security of the hunter by shooting well, she tries to do the same, perpetrating the death of her husband and her own final isolation in the attempt.

The most striking evidence of this role reversal is the way in which

Hemingway adapted the structure of the story to his thematic principle. The chronology of the first day is deliberately broken so that the opening scene of the story is set in the aftermath of the lion hunt. Francis has violated the code of the hunting fraternity by running from the lion, and he is presented as the object of Wilson's and Margot's contempt. Wilson assures him that he will not speak of the incident at the Mathiaga Club in Nairobi because, as he ironically says, "I have a living to make. You know in Africa no woman ever misses her lion and no white man ever bolts" (p. 106). Similarly, the final scene of the story is set in the aftermath of the buffalo hunt, but this time it is Margot who has broken the hunting code by shooting from the car. Wilson's contempt here is more bitter than before, as befits the more serious nature of her act, but he nonetheless assures her also of his silence: " 'Don't worry,' he said. 'There will be a certain amount of unpleasantness but I will have some photographs taken that will be very useful at the inquest. There's the testimony of the gun-bearers and the driver too. You're perfectly all right' " (pp. 135-136). Thus in both the opening and closing scenes, the chronologic setting in relation to the hunt and Wilson's reaction to the events of the hunt are the same, but in the concluding scene Margot has assumed the role played by Francis in the opening one. This balanced structure represents the fact of their reversed roles, and the two scenes are made to frame the process by which that reversal is brought about.

Here too structure is integral to theme as the process of reversal takes on a tragic inevitability from the arrangement of the intervening scenes. The long opening scene carries the action of the first day forward to late afternoon, after which the narrative returns to the previous night and runs in chronologic succession from that point to the conclusion of the lion hunt. The first day is set off from the second by the central flashback scene in which the Macombers' "sound basis of union" is presented. Then the second day begins and runs in uninterrupted chronologic sequence to the end of the story. In this way the opening scene is made to serve as a part of the frame without disrupting the dramatic symmetry between the first and second days. Read as a single narrative unit in two parts, the two days represent matched contraries balanced across the fulcrum of the central scene. As Carlos Baker has noted, "Part of the balance is achieved by the repetition of first effect: the buffalo, like the lion of the preceding day, is wounded, takes cover, and charges without warning."[14] Beneath the level of overt action, however, a subtle structural principle is at work which relies upon the same device. Both days begin with scenes that are fundamentally the same. In the first Francis is wakened at night by the lion and lies alone in his tent with his fear.

> It had started the night before when he had wakened and heard the lion roaring somewhere up along the river. It was a deep sound and at the end there were sort of coughing grunts that made him seem just outside the tent, and when Francis Macomber woke in the night to hear it he was afraid. He could hear his wife breathing quietly, asleep. There was no one to tell he was afraid, nor to be afraid with him, and, lying alone, he did not know the Somali proverb that says a brave man is always frightened three times by a lion ... (p. 110).

On the second night the same elements are present: the lion, Francis's fear, and his solitariness.

> It was now about three o'clock in the morning and Francis Macomber, who had been asleep a little while after he had stopped thinking about the lion, wakened and then slept again, woke suddenly, frightened in a dream of the bloody-headed lion standing over him, and listening while his heart pounded, he realized that his wife was not in the other cot in the tent. He lay awake with that knowledge for two hours. (p. 121).

Margot's sexual indifference to Francis, signified by her sleeping through the first night, is replaced by her active assertion of her femininity, signified by her sleeping with Wilson on the second night. She forsakes separate cots for a double cot and breaks her promise "that there would be none of that" (p. 122) because, between the first and second mornings, "the trip was spoiled" (p. 122). Yet if Francis's cowardice, prefigured by his fear on the first day at breakfast when "It's not light yet" (p. 112), spoils the trip for Margot and sends her to Wilson, so does her infidelity, the subject of Wilson's pun on "Topping" (p. 122), spoil the trip for Francis at breakfast on the second day "before daylight" (p. 122). What this structure makes preponderately clear is that Margot's infidelity is a symbolic repetition of Francis's cowardice and will inevitably result in driving him to Wilson also. Since both reactions toward Wilson are in response to unexpected isolation, both are commensurate with and dramatize the principle of dependence by which the Macombers are characterized in the central scene.

Finally, in addition to the beginning and end of each day, the internal structure of the two is also carefully balanced to project the reversal of roles between Francis and Margot. The primary example of this is to be found in Hemingway's treatment of the four brief scenes where Wilson, Francis, and Margot appear together in the hunting car. Baker has commented perceptively on the way in which Hemingway portrayed the changing relationship between the Macombers and Wilson by varying the seating positions in the car, but he sees this only as an incidental thematic device.[15] In fact, here as elsewhere in the story, theme and structure are inextricably related. Two car scenes occur on each day, before and after both the lion hunt and the buffalo hunt. As such, they frame the major action of each day in much the same way that the story itself is framed. Before the lion hunt Francis sits in the dominant front seat with Margot and Wilson behind him. After his display of cowardice, however, he is displaced by Wilson; Margot rejects his hand and symbolically joins Wilson in the front seat: "While they sat there his wife had reached forward and put her hand on Wilson's shoulder. He turned and she leaned forward over the low seat and kissed him on the mouth" (p. 113). This situation is directly reversed on the second day. Before the buffalo hunt Wilson sits in the dominant front seat with Francis and Margot behind him. After Francis's bravery, however, it is he who symbolically joins Wilson in the front seat, leaving Margot slumped alone in the back: "His wife said nothing and eyed him strangely. She was sitting far back in the seat and Macomber was sitting forward talking to Wilson who turned sideways talking over the back of the front seat" (p. 131).

What they talk about, moreover, is the "thing he [Wilson] had lived by" (p. 131), the Shakespearean quotation from which Wilson draws his courage and which he now shares with Macomber. The sexually innocent Francis, who did not know "the Somali proverb" (p. 110), thus undergoes "More of a change than any loss of virginity" (p. 131) and learns a corresponding Shakespearean "proverb". Whereas, in the car scene complementary to this one, Margot appeals for security, with a kiss, to "The beautiful red-faced Mr. Robert Wilson" (p. 120), Francis's relationship to him goes beyond sexual experience to the higher order of moral manhood, from which she is excluded. In addition to the reversal of roles which it projects, the consistency of motive with setting in this pattern may also shed light on Margot's apparently ambiguous motives for firing "at the buffalo" in the scene following Francis's initiation as a hunter. In all of the car scenes, the rear seat signifies isolation: first Margot and then Francis leans forward from the rear seat to join Wilson. While there is no evidence that Margot leans forward to fire her shot, she does fire from the rear seat where Wilson and Macomber have left her alone. Furthermore, she fires at a time when it appears that her isolation from Francis may be permanent: the buffalo "seemed about to gore Macomber" (p. 135). In light of the motivation toward security in each of the preceding scenes, it seems logical to assume that Margot's motives in this scene, similar to the others in every other way, are the same. Her shot represents a symbolic reenactment of her kiss from the back seat earlier: in both cases she is attempting to save herself. Although her beauty enables her to do so in the sexual terms of the first instance, however, she is unequipped to meet the moral imperatives which the second demands. The irony of hitting Macomber instead of the buffalo testifies not only to the extent of her failure as a hunter but also to the magnitude of her ultimate isolation.

The rendering of this theme does not, of course, rest with structure alone, yet even the imagaic patterns of the story follow the same balanced scheme and work toward the same end. A case in point is Hemingway's use of the colors red and white. As DeFalco has noted, Wilson's redness is emblematic of his passion and vitality. He writes.

> When Mrs. Macomber holds her husband in contempt and looks to Wilson as the husband-surrogate, Hemingway marks the attachment with further color symbolism by associating Mrs. Macomber with a near-color of red: "The rosé-colored, sun-proofed shirt she wore" or "looking pretty rather than beautiful in her faintly rosy khaki." When Macomber later gains his courage, a fact which his wife cannot reconcile, she is described several times over as "white faced".[16]

This is generally correct, but it fails to take into account the several other instances where these colors are employed and the intricacy with which the color motif is made to support the reversal of roles. In the story, red is associated not only with passion and vitality but also with courage, and it is the color of Wilson's courage that Francis assumes when he becomes, according to the guide, "a ruddy fire eater" (p. 130). White, on the other hand, is associated with fear when, after the lion hunt, Margot distinguishes between "the beautiful red-faced Mr. Wilson" and her cowardly husband by ironically calling Francis "my pearl" (p. 107). The colors are reversed when Francis's "pearly" whiteness on the first day becomes "ruddiness' on the second and Margot's "rosiness" gives way to her "very white" face (p. 128). Appropriately, both colors emanate from Wilson, to whose "standards" Margot and Francis are drawn by turns. Margot notices "where the baked red of his face stopped in a white line that marked the circle left by his Stetson hat" (p. 103). The white line symbolizes the fact that he is not absolutely fearless, and this is borne out when, after Francis has become "a ruddy fire eater", Wilson warns him, "Mind you, you'll be scared too, plenty of times" (p. 132). In the same way that Wilson controls his fear by the Shakespearean quotation, however, he hides the white line on his forehead with his hat. Thus Margot, dressed in a "rose-colored, sun-proofed shirt" (p. 104), is symbolically stating her willingness to accept him sexually when she asks, in the opening scene of the story, "Hadn't you ought to put your hat on even under the canvas at noon?" (p. 104). Because the sexual standards of American women "were his standards as long as they were hiring him" (p. 125), he accedes: "Might put it on,' said Wilson" (p. 104). In a reversal of this situation, in the final scene of the story, "ruddy" Francis accepts Wilson's "own standards about the killing" (p. 125) and bravely follows him into the bush after the wounded buffalo: "Wilson had his hat down over his eyes and his red neck showed just ahead of Macomber" (p. 134).

The emphasis on Wilson's face as his distinguishing feature suggests a final pattern of symbolism in the story by which the Macombers' alternate movement toward Wilson's standards is rendered. The pattern is based on the symbolic significance which Hemingway accords to the heads of beasts. Robert W. Lewis defines the animal symbolism in its larger context when he says:

> From Biblical times through the Middle Ages, two symbols of eros and agape had been a lion and a unicorn (or a hart, hind, etc. "Eland" is cognate with "elk," "stag," "hart," and "hind.") Macomber is capable of the unicorn—agape—but the lion—eros—frightens and eludes him. Not so Mr. Wilson .... Wilson wants Macomber to be good according to his code, and the white hunter is very happy when Macomber becomes a whole man and redeems the lion business by doing well on the buffalo hunt. (The buffalo he shoots are, of course, all bulls, traditional symbols of virility and fertility.)[17]

Within this larger context, however, Hemingway introduced a motif more particularly appropriate to his material by concentrating attention on the heads of animals. Just as Wilson's face contains the colors by which his character is judged, so big game animals are judged as trophies by their heads: the ferocity of the lion or buffalo is determined by the fullness of mane or spread of horn. In his African hunting story, Hemingway utilized the significance of trophy heads to distinguish between Margot's and Francis's relationship to Wilson and to mark the stages of Francis's emergence as a man and the course of his "short happy life."

After Francis's panic with the lion, Margot expresses her admiration for Wilson's physical beauty by reference to his red face but qualifies her praise for him as a hunter: she says, "You were lovely this morning. That is if blowing things' heads off is lovely" (p. 108). To Francis, however, who has begun to understand the significance of hunting for Wilson, the ritual is important. Wilson has instructed him in the hunter's "*shauri*" (p. 117), or responsibility to the beast, and the image of the lion, "horrible-looking now, with half his head seeming to be gone" (p. 119), returns to haunt his dreams in the form of "the bloody-headed lion" (p. 121). His isolation as lover as well as hunter is complete when he realizes, concurrent with the dream, that Margot is sharing Wilson's cot. Significantly, it is the ritualistic hunter-lover, Wilson, who blows things' heads off, who suggests the only way by which Francis can expurgate his fear and redeem himself as a man when he thinks, "Hope the silly beggar doesn't take a notion to blow the back of my head off " (p. 124). The association of Wilson with a virile bull, beginning with his pun on animal "Topping" (p. 122), concludes when Francis symbolically avenges his cuckolding by delivering the coup de grace to the bull buffalo according to Wilson's instructions: "Macomber aimed carefully at the center of the huge, jerking, rage-driven neck and shot. At the shot the head dropped forward" (p. 128). By firing the shot at the buffalo's head which he was unable to fire at the lion's, he symbolically rids himself of his psychological fear of heads and joins Wilson, and it is Margot who is afflicted with "a dreadful headache" (p. 128) as she watches "white faced." His fear is "gone like an operation" (p. 132), but hers is intensely felt, and she tries to conquer it by reenacting his symbolic head shot. When Francis stands firm to shoot at the head of the charging buffalo, Margot shoots at it also; but her fear of all "hateful looking" (p. 130) buffalo incapacitates her in the same way that Francis is incapacitated by his fear of the lion, whose roaring he "hates" (p. 112). Just as his panic wounded her figuratively and resulted in his isolation, so her fear of isolation wounds him literally and results in the same: shooting "at the buffalo" she instead "hit her husband about two inches up and a little to one side of the base of his skull" (p. 135). Ironically, the buffalo hunt is as she said it would be: "just like the lion" (p. 129). Francis's bloody head bears the same thematic relationship to Margot that the mutilated head of the lion bears to him: each is a symbol of fearful isolation, and the balance between them perfectly projects the reversal of the Macombers' roles.

The completeness with which Hemingway portrayed this rich symmetry makes it clear that Margot is neither a generic bitch nor a tragic heroine. Neither Richard B. Hovey's contention that she is "a Goneril-Regan in her bitchhood, more monster than woman"[18] nor Warren Beck's claim that she answers "the call to try once more to meet her husband's virtue and friendliness with a reasserted virtue and warmth of her own"[19] accords to the structural and imagaic demands of the story. In fact, at the end of the story, Margot is still the dependent individual striving to overcome isolation that she is presented as being at the thematic center, where her "sound basis of union" with Francis is described. When Francis becomes "awfully brave, awfully suddenly" (p. 133), he transcends the narrow limits of that former union, but, without his new found independence, she returns to it as the only thing she knows. She considers its wreckage bitterly "Because she had done the best she could for many years back and the way they were together now was no one person's fault" (p. 133). Her shot at the buffalo, then, is a symbolically standard reaction to the dictates of her orientation toward security and is motivated not only by bitchiness or nobility but by fear for herself. As Wilson correctly notes, "She was very afraid of something" (p. 133), and she says, "I've never been more frightened in my life" (p. 128). In this light the final shooting scene is the climax of a progressive structural and symbolic pattern in which Margot plays an unchanging but nonetheless integral role. Her failure to join the company of her hunter-lovers and her resultant hysteria give both scope and depth to the principle of ironic reversal, emphasizing the thematic centrality of the faulty marriage union, the extent of Francis's growth away from that inhibiting union, and the "happiness" of true self-sufficiency. The limitations to which Margot is subject, finally, dramatize and ennoble by contrast the magnitude of Francis's achievement of the "happy life."

University of Tulsa

---

[1] Robert B. Holland, "Macomber and the Critics," *Studies in Short Fiction*, 5 (Winter 1967), 171-178.

[2] Carlos Baker, *Hemingway: The Writer as Artist*, 3rd ed. (Princeton: Princeton University Press, 1963), pp. 189-190.

[3] *Ibid.*, p. 187.

[4] Ernest Hemingway, *The Fifth Column and the First Forty-nine Stories* (New York: Scribners, 1938), pp. 102-136. All subsequent references are to this edition and are in the text.

[5] Holland, p. 173.

[6] Virgil Hutton, "The Short Happy Life of Macomber," *University Review*, 30 (June 1964), 253.

[7] *Ibid.*, p. 262.

[8] Warren Beck, "The Shorter Happy Life of Mrs. Macomber," *Modern Fiction Studies*, 1 (November 1955), 37.

[9] Hutton, p. 254.

[10] Beck, p. 36.

[11] Joseph DeFalco, *The Hero in Hemingway's Short Stories* (Pittsburgh: University of Pittsburgh Press, 1963), p. 153.

[12] *Ibid.*

[13] *The Fifth Column and the First Forty-nine Stories.* All subsequent references are to this edition and are in the text.

[14] Baker, p. 189.

[15] *Ibid.*

[16] DeFalco, p. 205.

[17] Robert W. Lewis, *Hemingway on Love* (Austin: University of Texas Press, 1965), p. 84.

[18] Richard B. Hovey, *Hemingway: The Inward Terrain* (Seattle: University of Washington Press, 1968), p. 126.

[19] Beck, p. 35.

JOHN UNRUE

THE VALLEY OF BACA AND
A Farewell to Arms

"Psalm 121," says Professor Baker, "might do as a motto for Hemingway's collected works," and *A Farewell to Arms* is among the several Hemingway works he cites to show the relevance of the words "I will lift up mine eyes to the hills from whence cometh my help." He develops this point fully in his well-known essay on *A Farewell to Arms*, "The Mountain and the Plain," in which he equates the mountains with "home."[1]

More significant to the "home" which Lt. Frederic Henry and Catherine Barkley seek in Switzerland is not Psalm 121, however, but Psalm 84, the joyous song of one who fully understood the implications of deliverance. Hymns of praise like that of Psalm 84 were customary for the Hebrews to sing as they expressed their gratitude to Yahweh. Miriam, the sister of Moses, sang a similar song of thanks for the deliverance of the Israelites at the time they crossed the Red Sea.[2]

Verses three through six of Psalm 84 are strikingly applicable to the would-be-temple home for which Catherine Barkley and Frederic Henry sing their praises as they arrive in Switzerland. They have crossed a lake which they have mistaken for a threshold separating bondage from bliss. They are like the psalmist who praises the amiable tabernacles and pours out his heart to his God:

229

> Yea, the sparrow hath found an house, and the swallow a nest for herself, where she may lay her young, even thine altars, O Lord of hosts, my King and my God.
>
> Blessed are they that dwell in thy house; they will be still praising thee. Se-lah.
>
> Blessed is the man whose strength is in thee; in whose heart are the ways of thee.
>
> Who passing through the valley of Baca make it a well; the rain also filleth the pools.

It is the last of these verses that is most vital to the important Chapter XXXVII, for that clause describes precisely what Catherine and Frederic do when they arrive in Switzerland. The meaning of the phrase "valley of Baca" has troubled many scholars, but the most popular translation of the word *Baca* is tears—thus the well-known phrase "vale of tears."[3] In fact, the American Revised Version of the Bible renders this verse, "Who passing through the valley of Weeping they make it a place of springs, Yea the early rain covereth it with blessings."

One popular Bible commentary provides the following interpretation of verse six:

> The explanation of *Baca*, as meaning the valley of mulberry or Baca-trees is now very commonly abandoned for the one given in the ancient versions, the vale of weeping or of sorrow, a beautiful poetical description of the present life as one of suffering. To the *fons lacrymarum* is opposed the fountain of salvation or of joy, a figure so familiar in the scriptures, as to be readily suggested by the one word *spring* or *fountain*. The meaning of the clause, as thus explained, is that the persons pronounced happy in the foregoing verse convert the very vale of tears into a fountain of delight .... The valley through which they are advancing becomes green meadows and pastures, and fruitful fields by spring and rain.[4]

Another commentator adds that "the word [Baca] denotes a dry valley in which soft, gentle autumnal rain fell after the crops were sown."[5] Thus the vale of weeping becomes a vale of joy.

My point in elaborating upon this sixth verse of Psalm 84 is to show that Catherine and Frederic, too, have mistaken a vale of tears for a vale of joy upon their arrival in Switzerland. The rain that greets them is, in fact, the same foreboding, foreshadowing rain, symbolic of disaster, that Hemingway scholars have pointed to for years. But to the two lovers, blind to reality, it is not the rain that has threatened to engulf them as they have attempted to flee the constantly encroaching edge of doom. Rather they see it as a gentle, refreshing rain, the kind one would expect to find in "a place of springs."

Catherine and Frederic's ecstasy as they "stepped up" and "were in Switzerland together" is worth noting in this regard. As he approaches the shore, Frederic observes that "there was a fine November rain falling but it looked cheerful and clean even with the rain." Switzerland for Catherine is "a lovely country," and Henry loves the way it feels under his feet. And in a moment of Hemingway irony at its finest, Catherine says to her lover, "Darling, do you realize we're here and out of that bloody place?" Henry, also incapable of seeing the truth, answers, "I do. I really do. I've never realized anything before." As they continue to peruse the scene, they see that even the houses are better than other houses they have known.

But most relevant to the "valley of Baca" verse is Frederic's remark about the rain. "Isn't the rain fine?" he says. "They never had rain like this in Italy. It's cheerful rain." It is cheerful rain, of course, because he and Catherine are mistaking an ever-present vale of tears from which they have not truly escaped for a vale of joy. But Catherine, like the psalmist, wants to sing not a song of journey but a song of arrival, of deliverance. "And we're here, darling! Do you realize we're here?"

Like the sparrow who, says the psalmist, "hath found an house, and the swallow a nest for herself, where she may lay her young," Catherine, too, she believes, has found a refuge and, as Professor Baker says, "a home." Bible commentator F. C. Cook says of this verse in Psalm 84 that "the psalmist feels like a wandering bird, homeless, until he finds refuge in God's house." The latter half of the verse, says Cook, would have the psalmist saying, "The birds have their houses; my refuge and home, the place in which my heart finds all its comfort, is the altar of God."[6]

Catherine, too, wants to believe that she has found such a home, such a refuge, and like those whom the psalmist describes, she would make the journey to the place of deliverance pleasant, despite the difficult conditions under which it was taken. The journey through the night has not been bad for her. "I had a lovely time," she says to Frederic, "especially when you sailed with the umbrella." Switzerland is such a paradise to her that she fears that she might be dreaming. "I'm afraid I'll wake up and it won't be true," she says.

Frederic also is susceptible to delusion. He hopes that Catherine will not awaken, as she fears, to discover that she is merely driving him to the *stazione* in Milan to see him off to the war, but he is not capable of clear thinking. "I'm so groggy I don't know," he says. He is "very tired and vague in the head." He is so groggy that this joyous day of arrival is "like a comic opera."

Hemingway emphasizes the grogginess that prevents both Catherine and Frederic from seeing and feeling the dismal truth of their doom. Catherine is pregnant, and she is likewise hopeful as were those travellers, or those sparrows and swallows, for whom the temple area had become a refuge and a symbol of security.[7] Her faith, although she has no religion, is strong, and it is bolstered by her ability to hope. Indeed, her hope and Henry's hope endure because the lovers are kept groggy, if not by their own doing, then by someone else's.

As he brings the novel to a close, Hemingway provides numerous examples of the deception to which they have been prey. Prior to Catherine's going into the hospital, their hope is encouraged by the unseasonably warm weather which causes them to wish they were back in the mountains from which the rain had driven them. "On the days of false spring, it was very nice after boxing and taking a shower to walk along the streets smelling the spring in the air and stop at a cafe to sit and watch the people and read the paper and drink a vermouth; then go down to the hotel and have lunch with Catherine." Dazed by hope, they enjoy the refuge of the "false spring," and they are willing to make Switzerland a "place of springs."

Their final moments of false spring are spent in the hospital, where they are forced eventually to see and feel the truth to which they have been blind and numb. There, too, however, they would make this time of reckoning something other than what it is. Henry fears for Catherine, as he should, but for a while at least, he can escape his fear and go to prayer. Catherine's pains are very real, but the gas gives temporary relief. Drunk with gas, Catherine can regard Henry and her surroundings as "lovely." And her doctor becomes for her "the most wonderful doctor."

The merits of this doctor and the other doctors who attend Catherine are debatable, but there is no question about their keeping the fires of hope burning within Catherine and Frederic. "Things are going very well," a doctor says as Catherine is moved into a room where she can be given gas for the pains. Somewhat later, after he has made an examination, this doctor must answer Frederic's "How does it go, doctor?" with "It doesn't go." When the Caesarean is complete, another doctor assures Frederic that the child is all right. "He's magnificent. He'll weigh five kilos," the doctor says. Soon the child is dead—"the cord was caught around his neck or something." When the long incision is sewed up, the doctor who has performed the operation tells Frederic, "She is all right." Even when Frederic and Catherine are convinced that she is going to die, the truth continues to be clouded. Catherine's doctor assures her, "You are not going to die. You must not be silly." But she does die, and with her death comes the final, poignant proof of Catherine's and Frederic's folly, and proof that the rain in which Frederic walked back to the hotel was not different from the rain he had known in Italy.

No, Switzerland is not "a place of springs" no matter how much the lovers wanted it to be. There is some respite there, but it is only temporary. Catherine and Frederic are like those ants that Frederic mentions. Having escaped from the fire, their place of doom, they went to "the cool end," which they perhaps mistook for a place of springs, but from which they inevitably fell into the fire.

Hemingway's use of the Bible for title and symbol is well established. One should not be surprised, therefore, to discover that he saw in Psalm 84 great potential for dramatic irony and pathos, or that his two lovers who were sustained by hope and blinded to truth should mistake Switzerland for the place of joy and deliverance that such a place was to the psalmist. Finding out that Switzerland was not a place of springs made the discovery of inevitable doom all the more painful and the futility of the struggle all the more real.

University of Nevada—Las Vegas

---

[1] See, for example, Malcolm Cowley, "Introduction," *The Portable Hemingway* (New York: Viking, 1944), p. 16; E. M. Halliday, "Hemingway's Ambiguity: Symbolism and Irony," *American Literature,* 27 (1956), 57-63; John Killinger, *Hemingway and the Dead Gods* (Lexington: University of Kentucky Press, 1960), p. 47; Charles R. Anderson, "Hemingway's Other Style," *Modern Language Notes,* 76 (May 1961), 435; James F. Light, "The Religion of Death in *A Farewell to Arms,* "*Modern Fiction Studies,* 7 (Summer 1961), 171; Carlos Baker, *Hemingway: The Writer as Artist,* rev. ed. (Princeton: Princeton University Press, 1963), p. 95; Earl Rovit, *Ernest Hemingway* (New York: Twayne, 1963), p. 104; Robert W. Lewis, Jr., *Hemingway on Love* (Austin: University of Texas Press, 1965), p. 40; Philip Young, *Ernest Hemingway: A Reconsideration* (University Park: Pennsylvania State University Press, 1966), p. 91.

[2] Charles H. Patterson, *The Philosophy of the Old Testament* (New York: Ronald Press, 1953), p. 444.

[3] See Roy B. Chamberlin and Herman Feldman, eds., *The Dartmouth Bible* (Boston: Houghton Mifflin, 1961), p. 509n. See also George A. Buttrick, ed., *The Interpreter's Dictonary of the Bible* (New York: Abingdon-Cokesbury Press, 1952), I, 338; according to this source the Valley of Baca was a Palestinian valley, the name of which was probably taken from a species of gum-exuding (weeping) tree—perhaps the Balsam—which grew along its course; the word itself would seem to be a variant of the derivative from a root meaning "to weep"; the valley was presumably a rather arid and inhospitable route along which ran a toilsome pathway to Zion (Jerusalem), which pathway was made to appear much less forbidding because of the joyous faith and mission of the pious pilgrim travelling it.

[4] J. Glentworth Butler, ed., *The Bible-Work* (New York: Butler, 1892), V, 68. See also Matthew Black and H. H. Rowley, eds., *Peake's Commentary on the Bible* (London: Nelson, 1962), p. 431; here also the appearance-reality idea is expressed; although the valley was probably arid, "it seems to the expectant pilgrim to be well watered, since at the coming festival they will offer their prayers for rain"; the valley, therefore, the commentator continues, becomes "a place of springs."

[5] Butler, p. 69.

[6] Butler, p. 68.

[7] See Raymond E. Brown, S. S., Joseph A. Fitzmyer, S. J., and Roland E. Murphey, O. Carm., *The Jerome Biblical Commentary* (New Jersey: Prentice-Hall, 1968), I, 591.

DAVID J. WELLS

HEMINGWAY IN FRENCH

This study is designed to provide commentary on how translators have treated Hemingway's style in adapting him for a French audience. The Pléiade edition of Hemingway, printed by Editions Gallimard, was used for collation. Entitled *Oeuvres romanesques,*[1] this two-volume set also contains the same translations used for the "Livre de Poche" series, a very popular, inexpensive set of paperbacks, into which format several of Hemingway's novels have been set. The shorter pieces were issued in French for the first time by Gallimard in 1969 for inclusion in the Pléiade series. The short works, those which comprise *The Snows of Kilimanjaro and Other Stories* and *In Our Time,* will be used in this study, as they contain the most challenging concentration of syntactical problems.

A word on the *traduttore traditore* (translator=traitor) attitude seems in order before discussing specifics. The French translator must choose in certain instances between a phrase which will ring true to a Frenchman's ear and one which conveys the spirit of Hemingway's prose; in most cases the translator is likely to become a traitor—that is, in this case, acquiesce to commercial demands—and choose the former.

Hemingway's use of proletariat language provides numerous debatable choices in translation. In "The Killers" the waiter utters this colloquial sentence: "You can get that at six o'clock," which becomes "Je pourrai vous servir ça à six heures," (I will be able to serve you that at six o'clock.) The verb "get," always translates as the more formal "servir" in the lunchroom scenes, while the transfer from "you" to the more precise "je" seems equally unnecessary. The colloquial use of "on" ("one" in the sense of "you") seems more in order: "On peut vous donner ça à six heures," would have thus transmitted the proper mood. Conveying the flavor of the gangsters' speech also calls for special considerations: the translator emphasized "big" in the mocking "They all come here and eat the big dinner," with "grrrand." In a language which normally avoids stress in pronunciation, as does French, such an orthographic elaboration felicitously transmits some of the suppleness of oral English; the big-city thug's aggressiveness transforms the simple "grand" into a growl. A heavy-handed insult such as "None of your damn business," loses some of its harshness in the more colorful "C'est pas tes oignons" (None of your onions).

Substantives representing tangible objects, geographical locations, and other elements of "local color" indigenous to America show the translator's attitude toward precision even more clearly than his handling of idioms. A vocabulary item such as "ketchup" poses the choice of whether or not to translate; perhaps the endless malaise over "franglais" (the overuse of English by the French) dictated rendering "ketchup" as "sauce tomate." In the notes "jus de tomate" (tomato juice) is offered. Both of these translations obviously fail to evoke a feeling for the commonness of this American condiment. The interpretive possibilities of ketchup as a symbol for spilled blood perhaps prevented interpolating ketchup to the condiment most often found on French tables, mustard.

A more vexing problem occurs in dealing with deliberately awkward phrasing. For example, Hemingway often uses a sequence of verbs to create a tense, dry atmosphere, as in this choppy sentence: "George had cooked the sandwich, wrapped it up in oiled paper, put it in a bag, brought it in, and the man had paid for it and gone out." The translator divided the sentence into three sentences: "Georges prépara le sandwich, l'enveloppa dans du papier huilé et le mit dans un sac. Puis il sortit avec. Le client s'en alla après avoi payé." This reordering of conjunctions (et, then puis) makes the French less repetitive, hence more sophisticated, than the original. "The old man left after having paid," also smooths over the original English. A similar alteration occurs in "He had been a heavyweight prizefighter and he was too long for the bed," rendered by "Ancien poids lourd, il était trop long pour le lit," (A former heavyweight, he was too long for the bed.) In consistent fashion, the translator changes plodding English to flowing French, a transformation which establishes cause and effect not intended by Hemingway: *"Because* he was a former heavyweight . . . ."

When Hemingway's syntax becomes exceedingly difficult to handle, the translator often reverts to suppressing entire thoughts. In "A Clean, Well-Lighted Place" the first sentence presents problems: "It was late and everyone had left the cafe except an old man who sat in the shadow the leaves of a tree made against the electric light." The problem is solved by not mentioning the light: "Il était tard et il ne restait plus dans le cafe qu'un vieil homme assis à l'ombre d'un arbre," (It was late and there no longer remained anyone in the cafe except an old man seated in the shadow of a tree.) The original text forces the reader to slow his eye and to reconstruct the images in the sentence, thus creating a static atmosphere, some of which is lost in the translation. The next sentence, which ends with " . . . because he was deaf and now at night it was quiet and he felt the difference" loses much of its studied simplicity in the French which replaces coordination with subordination: ". . . car il était sourd et d'autant plus sensible au calme de la nuit" (. . . because he was deaf and therefore that much more sensitive to the calm and the night). A French audience would understand the translation far more easily than the American audience understands the original, thanks largely to the logical link provided by "d'autant plus." Furthermore the word "sensible" gives the old man an Epicurean air consistent with French taste.

"Big Two-Hearted River" contains a paragraph in which repeated use of short sentences creates a mood of simplicity and harmony: "It was a good place to camp. He was there, in the good place. He was in his home where he had made it." The translator evidently ran short on patience and omitted the second sentence quoted above: "C'était un bon coin. Il était chez lui dans sa maison, là où il l'avait construite," (It was a good spot. He was at home in his dwelling, there where he had made it.) In the next paragraph a parallelism created by "was"—an important contrast of dark and light—is lost in the French: "It was quite dark outside. It was lighter in the tent." "Il faisait noir comme tout dehors. On y voyait mieux sous la tente," (It was dark as anything outside. One saw better in the tent.) "One saw better" disturbs the repetition and robs the original of the stylistic opposition of the chaos of the dark night and the security of the lighted tent. Furthermore the pronoun "one" opens up Nick Adams' world which Hemingway intended to be private.

The variations cause only slight loss of sense when the bulk of the story is considered, yet the overall atmosphere is altered. A complete loss of sense occurs only rarely such as this gaffe found in "Chapter IV" of *In Our Time*: "We were frightfully put out ... " which becomes: "Il y eut un moment de grande stupeur ... " (There was a moment of great stupor ...).

Few liberties were taken in translating titles. with one notable exception. "The Short Happy Life of Francis Macomber" is interpreted as "L'heure triomphale de F. M." (The Triumphal Hour of F. M.), a rendering which eliminates the enigmatic possiblities of the original title, while substituting a more limited metaphor. The choice is made by the translator: "life" means "that moment of Macomber's courage."

Alterations of this nature are bound to occur when a work is adapted so as to have commercial appeal in a different culture. Anyone purporting to study a work closely will read it in the original. It goes without saying that in comparing *The Snows of Kilimanjaro and Other Stories* and *In Our Time* with the Pléiade edition, the accurately translated passages predominated. Nevertheless some of Hemingway's most distinctive prose loses its character, hence much of its significance, in translation.

Loyola University, New Orleans

---

[1] Ernest Hemingway, *Oeuvres romanesques. Reportages de Guerre. Poèmes à Mary*. Edition présentée, établie, annotée par Roger Asselineau. Traduction par J. Delpech, M. Duhamel, H. Robillot, V. Llona, O. de Weymer, G. Magnane, D. Van Moppès, R. Asselineau, P. de Beaumont, J. Dutourd. Paris: Gallimard, 1969. Names of the translators for individual short stories are not specified.

DAVID McCLELLAN

Is Custer a Model for the Fascist Captain in
For Whom the Bell Tolls?

Does General George Armstrong Custer forever charge blindly to his death as a model for the foolish Fascist captain in Chapter 27 of *For Whom The Bell Tolls*?

A case can be argued.

The captain looks and acts a lot like Custer. And Hemingway was a student of the final fight of Custer's life.

The captain "had a red face and a blond, British-looking moustache and there was something wrong about his eyes. They were a light blue and the lashes were light, too. As you looked at them they seemed to focus slowly." This could be a description of Custer's countenance as it emerges from accounts of his appearance or stares from the selection of photographs in Jay Monoghan's *Custer: The Life of General George Armstrong Custer* (Boston: Little Brown, 1959).

The wrongly-focusing eyes of both the captain and the general match fatal flaws in intellectual perception.

The captain fails to truly perceive his strategic situation in relation to El Sordo and his four Loyalist followers whom the captain's cavalry company has surrounded, and this failure of insight brings the captain's death. Concealed atop a besieged hill, El Sordo shoots

239

into the ground and into his dead horses, with the five shots intended to trick the captain into believing the surviving Loyalists have committed suicide. Although twice warned by his lieutenant that the shots might really signal a trap, the captain strides up the hill into El Sordo's gunsights, after implying the lieutenant is a coward.

Custer also charged wrong-eyed into a trap. On the day of his death, he was twice warned by his chief scout that the Little Big Horn Valley swarmed with Sioux and Cheyenne warriors vastly outnumbering his own Seventh Cavalry. Calling his scout a coward, Custer disregarded both warnings and was cut down on a hillside by Indian bullets.

It is interesting to note that there are similarities between El Sordo and Sitting Bull, the Indian chief who defeated Custer. In Chapter II of *FWTBT* El Sordo is described as " . . . short and heavy, brown-faced, with broad cheekbones . . . wide-set yellow-brown eyes, a thin-bridged, hooked nose like an Indian's, a long upper lip and a wide, thin mouth." Photographs of Sitting Bull in Chapter 5 of *The Custer Myth* by Col. W. A. Graham (Harrisburg, Pa.: Stackpole, 1953) are visual equivalents of Hemingway's description of El Sordo.

What is the evidence that Hemingway was a student of Custer and his last fight?

"And I know the exact details of how He [God] killed George Armstrong Custer, which nobody else knows . . . ", Hemingway once wrote Arthur Mizener (excerpt from letter in the *Washington Post* [30 October, 1972], B1-2).

In Chapter 30 of *FWTBT*, Robert Jordan recalls that while his own grandfather fought on the Union side in the Civil War along with Custer, the grandfather considered Custer a stupid man who "just had the ability to get himself in and out of trouble . . . and on the Little Big Horn he got into it but he couldn't get out."

In Chapter 16 of *Across the River and Into the Trees*, Colonel Cantwell thinks of Custer as a horse-cavalry man with "sawdust for brains" who on the Little Big Horn hill "made one real mistake, finally, and for good . . . ."

Hemingway included in his anthology of outstanding writing about combat, *Men at War* (New York: Crown, 1942), the section of Frederick F. Van De Water's book about Custer, *Glory Hunter* (Indianapolis: Bobbs-Merrill, 1934) which describes the Little Big Horn battle. This was a pioneer work in correcting the widely-believed legend of Custer as a daring but smart soldier who died through the incompetence of his subordinates and ill luck—instead of through his own stupidity.

East Tennessee State University

GEORGE MONTEIRO

HEMINGWAY ON DIALOGUE IN
"A CLEAN, WELL-LIGHTED PLACE"

Cleaning up the "messy" dialogue in "A Clean, Well-Lighted Place" has become a promising light industry in Hemingway studies. At last check there were no less than a dozen such proposals, including one plea for a return to the sanity of the Scribners original 1933 text. Rather remarkably, moreover, Scribners has responded to the wisdom of such scholarship (or the main thrust of it) by altering, without authorial sanction, the text of the story.

Given such scholarly concern, therefore, not to mention the present situation regarding the text, it might prove useful to point out that Hemingway himself was once asked to comment on the confusion in the story arising from the "messy" dialogue. This professional query brought forth a forthright reply of thirteen words. The Assistant Professor's note had sent Hemingway back to the story and the result—he was oh so sorry to disappoint—was that the story as originally published continued to make perfect sense to him.[1]

Brown University

---

[1] ALS, Hemingway to Judson Jerome, n.d., scrawled in at the bottom of Jerome's TLS to Hemingway, November 31, 1956. Special Collections, Mugar Library, Boston University. Paraphrased with the kind consent of Dr. Howard Gottlieb.

REVIEWS

It wouldn't be so."

"Why there are things between Daisy ~~and me~~ that
you'll never know," said Tom, "Things that neither
of us will never forget."

But Gatsby was looking at Daisy.
"I don't ask you, to say anything. I only want you, ~~Daisy now~~."
She didn't answer and he turned ~~miserably~~
to Tom, "She never loved you. I have a way — I
have reasons for knowing she never loved you. Good
reasons. She only married you because you were
rich and she was tired."

Those ~~tragic~~ eyes of Gatsby's ~~were the victory of~~ criterion
~~signified Tom's~~ triumph ~~history~~ but the dead dream
~~fought on through the head~~ struggled ~~for awhile~~ striving ~~to communicate~~ touch
what was no longer ~~communicable~~ tangible, struggling
unhappily, ~~undespairingly~~, ~~toward~~
that lost voice across the room. ~~Jordan~~
was crying.
"She's never stopped ~~loving me~~," ~~said~~ Tom and his
words seemed to lean ~~on now roughly~~ down over Gatsby,
"Certainly not for a common swindler who'd have to
steal the ring he put on her finger."

But Gatsby was too stunned to hear or care
and Tom, who was never a bully except in liquor,
saw that he had gone far enough. He could ~~afford~~
be magnanimous, and a little contemptuous

Page from *THE GREAT GATSBY: A Facsimile of the Manuscript.*

BUDD SCHULBERG

THE GREAT GATSBY:
A Facsimile of the Manuscript
Edited with an Introduction by Matthew J. Bruccoli
Washington: Bruccoli Clark/
Microcard Editions Books, 1973. $45.00

Surely it is no fault of F. Scott Fitzgerald's that the Fitzgerald *phenomenon*—from the success of his youthful first novel to the down-and-almost-out days in the ebbing years in Hollywood, from the serious revival in the early 50's to the current merchandizing hype of *The Gatsby Look*—has tended to obfuscate the literary genius of Fitzgerald. Unfortunately even more obscure, except to a handful of Fitzgerald scholars, is the infinite patience of the master craftsman with which Fitzgerald—in his finest work—shored up this genius. It is fashionable, as well as rather true, to think of Scott Fitzgerald as having squandered his genius. And he himself, in the painful self-examination of the middle 30's, realized what his stature would have been if he had pressed on from the impressive literary discipline of *Gatsby* and "never taken a backward look." But there have been other writers of genius who, quite the opposite of Fitzgerald, have succeeded in finding a discipline for their lives that they were unable to carry over into their literary work. This kind of squandering, in all of his novels from *Gatsby* to the unfinished *The Last Tycoon*, Fitzgerald never indulged. He may have had trouble getting to and staying at his desk, but once he got there, he stayed there, he worked and reworked, and then reworked again, with a dedication to craft that with every erasure, every word change, every rewriting of a paragraph, every shift of content from one chapter to another, refutes for all the time the stereotype of Fitzgerald the playboy, Fitzgerald the spendthrift of time and talent, Fitzgerald the panderer to current taste.

If you are one of the devoted Fitzgerald readers who resists the steamroller methods of go-for-broke Hollywood moguls determined to foist on a media-battered public the "Gatsbyization" of America, there is no better antidote to the recent hoopla than to return, studiously and reflectively, to the real thing. There is, of course, the novel itself, to be read in the peace of one's own study, far from the panting crowds who surged against police barricades for a glimpse of Robert Redford. In his immaculate pinks, this latest "interpreter" of Jay Gatsby struggled against the stream of miscasting and misunderstanding like a pink salmon destined for no more heroic ending than to be carved up on the critics' deli counter as lox. Mia Farrow, Hollywood-born and Hollywood-created, dressed to her beautiful teeth as Gatsby's Daisy, was a lovely symbol of filmdom's consistent failure to grasp the spirit of Fitzgerald's original and elusive work.

Behind the lavish movie that doesn't work is the novel that does, and behind the novel is the manuscript, the work-in-progress, now available in a facsimile of the Fitzgerald holograph itself. Thanks to prodigious and innovative scholarship on the part of Professor Matthew J. Bruccoli, serious students of Fitzgerald can now go directly to the source, to the first hand-written draft, to the inserts, the paragraph cuts, the rearrangement of entire chapters, a work of such fastidious craftsmanship that it was not even completed, as are most books, when it went to galley proof. In addition to the holograph is a generous sampling of galley-proofs, not merely corrected but often entirely rewritten, as Fitzgerald continued to pursue the grail of perfection.

Without exception, every page of the holograph contains corrections, erasures, inserts and cuts—from a single word to an entire page—that provide students of modern fiction with enough examples of the craft of the novelist to stimulate a full term's course, if not a lifetime of study. This reviewer read the facsimile of the holograph and the sampling of corrected galleys, with the published novel alongside, turning page by page to test the work-in-progress against the relatively short novel Scribners published in 1925. To do so is to understand in detail where inspiration ends and perspiration begins. "Hard work sets in," Fitzgerald had warned himself in his *Ledger*, upon finishing the handwritten draft. His method was to revise the typescript, and then, when this carefully reworked version went to the printers, revise the galleys with a scrupulous ferocity that few, if any, American novelists have applied to their work.

How easy it is for those of us who have admired Fitzgerald through seasons hot and cold to think of him as being at the top of his game, the peak of his control when he was addressing himself to the novel that was to raise his reputation from boy wonder (with the *succès scandale* of *This Side of Paradise)* to youthful maturity with the enduring achievement of *Gatsby*. But when you examine this facsimile you learn something that not even the most sage and scholarly generalization can provide.

Comparing the holograph to the galley-proof revisions to the published result, one is reminded of the celebrated exchange between Fitzgerald and his slightly younger contemporary, Thomas Wolfe. What a study in opposites they present: Fitzgerald, the ever-scrupulous putter-inner-and-taker-outer vs. Wolfe, the great pourer-inner—Let it flow like a river, with its improbable turns, its depths and shallows, its beauties and defects, the whole fluid works! In a characteristically evangelistic letter from (of all places!) The Garden of Allah Hotel in Hollywood, Fitzgerald had dared to caution Wolfe against his excesses:

> Now the more, the stronger, man's inner tendencies are defined, the more he can be sure they will show, the more necessity to rarefy them, to use them sparingly. The novel of selected incident has this to be said: that the great writer like Flaubert has consciously left out the stuff that Bill or Joe (in his case, Zola) will come along and say presently. He will say only the things that he alone sees. So *Madame Bovary* becomes eternal, while Zola already rocks with age ...
>
> That, in brief, is my case against you ...

Wolfe's rebuttal was combative. Questioning that there was such a place as *The Garden of Allah* Hotel, he held to his own conviction in "the *unselective* novel that boils and pours." Taking his stand with the putter-inners as against the leaver-outers, he told Fitzgerald to "Flaubert me no more Flauberts ...."

Here is a classic confrontation between two gifted American writers at opposite ends of the novel's spectrum: Wolfe, the compulsive putter-inner, in love with everything he wrote; Fitzgerald, the compulsive reviser, constantly questioning, changing and refining. He could agonize over changing *resemble* to *look like*, or *he interrupted* to *he suggested* or *looked* to *glanced*, or *quickly* to *vigorously*, or *a sort of joy* to *a joyous exaltation*. Or, *My house was on the tip of West Egg* to the more direct *I lived at West Egg* ....

It is a fascinating game one can play by the hour. But of course the dedicated tedium of revision cuts much deeper than a search for the *mot juste*, or even the *phrase juste*. One could devote a full day to the study of the elimination of adjectives and adverbs that clutter the picture or arrest the narrative flow. And one could devote another informative day to a rereading of the block cuts, one hundred to two-hundred-and-fifty-word passages long buried in library vaults, but still aglow with the kind of evocative prose that only Fitzgerald could write. It is always difficult for an author to blue-pencil what he thinks of as lovely language. But when you ponder the motive for Fitzgerald's deletions, you find a superbly self-critical author aware that he has told too much too soon. The masterful unfolding of the plot and theme, through the eyes of the carefully uninvolved and yet sympathetic narrator, Nick Carraway, is precious and delicate. The narrator is sufficiently far removed and yet exactly close enough to provide the perfect balance wheel for the novel's subtle machinery. The relationship of the narrator to the principal characters revolving around him is flawless. But as one learns from a study of the block-cuts and major rearrangements to be found in this facsimile, the seeming effortlessness of *Gastby* evolved from exhaustive effort.

One wishes there were space to examine all the telling examples of "hard work" that bear out the author's purpose in not jumping his own carefully loaded and accurately aimed hunting gun. He was able to block out a passage or a page or an entire section because it told us too much about Nick and therefore brought his narrator too close to stage center; or too much about the Buchanans before they came east from their natural habitat in the middle west, instead of allowing their geographical and cultural dislocation to reveal themselves organically in the course of their scenes and their dialogue as they reign in one of the grandest of the white places of fashionable East Egg; or too much about Gatsby himself, that mysteriously cultivated rough-neck who is brought so slowly into focus at his first party, through the curious but circumspect eyes of Nick Carraway, that at first you don't see him at all, although he is literally all around you. Study the cuts and rewriting of Gatsby's introduction to the novel, and you find yourself drawn closer to the critical intelligence of Fitzgerald the great taker-outer. Tricks of magic are being performed here, and like the work of all master magicians, what appears as

magic to the viewer is produced only through infinite patience with
the refinements of technique.

It was Dorothy Parker who said of Fitzgerald that he was
incapable of writing a bad line. It is doubtful that anyone ever has
enjoyed that incapability, from Shakespeare to Salinger. Fitzgerald
was a perfectionist rather than the embodiment of perfection. Of
course he was capable of bad lines. You will find some of them in the
holograph. You also will find them, in nearly every case, deleted or
refined.

One of the most significant changes to be found in the facsimile is
to compare the haunting coda of the novel, in its closing two pages
(217-218) as published, with the original passage and placement. I
have known Fitzgerald students who could quote that ending:

> Most of the big shore places were closed now and there were hardly any
> lights except the shadowy, moving glow of a ferryboat across the Sound.
> And as the moon rose higher the inessential houses began to melt away
> until gradually I became aware of the old island here that flowered once
> for Dutch sailors' eyes—a fresh, green breast of the new world. Its vanished
> trees, the trees that had made way for Gatsby's house, had once pandered
> in whispers to the last and greatest of all human dreams; for a transitory
> enchanted moment man must have held his breath in the presence of this
> continent, compelled into an aesthetic contemplation he neither under-
> stood nor desired, face to face for the last time in history with something
> commensurate to his capacity for wonder.
>
> And as I sat there brooding on the old, unknown world, I thought of
> Gatsby's wonder when he first picked out the green light at the end of
> Daisy's dock. He had come a long way to this blue lawn, and his dream
> must have seemed so close that he could hardly fail to grasp it. He did not
> know that it was already behind him, somewhere back in that vast
> obscurity beyond the city, where the dark fields of the republic rolled on
> under the night . . . .

What a provocative surprise it is to come across an earlier version
of this passage in the holograph at the end of Chapter One! When
Nick returns from his visit with the Buchanans and looks out from
his lawn to see his mysterious neighbor in the moonlight stretching
his arms seaward toward the green light at the end of Daisy's dock
across the bay, Fitzgerald had concluded the opening chapter with
these two paragraphs:

> The sense of being in an unfamiliar place deepened on me and as the
> moon rose higher the inessential houses seemed to melt away until I was
> aware of the old island here that flowered once for Dutch sailors eyes—a

> fresh green breast of the new world. Its vanished trees, the very trees that had made way for Gatsby's house, had once pandered in whispers to the last and greatest of all human dreams—for a transitory and enchanted moment man must have held his breath in the presence of this continent, compelled into an aesthetic contemplation he neither understood nor desired, face to face for the last time in history with something commensurate to his capacity for wonder.
>
> And as I sat there brooding on the old unknown world I too held my breath and waited, until I could feel the motion of America as it turned through the hours—my own blue lawn and the tall incandescent city on the water and beyond that the dark fields of the republic rolling on under the night.

The rephrasing is instructive, but far more impressive is his realization that he has anticipated, in this opening chapter, his inevitable conclusion: that Gatsby is larger than life, that he has come to represent nothing less than the American dream, and that the loss of Daisy, and his tragic failure to win her away from Tom Buchanan, is symbolically linked to a green and enchanted America that held forth a promise of "the last and greatest of all human dreams." Placed as it was originally, that shining passage threatens to make of *The Great Gatsby* the thing that Fitzgerald the moralist abhorred, "a moral story." Moved to the end of the published version, after the story has been so brilliantly told, it is revealed as a story with a moral, which is something else again. Studying the sensitive rewording and the daring rearrangement of this coda, one of the most moving passages in modern American literature, we are thankful to Matthew Bruccoli for his resourceful scholarship. His admirably precise Introduction is a feast of inside knowledge and informed insights that opens us to intriguing new fields of Fitzgeraldiana. Our only quibble is that the opening hand-written chapters of the holograph might not have been darkened so as to be more legible. There were times when these old eyes watered and strained. But that is a small price to pay for this rare opportunity to meet Scott Fitzgerald, the tireless literary craftsman whose artistic conscience will outlive the myths, the romances, and the rip-offs.

BRYANT MANGUM

F. Scott Fitzgerald's Ledger
A Facsimile.
Introduction by Matthew J. Bruccoli.
Washington: Bruccoli Clark/NCR
Microcard Editions, 1972. $35.00.

Fitzgerald was a literary artist who was also a professional writer, and the ledger in which he kept his records between 1919 and 1938 is the best gauge there is—or is likely ever to be—of the degree of concern Fitzgerald had for the professional aspects of his career. It shows that he cared about everything he wrote, whether he wrote it for love, for money, or for both. It shows that, in addition to concerns with each work which were purely literary, he cared where it appeared first, how much it earned, where it was reprinted, what people along the way thought about it, and what ultimately became of it. *F. Scott Fitzgerald's Ledger* is a facsimile of the meticulous record that he kept, a scorecard for himself and a permanent account for posterity, of each literary transaction. And while this record is clearly not for those who would prefer to believe that Fitzgerald's "serious work," as opposed to his "commercial writing," was hatched in an economic vacuum, it will be an indispensible resource tool for those interested in exploring the integral relationship between the professional author/literary artist sides of Fitzgerald's career.

Sections one and three of the *Ledger*, "Record of Published Fiction—Novels, Plays, Stories" and "Published Miscelani (including

103

NAME	DESCRIPTION	MAGAZINE	DATE	REMARKS
Published Miscelani [inclusive movies] for which I was Paid				
A Dirge	Parody Verse	Judge	Dec. 1919	
"Predjudices 2 Genos"	Review	Bookman	March 1921	
This is a Magazine	Sketch	Vanity Fair	Dec. 1920	
"Brass"	Review	Bookman	Oct 1920	
When the Movies Own The Publishers	Suggestion	Life		

Page from *F. Scott Fitzgerald's LEDGER.*

movies) for which I was paid," are companion sections which, taken together, comprise Fitzgerald's annotated autobibliography. These sections indicate how conscious Fitzgerald was of using all available markets for his writings. First magazine appearances in his "Record of Published Fiction," for example, are followed by subsequent reprintings which earned additional money. The practical function that such a record served for Fitzgerald is clear: he always knew whether he had used all available markets for a work or if it was still potentially salable. For the Fitzgerald scholar these autobibliographical sections are useful on several counts. Because they are bibliographies in preliminary form, they have made, and will continue to make, Fitzgerald bibliographies more complete. Also, in indicating the dates of composition of various works, both sections are essential in any study of Fitzgerald's development as a writer. Among the most useful features of these sections is Fitzgerald's designation of "Stripped and—Permanently Buried" in "Record of Published Fiction." This notation provides a starting point for analyses of his methods of composition, particularly in the case of various novel related stories. The thirty stories which Fitzgerald "Stripped" for possible use in novels indicate what to look for in Fitzgerald's longer works. And there is much yet to be found.

Section two, "Money Earned by Writing since Leaving Army," and the single-page section four, "Zelda's Earnings," are complete financial records of the Fitzgeralds' earnings from writing. Section two, after all the yearly totals are added, shows that Fitzgerald's earnings from his profession before he went to Hollywood in 1937 amounted to slightly less than $400,000, a figure that, to many, will be surprisingly small. In addition, it indicates the relative importance of Fitzgerald's various outlets for his work. The short stories, for example, obviously less important to Fitzgerald from a literary standpoint than the book market, earned more than $225,000, over three times the amount of his novel advances and royalties. While these figures suggest superficially that the financial incentive provided by the slick magazine fiction market might have lured Fitzgerald into the trap of writing stories for magazines that payed high prices at the expense of writing more books, a closer look indicates that the relationship is much more complicated than this: Fitzgerald was usually at his best artistically during periods of his greatest earnings from short stories.

While the first four sections of the *Ledger*, then, suggest studies that deal primarily with the professional side of Fitzgerald's career, the fifth section, "Outline Chart of My Life," invites analyses that are more directly literary—specifically, studies involving Fitzgerald's use of autobiographical details for his fiction. The "Outline Chart" is a year by year catalog of highly charged emotional episodes in Fitzgerald's life, written, with very few slips, in the third person. Reading this section is like walking through a corridor filled with familiar people. Amory Blaine is there; Basil, probably more than anyone, is there; Dexter Green and Gatsby are there. Rudolph Miller is there in confession; and so is Nick Carraway there, judging the years and people in the upper-left-hand margins. The names are different, but the people are easily recognizable. One interesting study that this section suggests is a comparison of Fitzgerald's artistic detachment in the adolescence episodes of the *Ledger* with that in the Basil Duke Lee stories. There are, however, many others.

Fitzgerald's *Ledger* poses all of these questions and many more; and its publication in facsimile, because it is apt to set a precedent for the publication of similar documents for other authors, raises questions of a different sort. The *Ledger,* contains a useful introduction by Prof. Bruccoli, which provides historical background and suggests various reasons for the importance of this document to Fitzgerald scholarship; there is a textual note preceding the text; and there is a headnote to the "Appendix"—to some additional 1934, 1935, and 1936 entries which Fitzgerald apparently wrote when the *Ledger* was not accessible. But this is the only apparatus. Should there be footnotes in the text to point out to the reader Fitzgerald's errors in addition, for example? Or should there be guides which indicate probable composition dates for entries in Fitzgerald's "Outline Chart?" And is a facsimile the best way of making Fitzgerald's records available to researchers? The casual reader, of course, will have more difficulty reading Fitzgerald's handwriting than he would reading a typescript, and he may be annoyed at the absence of guides to help him interpret the enormous amount of data in the text. But this is not the casual reader's book. It is Fitzgerald's permanent record for himself and for those who have more than a passing interest in his career. Anything less than a facsimile could have distorted the record; anything more—a facsimile or a typescript plus footnotes, for example, would have pushed the record into the background. It belongs in the foreground; in the hands of the Fitzgerald scholar. Now that it is there as Fitzgerald wrote it, it can, and should, be interpreted.

Virginia Commonwealth University

DAVID J. NORDLOH

*Apparatus for a Definitive Edition of
F. Scott Fitzgerald's The Great Gatsby
[Under the Red, White, and Blue].*
Matthew J. Bruccoli
Columbia: University of South Carolina
Press, 1974. $14.95. Also 50 copies in
replica of original binding—$50.

This volume is the first in the series South Carolina Apparatus for Definitive Editions (SCADE), of which Professor Bruccoli is also series editor. It provides material whereby an interested reader, using commonly available printed editions of the novel, can construct a definitive edition—one which both fulfills the author's complete intentions and eliminates typographical error and various forms of editorial interference. The mechanics of the *Apparatus* and the intention for which it has been prepared are thus consistent with the standards and procedures established by the Center for Editions of American Authors of the Modern Language Association. Because *The Great Gatsby* is still protected by copyright, the fully edited text itself cannot be published, the way other CEAA editions are; but the *Apparatus* is offered as the next best thing, a "do-it-yourself kit" for preparing the definitive edition. In fulfilling CEAA requirements in this innovative way, this volume is the first to bear the seal of a CEAA "Approved Apparatus."

The major sections of the volume deal directly with the textual history of *The Great Gatsby* and the evidence necessary to edit it. The most important are the Historical Introduction, which details the genesis, composition and publication of the novel, and Editorial

Emendations in the Copy-Text, which indicates how published versions of the novel should be specifically altered to produce the definitive text as Professor Bruccoli envisions it. There are also Textual Notes, commenting on individual readings, both emended and unemended; a list of the revisions made by Fitzgerald in a copy of the first printing; a list of the differences between an extant set of galleys revised by Fitzgerald and the first-printing text ultimately produced from them; a full Historical Collation of variants among all printings; a list of Plate Alterations in the Second Printing of the first edition; a Collation of the Scribner Library Edition of the novel in selected printings; a list indicating how the end-line hyphenations in the first edition should be resolved; a pedigree of editions and printings; a section of Explanatory Notes.

The conception of this apparatus volume and the whole SCADE series is most laudable, and the elaborate presentation of the various kinds of textual evidence testify to Prof. Bruccoli's long interest and research in Fitzgerald's life and work. In fact, some portions of the *Apparatus* have appeared in other materials previously published by him, including his bibliography of Fitzgerald. This book and Prof. Bruccoli's other work are a remarkable example of the debt an author's reputation owes to a single scholar.

But though the pattern for such editing kits is solidly established here, and though the presentation of collation evidence seems generally complete, the volume seems finally cursory in its treatment of matters most significant to establishing a definitive text—in the choice of copy-text and in the articulation of a notion of the author's intentions and working methods which must be applied in selecting authoritative readings among variants and in making independent editorial changes.

The relationship of the theory of copy-text to modern editing is immensely complex. But the basic idea is that a definitive edition begins with the selection of the form of a given text which is complete, coherent, and closest to the author's hand and control. At any point after the completion of that form of the text—the copy-text—an author's ability to correct, revise, and supervise is more limited, and though he may in fact make changes later, his text is also likely to be edited by publishers, misread by compositors. There are few forms of *The Great Gatsby* from which to choose the copy-text. The manuscript (available in a full-scale facsimile published by Microcard Editions Books, also prepared by Prof. Bruccoli) is not a suitable choice, since it is vastly different from the finished text, and was probably followed by one or more extensively revised typescripts; it is simply too far removed from the complete, coherent novel finally printed. The other choices are a set of revised galleys, retained by Fitzgerald when he sent a master set (now lost), in most respects a duplicate of them, to Scribners, and the printed text. Prof. Bruccoli chooses the printed text as copy-text, and lumps the two "printed" forms, galleys and published book, together, thinking the difference between them insignificant: "The choice between galleys and first printing requires no defense since both are the same typesetting." The case is not that simple, as he elsewhere points out: Fitzgerald was sent second galleys or page proofs of the novel but is said not to have revised them; the galleys were extensively house styled and corrected by Scribner editors; and, because of Fitzgerald's extensive reworking, chapters 6 through 8 had to be almost completely reset. To refer to galleys and printed book as the "same typesetting" is to miss not only the physical but the authoritative differences they involve: the galleys derive from Fitzgerald's hand and control, the book is overlaid with editorial correction and stylistic sophistication. The extant revised galleys ought to have been more thoroughly considered as a possibility for copy-text, and the variants between them and the book more systematically examined. Prof. Bruccoli does comment upon some of those variants, but he fails to acknowledge the crucial importance of the pre-publication material.

Just as importantly, *Apparatus for F. Scott Fitzgerald's The Great Gatsby* fails to provide a coherent sense of Fitzgerald as author that ought to form the basis for individual editorial judgments in this volume. Fitzgerald is said to have been a weak speller and punctuator, and to have left a good many details to his editors. But he was also a careful craftsman, especially in revision, and immensely concerned with the choices of individual words, with the possibilities of connotation. How seriously then should an editor take his proposed change in the title of the novel, relayed to Scribners in a telegram: "CRAZY ABOUT TITLE UNDER THE RED WHITE AND BLUE STOP WHART WOULD DELAY BE." Prof. Bruccoli takes the message, which arrived too late to allow for the change, as evidence of what Fitzgerald "settled on," even though he had earlier considered a whole list of titles, including "Trimalchio" and "On the Road to West Egg." Comments about specific readings that Fitzgerald "meant" a certain word though he didn't supply it, that he "may have wanted the connotations," that "The misusage is deliberate" seem cavalier in the absence of an informing sense of Fitzgerald's intentions for his novel. Spellings like "Vladmir" and "*Tuolomee*" are altered because they are "impossible" or are inaccurate renditions of what are supposed to be Fitzgerald's precise references to fact; "Little Girl Bay" is even revised to "Little Girl Point" because no such bay exists. Prof. Bruccoli makes decisions about Fitzgerald's sometimes indeterminate revisions in a copy of the first printing without indicating the rationale for decision, even in the face of his own rumors that some of the contents of that copy are non-authorial. Of the 138 emendations he requires for the construction of the definitive edition, Prof. Bruccoli is the only authority for more than a hundred. And after this great number of alterations, questions about the published text remain: shouldn't "The telephone rang inside, startlingly ..." (19.21 in the first edition) be corrected? There are minor inaccuracies in the Editorial Emendations list: it fails to include Fitzgerald's deletion of a comma after "days" (at 28.4 in his marked copy of the first edition); several entries are misnumbered or misstated; the distinction between Fitzgerald's emendations and editorial corrections of those emendations isn't fully specified.

In some phases of scholarship, the remarking on details is pejoratively referred to as quibbling. In the case of textual editing, however, details are almost everything. *Apparatus for F. Scott Fitzgerald's The Great Gatsby* is remarkable for its intention, for the inclusiveness of its presentation of the raw evidence any editor must use. But for a more satisfactory result it needed more time, greater elaboration, more care.

Indiana University

KENNETH EBLE

The Basil and Josephine Stories.
Edited with introduction by John Kuehl
& Jackson Bryer.
New York: Scribners, 1973. $8.95

*Bits of Paradise: 21 Uncollected Stories
by F. Scott & Zelda Fitzgerald.*
Edited by Scottie Fitzgerald Smith &
Matthew J. Bruccoli with Foreword by
Scottie Fitzgerald Smith.
London: Bodley Head, 1973. £3.50.
New York: Scribners, 1974. $7.95.

Keeping up with Fitzgerald publications continues to be a task, a pleasant one, since these two recent collections are of Fitzgerald's own fiction. This much, then, in apologizing for the reviewer's delay in writing about these books, both published in 1973. Most of the content is familiar to the Fitzgerald scholar, thus simplifying the task of keeping up. To the ordinary reader, the two collections somewhat represent two sides of the Fitzgerald coin: the fiction in the one—*Basil and Josephine*—still rings true, but in the other—*Bits of Paradise*—the stories sometimes have a tinny sound.

I must admit a long-held prejudice in favor of the Basil Duke Lee stories which may not be shared by all readers. They fall into a category of stories which, though not purely American, embrace a number of interesting American writers and works of fiction. *Huckleberry Finn* stands at the head of the list, and not far behind are *Winesburg, Ohio*, and Hemingway's Nick Adams stories. Closer to Fitzgerald's actual acquaintance with the fiction of adolescence is

261

Booth Tarkington's *Penrod* and *Penrod and Sam* and Owen Johnson's Lawrenceville stories and *Stover at Yale*.

Most of the stories in which Basil Duke Lee is the central character already appeared in book form in *Taps at Reveille*, still to me the best single collection of Fitzgerald's stories. Five *Basil* stories and three *Josephine* stories comprise the opening section of that collection. Kuehl and Bryer have filled out the two series with this book and accompanied the stories with an excellent introduction.

Most of the *Basil* stories were written during Fitzgerald's return to the United States in 1927 and a frantic summer abroad in 1928. They represented a stern professional effort to return to the materials of his own early life both to keep the pot boiling and to regain a confidence that had dissipated in Europe as he tried unsuccessfully to bring another serious novel into being. Eight of them (one was rejected) appeared in the *Saturday Evening Post* from April 1928 to April 1929. They are as excellent in craftsmanship as any stories Fitzgerald ever wrote. And they are remarkably faithful to Fitzgerald's own experience and to the emotions and attitudes which were crucially shaping Fitzgerald's movement out of adolescence. Through all of the stories runs the theme of desires not quite satisfied, of last minute rescues from shame and despair. They are, of course, creations of a writer at the peak of his craft, and the tone with which Fitzgerald looks at his youthful self is one of the remarkable achievements of these stories.

Fitzgerald told Maxwell Perkins in the summer of 1928 that he planned to publish a book of these stories, referred to them as a "nice *light* novel," to run perhaps fifty or sixty thousand words. But the plans were set aside for a number of reasons, among them Fitzgerald's involvement with the serious novel that he couldn't seem to bring to completion and his uneasiness about what publishing the *Basil* stories as a novel might do to his reputation. Behind his reservations is an interesting and as yet unexplored story of his relation to Booth Tarkington, both the man and writer, and Tarkington's early, tremendously popular works dealing with American adolescence. The appearance of the Kuehl-Bryer collection gives these and the *Josephine* stories a chance to be read afresh by a new generation of Fitzgerald readers.

I am personally less fond of the *Josephine* stories and Fitzgerald himself seemed less committed to them than to the *Basil* ones. They, too, appeared as *Saturday Evening Post* stories, between 5 April

1930 and 15 August 1931. The central character relied heavily upon Fitzgerald's memory of Ginevra King, and the stories in age of characters and situation extend the *Basil* series. None of the stories is, I think, as totally successful as the much earlier story, *The Ice Palace*, in which Fitzgerald uses a girl, Sally Carrol Happer, as the protagonist of the story. Nevertheless, they are full of satisfying touches of precise characterization, wry observation, and Fitzgerald stylistic flourishes.

The stories in *Bits of Paradise* include nine previously published during Fitzgerald's lifetime (eight of these from the *Saturday Evening Post*), nine published stories by Zelda, one collaboration, and two stories by Scott, published posthumously. Scottie Fitzgerald Smith notes in the Foreword that "this is the last book which will ever be published devoted to previously uncollected writings of my parents .... Now everything that's fit to print—and even some that's borderline!—is out on the table for all to see."

This volume has its chief justification in the fact that the stories of Scott's which the editors selected are not far below the rank of those which Fitzgerald himself had included in collections. The writing is, as Prof. Bruccoli observes, "highly professional commercial writing for magazines that could afford the best that money could buy." I agree with him that "The Swimmers," "A New Leaf," and "What a Handsome Pair" are major Fitzgerald stories, deserving to be rescued from oblivion. The stories as a group save readers the trouble of thumbing through old copies of *The Post* to find the realities of Scott Fitzgerald as a popular magazine writer. The student now has easy access to a means of comparing Fitzgerald's more commercial writing with his more solidly established fiction. And the general admirer of Fitzgerald finds further elaboration of Fitzgerald's attitudes to the world and himself.

The stories written by Zelda are a kind of bonus in this volume. Through his agent, Harold Ober, in July 1930, Fitzgerald submitted three stories to Maxwell Perkins at Scribners, which he described as having been written "in the dark middle of her nervous breakdown. I think you'll see that apart from the beauty and richness of the writing they have a strange haunting and evocative quality that is absolutely new." The stories were rejected, but two others, "Miss Ella" and "A Couple of Nuts," appeared in *Scribner's* in 1931 and 1932. The others are a number of portraits of women done for *College Humor* in 1929 and 1930, a very short piece for *The New Yorker* in 1932, and *A Millionaire's Girl*. All of the *College Humor* pieces were credited to both Scott and Zelda. *A Millionaire's Girl* was prepared for that series, but according to Prof. Bruccoli, Harold Ober saved it from being printed there at $500 and sold it instead to *The Saturday Evening Post* for $4,000. In that form it appeared as by F. Scott Fitzgerald alone.

Readers of *Save Me the Waltz* will find that these shorter pieces have the same arresting, yet irritating qualities of the novel. They are full of metaphors and similes and personifications that might seem to be an extension of Fitzgerald's own stylistic habits but without his control. Maxwell Perkins wrote Scott with regard to one of the *Scribner's* stories: " ... I was going to ask Zelda if she would consider whether her figures of speech—I suppose they would be called similes—were not too numerous, and sometimes too remote." That Zelda's style constitutes one aspect of a literary talent is indisputable. But Prof. Bruccoli is probably right in saying "It is absurdly sentimental to equate F. Scott and Zelda Fitzgerald as writers. In literature, as in everything else, there is a crucial distinction between the gifted amateur and the professional."

University of Utah

WILLIAM WHITE

Hemingway at Auction 1930-1973
Compiled by Matthew J. Bruccoli and
C. E. Frazer Clark, Jr.
Introduction by Charles W. Mann
Detroit: Bruccoli Clark/Gale
Research Company, 1973. $25.00

For a variety of reasons many authors prefer not to have their correspondence published, but sooner or later—if interest in the author remains high—such letters will be published after his death. *The Letters of A. E. Housman*, for example, did not appear until 1971, thirty-five years after he died; he would far rather their having been uncollected and unpublished. As for Ernest Hemingway, he left a note, dated 20 May 1958, for his executors: "It is my wish that none of the letters written by me during my lifetime shall be published. Accordingly, I hereby request and direct you not to publish or consent to the publication by others, of any such letters" (Audre Hanneman, *Ernest Hemingway: A Comprehensive Bibliography* [Princeton 1967], p. 256. Nevertheless, the Hanneman bibliography lists (pp. 256-266) no less than 110 letters published in full or partially quoted, and many more have been published since 1967. One day there will be a collected edition of Hemingway letters.

Meanwhile, in *Hemingway at Auction 1930-1973*, Bruccoli and Clark include more than 150 Hemingway letters, some in full, some in facsimile, some in bits and pieces. And though for many readers this is the most readable and valuable aspect of this second volume in the *Authors at Auction* Series, it is not the principal reason for the new book's publication—which is to present a comprehensive, fully illustrated record of Hemingway collecting since its beginning in 1930. This is done by reproducing (in facsimile) pages from sixty auction sale and fifty-five dealers' catalogues containing books, letters, and MSS. of Ernest Hemingway, each entry appearing exactly as it did when first printed, with the addition (in the margin) of the prices which the items fetched at auction.

Most readers of *Hemingway at Auction*—though "users" of this remarkable and fascinating reference work is a more precise term—will follow the rise in prices of Hemingway material during the past forty-four years, from the $160 that *in our time* brought in 1930 (a depression year, when its author was thirty-one years old and the book only five years old) to the $2800 for the Sylvia Beach copy in 1968 (House of Books sold another copy for $2750 in 1973). Prices that an author's books and manuscripts command are one, though only one, indication of his reputation, particularly among collectors; but there is a high correlation between these prices and his reputation among the general readers and critics, professors and scholars. There are, of course, writers of small literary merit whose works bring high prices, and there are reasons for this other than the novelist's or poet's purely literary ability and fame. In Hemingway's case, the number of books and articles being produced year in and year out about him, plus the sales of his books and the printing of new editions and translations and posthumous work all show his high standing in both the popular and scholarly areas. Thus those studying the reputation of the author of *The Sun Also Rises* and *A Farewell to Arms* will certainly welcome this new Bruccoli Clark Book which follows *Hawthorne at Auction.*

The prices that Hemingway material brought at auction vary from $13,000 for 303 leaves of *Death in the Afternoon* manuscript—18 typed and 285 in the author's hand—to $1.75 for Louis Henry Cohn's *Bibliography of the Works of Ernest Hemingway* in 1931. And Charles W. Mann sums this up in his Introduction: "The total figure for all auction sales so far has been $130,342.75, much of it in inflated dollars, which indicates appreciation of one kind or another. One would like to hear Ernest Hemingway's reaction to it."

While this aspect of *Hemingway at Auction* will greatly interest the collector and the followers of Hemingway's reputation as they leaf through these facsimile pages of auction record and dealers' catalogues that are, in Mr. Mann's view, "often uneven, selective, and even inaccurate in transcription and description," it is Hemingway's letters that I find the most rewarding appeal of the 308-page volume. Of these, Mr. Mann writes: "Hemingway, with his guard down in his letters remains a startling, aggressive, compelling writer. As we will never read his collected letters, these pages will remain the only medium through which, however fragmentarily, we can still occasionally hear his voice." (I do not wish to quarrel with Mr. Mann, but "never" is a strong word.)

In more than 150 letters Hemingway discusses with considerable candor his writing problems, his reactions to book reviewers and others about his works, his communications with friends and members of his family on a wide variety of subjects, his frank—Hemingway is frank, if nothing else—comments on Scott Fitzgerald and other authors, and often scathing retorts to such critics as Malcolm Cowley. In fact, there is so much first-hand Hemingway material "buried" in *Hemingway at Auction* one is almost tempted to list the book as a primary source (*by* Hemingway) instead of secondary (*about* Hemingway). And again and again, a reviewer would like to quote from the swatches which the Charles Hamilton and the Parke-Bernet auction catalogues print.

In going through this Bruccoli Clark Book, one is tempted to ask numerous questions about MSS. offered for sale: What has become of the five-page typescript for a stage reading of Hemingway's short story, "The Sea Change"? Should it be published? Two other stage readings of short stories, "Cat in the Rain" and "Hills Like White Elephants": where are they? is publication possible?

As tantalizing as all this is, it is perhaps best here to return to Mr. Mann's introductory remarks: "A writer's career is his books, and his reputation is mirrored by how others view them. The fortunes of the sales room in their ups and downs and haphazard selection are an important part of the record; but the record also reveals how the collector gathers the material to which the scholar turns his attention, and from which reputations are maintained, rebuilt, or rediscovered."

So, no matter whether it's Hemingway's reputation or those letters, inscriptions and MSS. you're most attracted by—and one is also thankful for Linda Berry's full and detailed forty-page index—*Hemingway at Auction* is a work no Hemingway enthusiast or serious student can afford to miss, even at $25.00.

Oakland University

RICHARD LAYMAN

Ring Around Max.
Dekalb: Univ. of Northern Illinois Press,
1973. Cloth, $8.50; Paper, $5.00.

Ring Around Max is indispensable to anyone seriously interested in the last ten years of Ring Lardner's career. Editor Caruthers has collected "all existing correspondence" between Lardner and Maxwell Perkins, a correspondence which contains much valuable information unavailable elsewhere. There are sales and royalty figures on Lardner's books as reported by Perkins to the author, supplemented by Caruthers' interstitial comments. Lardner's friendship with Fitzgerald, who introduced him to Scribners, is the subject of many of the early letters in which Lardner seems more interested in news about his friend than in the details of publishing his books. His interest in the publication of his work in book form, yet reluctance to transform himself from journalist to novelist, reveals Lardner's attitude toward himself as an author. Ring Lardner's reserved, even shy, dignity and sincere interest in the well-being of others is illustrated here as it is nowhere else. Yet, because some information in the foreword and the interstitial comments is questionable, and annotation and documentation are inadequate, the book is not as useful as it should be.

In the foreword Caruthers writes: "During the twenties, Lardner earned up to $30,000 annually from his Bell Syndicate column, and supplemented this income by as much as another $25,000 a year from his work in the theater and in Ziegfeld's Follies, and from the publication of his fiction in periodicals." Although $25,000 may represent an average year's earning from his magazine and theater work, according to a record Lardner himself kept in which he listed his income for 1926, 1927, and part of 1928, he made $44,930 from magazines alone in 1927. This apparently includes payment for four stories which appeared in *Cosmopolitan* during 1928.

The next paragraph of the foreword continues, "His stories were much in demand: he eventually obtained the top price from the *Post*, which was then [when?] $1250 a story, and he received as much as $3500 for each story accepted by *Cosmopolitan*." In a letter from F. Scott Fitzgerald to Harold Ober dated 29 December 1922 (*As Ever, Scott Fitz*–, p. 51), Fitzgerald writes that he knows "confidentially" that Lardner gets $1500 per story from the *Post*. And according to Lardner's list of his income referred to above, by July 1926 he was receiving $4000 per story from *Cosmopolitan*; by March 1927, $4500.

Also in the foreword Caruthers states that *Round Up* (1929) "sold about 100,000 copies in the first year of publication." In his interstitial comments he cites sales records of Lardner's books as of 1932, indicating that 85,261 copies of *Round Up* had been sold.

In the interstitial comments the dates of Lardner's involvement with the "You Know Me Al" comic strip are listed as "from September 1922 to the fall of 1924." This is contrary to a letter from Lardner to Perkins dated 2 December [1924] in which he writes, "I think I am going to be able to sever connections with the daily cartoon early next month;" and a letter from Lardner to Fitzgerald dated 9 January 1925 which reads, "I have quit the strip and Dick Dorgan is doing it, with help from Tad" (Elder, *Ring Lardner*, p. 197). The dates of Lardner's involvement with the comic strip have never been correctly listed in print. It appeared with the credit "by Ring Lardner" from 26 September 1922 to 26 September 1925. Whether the credit was given Lardner between January and September 1925 to capitalize on his name or he was nine months ahead in his work when he quit the strip is undetermined.

A perhaps minor and moot point is that Caruthers refers to the strip as "You Know Me, Al," inserting a comma after "Me." The illustrations he includes from the strip, from an unidentified *Gazette Times*, also carry the title with a comma. But when the title is referred to in a frame of an advertisement for the series released by the Bell Syndicate (reproduced on the inside front cover of the paperback edition of *Ring Around Max* only), the title appears without the comma; and in the *Milwaukee Journal*, which also carried the syndicated series, the comma is used on the first day the strip appears only and is dropped after that. It is, furthermore, difficult to believe that Lardner would have participated in reinforcing this error commonly made in referring to his book.

Ring Around Max includes "A Chronological Listing of First Publications Of Ring Lardner's Books and Magazines Pieces," the most complete list of its kind to appear in print. Among items absent from the list, however, are: "Gas, Oil and Air" (story), *Milestones*, June 1917; John Wheeler, "Ring Lardner" (article), *Collier's*, 17 March 1928, for which Lardner wrote an introduction; "This Play's the Thing—JUNE MOON" (play), *Theatre Magazine*, February 1930; and, "A Reporter In Bed" (article), *New Yorker*, 26 September 1931.

I would take issue with Caruthers on one final point. He ends his foreword with the statement: "This correspondence strongly implies, however, that Perkins probably succeeded in obtaining far more fiction from Lardner than anyone else would have been likely to do." There is little evidence that Lardner ever wrote anything at Perkins' request except some prefaces, and short comments on the stories in *How To Write Short Stories*. That seems, in fact, to be the major critical lesson to be learned from *Ring Around Max*: Ring Lardner wrote stories and articles for magazines, and columns for newspapers; Max Perkins molded that material into books.

If *Ring Around Max* is not a complete success, it is perhaps more an indication of the inadequacy and inaccuracy of previous scholarship than the insufficiency of the present volume. There is currently precious little reliable material on the life and career of Ring Lardner. If the errors and shortcomings of this volume are eliminated, Caruthers' "The Complete Correspondence of Ring Lardner," advertised on the dust wrapper for publication in Fall 1973, can go far to fill the void. It will be an excellent place to begin serious examination of this much neglected author's work.

University of South Carolina

BIBLIOGRAPHICAL MATERIAL

BRUCCOLI
ADDENDA II

The following items were either omitted from Matthew J. Bruccoli's *F. Scott Fitzgerald: A Descriptive Bibliography* (Pittsburgh: University of Pittsburgh Press, 1972) or appeared after the bibliography was published.

M.J.B.

SECTION A

A5.1.a   *Correction:* entry for 176.36 on p. 17 should read: Johnston [Johnson

A5.1.c   *Correction:* The ViU copy (PS 3511.19 T45. 1920b. 709285) is bound in blue boards with orange cloth spine and printed paper label.

A5.3   1950 second printing reported but not seen.

A5.4   *Correction:* Date of publication was 1954, not 1948.

A5   Excerpts from *TSOP:*
Modern Women in Love, ed. Christina Stead & William Blake. New York: Dryden Press, [1945], pp. 131-143.
"The Jazz Age," *Swank* (January 1946), 64-66.
Approaches to Prose, ed. Caroline Shrodes & Justine Van Gundy. New York: Macmillan, 1959, pp. 561-578.

A6.3   Reprinted in Scribner Library, #371. A.8.72 (C).

A7.1.b   Included in A32.

A8   Excerpts from *B & D:*
The American Treasury, 1455-1955, ed. Clifton Fadiman & Charles Van Doren. New York: Harper, 1955, p. 954.
The Classic Woman, ed. James Sterling Moran. Chicago: Playboy Press, 1971. Reported but not seen.

A8.1.b$_1$ *Correction:* In copyright notice the year 1929 should be 1921.

A8.1.d   *Note:* The title page is integral.

A8.1.f   This Grey Walls reprint is repaged, and the preliminary matter is reset.

A9.2.a   *Correction:* This entry becomes A9.2.a$_1$ (first state).
There are 191 variants between the Scribners first printing and the Collins first printing (first state), of which two are substantives:
39.4 hump [39.1 lump
114.12 you're [113.33 your

New entry: A9.2.a$_2$ (second state).
A^8 B^8 ($\pm$B$_6$,$_8$) C^8 ($\pm$C$_2$) D-I^8 K-U^8 X^8
16.2; 16.31; 20.23; 24.24 Diana Manners [Cynthia Manley
Locations: MJB (review copy); BM; Bodleian.

A11   A page of MS is facsimiled in *The Princeton University Library Chronicle,* XII (Summer 1951), 183.

A11   Excerpts from *GG:*
           Taken at the Flood, ed. Ann Watkins. New York:
           Harper, 1946, pp. 32-43.
           Better Reading 2: Literature, ed. Walter Blair & John
           C. Gerber. Chicago: Scott Foresman, 1948, pp.
           172-176.
           The American Treasury 1455-1955, ed. Clifton Fadi-
           man & Charles Van Doren. New York: Harper, 1955,
           pp. 954-955.
           An Anthology of American Humor, ed. Brom Weber.
           New York: Crowell, [1962], pp. 523-532.
           American Heritage, XVI (August 1965). Special
           Issue: "the Twenties," ed. Oliver Jensen. New York:
           American Heritage Publishing, 1965, pp. 36-37.
           *New York Proclaimed, ed. V.S. Pritchett. London:
           Chatto & Windus, 1965. New York: Harcourt, Brace &
           World, 1965, p. 64.
           Advanced Spanish Prose Composition, ed. Cyril A.
           Janes & Alec Payne. London: Oxford University Press,
           1971, pp. 93-94.
           *In the Presence of this Continent American Themes
           and Ideas,* ed. Robert Baylor & James Moore. New
           York: Holt, Rinehart and Winston, [1971]. Epigraph.

A11   *Note: Apparatus for F. Scott Fitzgerald's The Great
           Gatsby [Under the Red, White, and Blue],* by Matthew J.
           Bruccoli. Columbia: University of South Carolina Press,
           [1974]. Apparatus for a definitive edition. Also 50
           boxed copies in facsimile of original *GG* binding.

A15   Excerpt from *TITN:*
           Reading Writing and Rewriting, ed. W.T. Moynihan,
           et al. Philadelphia & New York: Lippincott, [1964], p.
           180.

A18   Excerpt from *LT:*
           *In the Presence of this Continent American Themes
           and Ideas,* ed. Robert Baylor & James Moore. New
           York: Holt, Rinehart & Winston, [1971], pp. 200-203.

A19   *Note: The Crack-Up* was announced for publication by
           the Colt Press in 1942 (see *Publishers' Weekly,* 31
           January 1942), but this edition was never published.

A26   *Correction:* Printings should be re-numbered, thus:
A26.1.d [A26.1.e
A26.2 [A26.1.d
A26.3 [A26.2
A26.4 [A26.3
A26.5 [A26.4
The Letters of F. Scott Fitzgerald was distributed by the Book-of-the-Month Club in 1974. Copyright page: B-10.63[V].

A28   Printed from the plates of *The Princeton University Library Chronicle,* XXVI (Winter 1965). See C316.

A31   *Note:* Although the title page is dated 1969, the first copy was sold 24 February 1970. There was no formal publication date.

A33   Reprinted in Scribner Library, 1973. #460. Copyright page: 1 . . . 19 c/p 20. . . 2

A34.1.a   *Correction:* The title-page facsimile on p. 162 was made from a proof on which Ober's first name was incorrectly printed as *Howard.* The first printing of the book correctly prints *Harold.*

A35   *Note:* Promotional brochure for *Ledger.* Facsimiles 6 pages. Washington: Bruccoli Clark/Microcard Editions Books, 1973.

A36   *Note:* Promotional brochure for *GG* manuscript. Facsimiles 2 pages. Washington: Bruccoli Clark/Microcard Editions Books, 1973.

A37   *New Entry: The Basil and Josephine Stories by F. Scott Fitzgerald,* ed. Jackson R. Bryer & John Kuehl. New York: Scribners, [1973]. Copyright page: 1. . . 19 H/C 20. . . 2
†"That Kind of Party," "The Scandal Detectives," "A Night at the Fair," "The Freshest Boy," "He Thinks he's Wonderful," "The Captured Shadow," "The Perfect Life," "Forging Ahead," "Basil and Cleopatra," "First Blood," "A Nice Quiet Place," "A Woman With a Past," †"A Snobbish Story," †"Emotional Bankruptcy." Daggers indicate first book appearances.

An unknown number of review copies were prepared from Xerox of page proof.

A38.1.a   *New Entry: Bits of Paradise 21 Uncollected Stories by F. Scott and Zelda Fitzgerald,* selected by Scottie Fitzgerald Smith & Matthew J. Bruccoli with a foreword by Scottie Fitzgerald Smith. London: Bodley Head, [1973]. Includes †"The Popular Girl," †"Love in the Night," †"Our Own Movie Queen" (ZF and FSF), †"A Penny Spent," "The Dance," †"Jacob's Ladder," †"The Swimmers," †"The Original Follies Girl" (ZF), †"The Southern Girl" (ZF), †"The Girl the Prince Liked" (ZF), †"The Girl with Talent" (ZF), "A Millionaire's Girl" (ZF), †"Poor Working Girl" (ZF), †"The Hotel Child," †"A New Leaf," †"Miss Ella" (ZF), †"The Continental Angle" (ZF), †"A Couple of Nuts" (ZF), †"What a Handsome Pair!," "Last Kiss," "Dearly Beloved." Daggers indicate first book appearances.

An unknown number of review copies in printed paper wrappers stamped *UNCORRECTED PROOF COPY* were prepared.

A38.1.b   *Bits of Paradise.* New York: Scribners, [1974]. Copyright page: 1. . . 19 C/C 20. . . 2 Reprint of English edition.

Section AA

New Entry: F.S. Fitzgerald e E. Hemingway Selected Short Stories, ed. P. Costa and D. Caldi. Torino: Petrini, 1973. With Italian notes. Includes "The Sensible Thing," "The Baby Party," "The Bridal Party," "Babylon Revisited," "Financing Finnegan," "Pat Hobby Himself." No first book material.

New Entry: Three Hours Between Planes. Agincourt, Ontario: Book Society of Canada, [1970]. Book Society Searchlight #116. Caption title. Folio for loose-leaf binder, with separate 1-leaf commentary. See C303.

SECTION B

B32   *The Far Side of Paradise* was serialized in the *Atlantic Monthly,* CLXXXVII (December 1950, January-February 1951). Two chapters were published as "Fitzgerald in the Twenties," *Partisan Review,* XVII (January 1950).

Love and Revolution, by Max Eastman. New York: Random House, [1964]. On copyright page: *'First Printing'* Quotes part of a letter, p. 501; reports conversation, pp. 465-468.

Wives and Lovers, ed. Alex Austin. New York: Lion, [1956]. Lion Library #111. "Flight and Pursuit." See C 223.

Fitzgerald/Hemingway Annual 1972. [Washington, D.C.]: NCR Microcard, [1973]. Includes the following previously unpublished material: "Fitzgerald on *Ulysses:* A Previously Unpublished Letter to Bennett Cerf," Fitzgerald's annotations in his copy of *Ulysses,* "Six Previously Unpublished Fitzgerald Letters to Hunt Stromberg," "An Additional Lyric for 'It is Art,' " "A Fitzgerald Auto-Bibliography," "Fitzgerald to Roger Burlingame: A New Letter." First book publication for "Fitzgerald on 'The Ice Palace': A Newly Discovered Letter" and "10 Best Books I have Read."

Note: Alan R. Margolies' "A Note on Fitzgerald's Lost and Unpublished Stories," *Fitzgerald/Hemingway Annual 1972,* discusses typescripts of "The Pearl and the Fur" and "Temperature" ("The Woman in the House").

The Romantic Egoists, ed. Scottie Fitzgerald Smith, Matthew J. Bruccoli & Joan P. Kerr. New York: Scribners, [1974]. Includes previously unpublished letters and notes; first publication for "The Pampered Men." Also limited issue of 500 numbered copies signed by Scottie Fitzgerald Smith—published simultaneously with trade issue.

The Garden of Allah, by Sheilah Graham. New York: Crown, [1970]. Poem, p. 188.

SECTION BB

This Is Where I Came In The Impromptu Confessions of Edward Anthony. New York: Doubleday, 1960. Reports conversation, pp. 129-130.

SECTION C

C108   "The Popular Girl" is excerpted in *A Collection of Travel in America by Various Hands,* ed. George Bradshaw. New York: Farrar, Straus, 1948, pp. 288-289.

C168   *Correction:* The year 2927 should be 1927.

C195   "The Swimmers" is excerpted in *The American Treasury 1455-1955,* ed. Clifton Fadiman & Charles Van Doren. New York: Harper, 1955, p. 17.
Also epigraph for John Gunther, *Inside U.S.A.* New York: Harper, 1947.

C209   "A Snobbish Story" is part of the Josephine series.

C280   "Design in Plaster" is included in *Afternoon of an Author.*

"Infidelity." *Esquire,* LXXX (December 1973), 193-200, 290-304. Screenplay.

SECTION D

Bernice Weiss, Books. . . Catalog Number 46 (1973). #177: *F & P* inscribed: "To Caroline Pfeiffer from F. Scott Fitzgerald (on a most embarrasing occasion)".

Modern First Editions. . . February 20, 1973. . . Sotheby Parke-Bernet Sale E 3476. #207:
1- ALS to Marie Hersey, January 1915: "The letter

that you sent, Marie, / Was neither swift nor fair. / I hoped that you'd repent, Marie, / But Lent could not prevent Marie / From being debonnaire / . . . So write me what you will, Marie, / Altho' I will it not. / . . . . And tho' you treat me ill, Marie, / Believe me I am still, Marie, / Your fond admirer / Scott."
2- Collage, 8 pp, for Marie Hersey. Illustrated in catalogue.
3- ALS, 1 p. Headed: "Sacred to the memory of Xmas 1911. . . for Marie Hersey."
4- ALS, 1 p. Ginevra King to Fitzgerald, asking him to phone.
5- Ginevra King's card with "Scot Fitz" signed for 2 dances. With calling cards of Fitzgerald and Miss King.
Sold as a lot and purchased by Quaritch, which subsequently recatalogued as separate items (*Autographs & Manuscripts*. . . 931; #176, #177, #178).

Catalogue 20. . . Black Sun Books (1973), #70: Fitzgerald's Newman School textbook, with notes and marginalia. The Gateway Series of English Texts—Washington's Farewell Address and Webster's First Bunker Hill Oration (New York, 1911). With autobiographical comments on rear endpaper: "With apologies for living Francis Scott Fitzgerald."
#71. *TSOP*, inscribed.

Catalogue 118. . . Heritage Bookshop (1973). #789: *TITN*, inscribed: "For. . . from his friend F. Scott Fitzgerald This story of a Europe that is no more. Sept. 1940".

SECTION F

Cowley, Malcolm. "Fitzgerald's 'Tender'—The Story of a Novel," *New Republic*, CXXV (20 August 1951), 18-20. Quotes from letters, notes, and conversation. Reprinted as part of introduction to revised *TITN* (A 15).

The Princeton University Library Chronicle, **XXXIV** (Spring 1973), 183. List of recent acquisitions includes *GG*, inscribed: "For Telulah, from her admiring friends Scott & Zelda. Paris, November 1925."

West, James L.W., III. "F. Scott Fitzgerald to Arnold Gingrich: A Composition Date for 'Dearly Beloved,'" *PBSA*, LXVII (#4, 1973), 452-454. Includes Fitzgerald's 23 February 1940 letter to Gingrich.

West, James L.W., III. "Notes on the Text of F. Scott Fitzgerald's 'Early Success,'" *Resources for American Literary Study*, III (Spring 1973), 73-79. Facsimiles 2 pages of TS and quotes unpublished material. See C 274.

SECTION I

Copies of the 1972 Book-of-the-Month Club reprint of the Southern Illinois University Press edition of *SMTW* are not so identified, but they can be recognized by the following points:

BOMC omits card page.

BOMC has 13-lines on copyright page.

BOMC bound in black cloth, with blindstamped square on back.

BOMC dustjacket has '0633' on back.

New Entry: Bits of Paradise (London: Bodley Head, [1973]; New York: Scribners, [1974]). Includes 10 stories by Zelda Fitzgerald. See A 38.

REPRINTINGS
OF
FITZGERALD

The following list includes all located reprintings of work by Fitzgerald—including letters. These items were excluded from *F. Scott Fitzgerald: A Descriptive Bibliography*. It is anticipated that supplements to this list will be published. Addenda are earnestly solicited. An asterisk indicates that the entry has not been examined by the compiler.

"ABSOLUTION" (STORY)

A College Book of Modern Fiction, ed. Walter B. Rideout and James K. Robinson. Evanston & Elmsford: Row, Peterson, 1961.

The Dimensions of the Short Story, ed. James E. Miller, Jr. and Bernice Slote. New York & Toronto: Dodd, Mead, 1964.

Studies in the Short Story, revised edition, ed. Adrian H. Jaffe and Virgil Scott. New York: Holt, Rinehart & Winston, 1966; third edition, 1968. (First edition not seen.)

Introduction to Literature: Stories, second edition, ed. Lynn Altenbernd and Leslie L. Lewis. New York: Macmillan, 1969. (First edition not seen.)

Twelve Short Stories, second series, ed. Marvin Magalaner and Edmond L. Volpe. New York: Macmillan, 1969. (First series not seen.)

"The Adjuster" (story)

A Lady's Pleasure, ed. J.L. Collins. New York: William Penn, 1946.

"At Your Age" (story)

Husbands and Lovers, ed. Joseph Greene and Elizabeth Abell. New York: Bantam, 1949.

"Babylon Revisited" (story)

50 Best American Short Stories 1915-1939, ed. Edward J. O'Brien. Boston: Houghton Mifflin, 1939; New York: The Literary Guild of America, 1939.*

A Quarto of Modern Literature, ed. Leonard Brown and Porter G. Perrin. New York: Scribners, 1940. "The Rich Boy" was substituted for this story in the third edition of 1950.

Present-Day Stories, ed. John T. Frederick. New York: Scribners, 1941.

Great Modern Reading, ed. W. Somerset Maugham. Garden City: Doubleday, 1943.

Introduction to Modern English and American Literature, ed. W. Somerset Maugham. New York: New Home Library, 1943.

The Pocket Book of Modern American Short Stories, ed. Philip Van Doren Stern. New York: Washington Square, 1943*; Philadelphia: Blakiston, 1943*; New York: Pocket Books, 1945.

*A Treasury of Short Stories, ed. Bernadine Kielty. New York: Simon & Schuster, 1947.

The College Short Story Reader, ed. Harry W. Hastings, New York: Odyssey Press, 1948.

Introduction to Literature, ed. L.G. Locke, W.M. Gibson, and George Arms. New York: Rinehart, 1948.

American Literature An Anthology and Critical Survey from 1860 to the Present, Vol. II., ed. Joe Lee Davis, John T. Frederick, and Frank Luther Mott. New York: Scribners, 1949.

The Critical Reader, ed. Wallace Douglas, Roy Lamson, and Hallett Smith. New York: Norton, 1949.

The College Miscellany, ed. Samuel N. Bogorad and Jack Trevithick. New York: Rinehart, 1952.

Short Stories in Context, ed. Woodburn O. Ross and A. Dayle Wallace. New York: American Book Co., 1953.

*Stories: British and American, ed. J.B. Ludwig and W.R. Poirier. Boston: Houghton Mifflin, 1953.

Contemporary Short Stories Representative Selections, Vol. II., ed. Maurice Baudin, Jr. Indianapolis & New York: Bobbs-Merrill, 1954*; New York: Liberal Arts Press, 1954.

The Saturday Evening Post Treasury, ed. Roger Butterfield. New York: Simon & Schuster, 1954.

American Short Stories; Isolated People in the Modern World, VI, ed. Theodor Wolpers. Paderborn: Verlag Ferdinand Schöningh, [1956].

A College Treasury Vol. II. Fiction, Drama, Poetry, ed. Paul A. Jorgensen and Frederick B. Shroyer. New York: Scribners, 1956.

A College Treasury, Prose, Fiction, Drama, Poetry, ed. Paul A. Jorgensen and Frederick B. Shroyer. New York: Scribners, 1956.

American Poetry and Prose, fourth edition, ed. Norman Foerster. Boston: Houghton Mifflin, 1957. This story did not appear in the third edition. (Earlier editions not seen.)

More Stories to Remember, II., ed. Thomas B. Costain and John Beecroft. Garden City: Doubleday, 1958; Vol. IV, New York: Popular Library, 1958*.

Short Fiction: A Critical Collection, ed. James R. Frakes and Isadore Traschen. Englewood Cliffs, N.J.: Prentice-Hall, 1959.

Literature: An Introduction, ed. Hollis Summers and Edgar Whan. New York: McGraw-Hill, 1960.

Stories of Modern America, ed. Herbert Gold and David L. Stevenson. New York: St. Martin's, 1961.

Modern Short Stories: The Uses of Imagination, ed. Arthur Mizener. New York: Norton, 1962.

Fifty Best American Short Stories: 1915-1965, ed. Martha Foley. Boston: Houghton Mifflin, 1965.

A College Treasury Fiction, Drama, Poetry, second edition, ed. Paul A. Jorgensen and Frederick B. Shroyer. New York: Scribners, 1967. (First edition not seen.)

The American Tradition in Literature, Vol. II., third edition, ed. Sculley Bradley, Richmond Croom Beatty, and E. Hudson Long. New York: Norton, 1967. (Earlier editions not seen.)

Galaxy, ed. Mark Schorer. New York: Harcourt, Brace & World, 1967.

Reading Modern Fiction: 31 Stories with Critical Aids, fourth edition, ed. Winifred Lynskey. New York: Scribners, 1968. (Earlier editions not seen.)

Stories from the Quarto, ed. Leonard Stanley Brown. New York: Scribners, 1968.

American Literature Vol. II, ed. Richard Poirier and William L. Vance. Boston: Little, Brown, 1970.

Great Short Stories of the World. Pleasantville, N.Y.: The Reader's Digest Association, 1972.

"THE BABY PARTY" (STORY)

Editor's Choice, ed. Alfred Dashiell. New York: Putnam, 1934.

*A World of Great Stories, ed. Hiram Haydn and John Cournos. New York: Crown Publishers, 1947.

*Welcome to Life, ed. H.S. Burnett and Eleanor Gilchrist. New York: Frederick Fell, 1948.

*Modern American Humor, ed. B. Cerf. Garden City: Doubleday, 1954.

The Story at Work: An Anthology, ed. Jessie C. Rehder. New York: Odyssey, 1963.

American Short Stories: 1820 to the Present, revised edition, ed. Eugene Current-Garcia and Walton R. Patrick. Chicago: Scott, Foresman, 1964. (Earlier edition not seen.)

"BENEDICTION" (STORY)

*The Smart Set Anthology, ed. B. Rascoe and G. Conklin. New York: Reynal & Hitchcock, 1934.

Great Modern Catholic Short Stories, ed. Sister Mariella Gable. New York: Sheed & Ward, 1942

*They Are People, ed. Sister Mariella Gable. London: Sheed & Ward, 1943; New York: Sheed & Ward, 1947.

*Bachelor's Companion, ed. B. Rascoe and G. Conklin. New York: Grayson, 1944.

Twelve Great Stories A New Anthology [*Avon Short Story Monthly*, No. 31] (June 1946).

Golden Legends, ed. Samuel Cummings. New York: Pellegrini & Cudahy, 1948.

"BERNICE BOBS HER HAIR" (STORY)

*Stories, ed. Frank G. Jennings and Charles J. Calitri. New York: Harcourt, Brace, 1957; also a teacher's edition.

"THE BOY WHO KILLED HIS MOTHER" (POEM)

Ellery Queen's Mystery Magazine, XLIV (November 1964).

"THE CAMEL'S BACK" (STORY)

Best American Stories, 1919-1924, Vol. I., ed. Blanche Colton Williams. Garden City: Doubleday, Page, 1926.

"THE CAMEO FRAME I" (POEM)

"Past Poetic," *University*, VIII (Spring 1961).

"THE CAMEO FRAME II" (POEM)

"Past Poetic," *University*, VIII (Spring 1961).

"THE CAPTURED SHADOW" (STORY)

The Scholastic, XXVII (12 October 1935).

*Short Stories for English Courses, revised edition, ed. Rosa Mary Mikels and Helen T. Munn. New York: Scribners, 1960. (Earlier edition not seen.)

Short Stories for English Courses, ed. R.M.R. Mikels. New York: Scribners, 1963.

"THE CRACK - UP" (ESSAY)

The American Treasury 1455-1955, ed. Clifton Fadiman and Charles Van Doren. New York: Harper, 1955, pp. 955-956. Excerpts.

Major Writers of America II, ed. Perry Miller. New York: Harcourt, Brace & World, 1962.

A New Directions Reader, ed. Hayden Carruth and J. Laughlin. New York: New Directions, 1964.

American Literary Masters Volume Two. ed. Charles R. Anderson. New York: Holt, Rinehart & Winston, 1965.

"From *The Crack-Up*," *Twentieth Century American Writing*, ed. William T. Stafford. New York: Odyssey Press, 1965, pp. 193-194. Excerpt.

Major Writers of America, Shorter edition, ed. Perry Miller. New York: Harcourt, Brace & World, 1966.

Essays Classic & Contemporary, ed. R.W. Lid. Philadelphia: Lippincott, 1967.

American Perspectives, ed. Harold P. Simonson. New York: McGraw-Hill, 1968.

American Literature The Makers and the Making Volume II, ed. Cleanth Brooks, R. W. B. Lewis, and Robert Penn Warren. New York: St. Martin's, 1973.

"CRAZY SUNDAY" (STORY)

The American Mercury Reader, ed. Lawrence E. Spivak and Charles Angoff. Philadelphia: Blakiston, 1944; Garden City: Blue Ribbon Books, 1946.

*Avon Short Story Monthly, No. 42 (July 1948).

*Great Stories about Show Business, ed. Jerry D. Lewis. New York: Coward-McCann, 1957.

Concerning a Woman of Sin and Other Stories of Hollywood, ed. Daniel Talbot. Greenwich, Conn.: Fawcett Publications, 1960.

*Story: An Introduction to Prose Fiction, ed. Arthur Foff and Daniel Knapp. Belmont, Cal.: Wadsworth, 1964.

Twentieth Century American Writing, ed. William T. Stafford. New York: Odyssey Press, 1965.

"THE CURIOUS CASE OF BENJAMIN BUTTON" (STORY)

Pause to Wonder, ed. Marjorie Fischer and Rolfe Humphries. New York: Julian Messner, 1944.

*Avon Ghost Reader, No. A-90 (September 1946).

Travelers in Time: Strange Tales of Man's Journeyings into the

Past and Future. ed. Philip Van Doren Stern. New York: Doubleday, 1947.

*The Treasury of Science Fiction Classics, ed. Harold W. Kuebler. Garden City: Hanover House, 1954.

"THE DANCE" (STORY)

14 Great Stories by 14 Great Authors [*Avon Modern Short Story Monthly,* No. 7]. New York: Avon, 1943.

*"Georgia," The Fabric of Fiction, ed. Douglas Bement and R. M. Taylor. New York: Harcourt, Brace, 1946. pp. 201-204. Excerpt.

*Coming Aphrodite. New York: Avon, 1955.

Ellery Queen's 1963 Anthology, ed. Ellery Queen. New York: Davis, 1962.

The Saint Mystery Magazine, No. 3 (May 1963)—London; No. 1(July 1963)—New York.

"DEARLY BELOVED" (STORY)

New York Times (20 August 1969).

Louisville Courier-Journal (21 August 1969).

Paris International Herald-Tribune (21 August 1969).

Akron Beacon Journal (14 September 1969).

San Francisco Examiner (21 September 1969).

London Daily Telegraph Magazine (28 November 1969).

NCR World, II (Nov.-Dec. 1969).

"The Debutante" (Story)

Nassau Lit. 1842-1942, C (1942).

"The Diamond as Big as the Ritz" (Story)

Modern American Prose, ed. Carl Van Doren. New York: Harcourt, Brace, 1934; New York: The Literary Guild of America, 1934.

*The Moonlight Traveler; Great Tales of Fantasy and Imagination, ed. Philip Van Doren Stern. Garden City: Doubleday, Doran, 1943.

11 Great Modern Stories/The Avon Annual 1947. New York: Avon, 1947.

*Great Tales of Fantasy and Imagination, ed. Philip Van Doren Stern. New York: Pocket Books, 1954.

*The Short Story: Fiction in Transition, ed. John Chesley Taylor. New York: Scribners, 1969.

"Early Success" (Essay)

Modern Prose Form and Style, ed. William Van O'Connor. New York: Crowell, 1959.

Metronome, LXXVII (September 1960).

The Modern Age Literature, ed. Leonard Lief and James F. Light. New York: Holt, Rinehart & Winston, 1969.

"Echoes of the Jazz Age" (Essay)

These Were Our Years, ed. Frank Brookhouser. Garden City: Doubleday, 1959.

Major Writers of America II, ed. Perry Miller. New York: Harcourt, Brace & World, 1962.

Off Campus, I (December 1962).

20th Century American Authors, ed. K. Ohashi and T. Koyama. Tokyo: Kinseido, 1964.

Vogue, CLXII (December 1973).

American Literature, Volume II, ed. Richard Poirier and William L. Vance. Boston: Little, Brown, 1970.

The Culture of the Twenties, ed. Loren Baritz. Indianapolis & New York: Bobbs-Merrill, 1970.

"THE EVIL EYE" (SONG LYRIC)

"The Girl of the Golden West," *Funny Side Up*. Program of the Triangle Club's 75th Anniversary production, 1963.

"FAMILY IN THE WIND" (STORY)

A Treasury of Doctor Stories by the World's Great Authors, ed. Noah D. Fabricant and Heinz Werner. New York: Frederick Fell, 1946.

"THE FOUR FISTS" (STORY)

For Men Only; A Collection of Short Stories, ed. James M. Cain. Cleveland: World, 1944.

"THE FRESHEST BOY" (STORY)

The Story; A Critical Anthology, ed. Mark Schorer. New York: Prentice-Hall, 1950.

The Story Survey, revised edition, ed. Harold William Blodgett. New York & Philadelphia: Lippincott, 1953. (Earlier edition not seen.)

Selection A Reader for College Writing, ed. Walter Havighurst, Robert F. Almy, Gordon D. Wilson, and L. Ruth Middlebrook. New York: Dryden Press, 1955.

Reading for Pleasure, ed. Bennett Cerf. New York: Harper, 1957.

An Introduction to Literature: Reading the Short Story, ed. Herbert Barrows. Boston: Houghton Mifflin, 1959.

Modern Short Stories: The Fiction of Experience, ed. M. X. Lesser and John N. Morris. New York: McGraw-Hill, 1962.

Papertexts, advanced series. New York: Simon & Schuster, n.d.

"INTRODUCTION TO THE GREAT GATSBY"

A Little Treasury of American Prose, ed. George Mayberry. New York: Scribners, 1949.

"HANDLE WITH CARE" (ESSAY)

The American Treasury 1455-1955, ed. Clifton Fadiman and Charles Van Doren. New York: Harper, 1955, p. 955. Excerpt.

"HOT AND COLD BLOOD" (STORY)

Today's Woman, XIV (September 1946).

"HOW TO LIVE ON $36,000 A YEAR" (ESSAY)

75 Prose Pieces, second edition, ed. Robert C. Rathburn and Martin Steinmann, Jr. New York: Scribners, 1967. (First edition not seen.)

"How to Waste Material: a Note on My Generation" (Essay-Review)

The Griffin, VII (Summer 1958).

"The Ice Palace" (Story)

Trumps: A Collection of Short Stories. New York, London: Putnams, 1926.

*The Fabric of Fiction, ed. Douglas Bement and R. M. Taylor. New York: Harcourt Brace, 1946, pp. 165-167. Excerpt.

Major Writers of America, Shorter edition, ed. Perry Miller. New York: Harcourt, Brace & World, 1966.

"An Interview with F. Scott Fitzgerald" (Self-Interview)

Books and Bookmen, IX (June 1964).

"The Jelly Bean" (Story)

*Contemporary Types of the Short Story, ed. G. H. Gerould and Charles Bayly, Jr. New York: Harper, 1927.

Contemporary Trends: American Literature Since 1914, ed. John Herbert Nelson. New York: Macmillan, 1933.

Reading the Short Story, ed. Harry Shaw and Douglas Bement. New York, London: Harper, 1941.

*The Fabric of Fiction, ed. Douglas Bement and R. M. Taylor. New York: Harcourt Brace, 1946.

*Craft of the Short Story, ed. Richard Summers. New York: Rinehart, 1948.

College Reading A Collection of Prose, Plays, and Poetry, second edition, ed. George Sanderlin. Boston: D.C. Heath, 1958 (First edition not seen.)

*Fifty Modern Stories, ed. Thomas Marshall Howe. Evanston, Illinois: Row, Peterson, 1960.

"JEMINA" (STORY)

Nassau Lit. 1842-1942, C (1942).

"THE LAST KISS" (STORY)

A Cavalcade of Collier's, ed. Kenneth McArdle. New York: Barnes, 1959.

*Great Tales of the Far West, ed. Alex Austin. New York: ALMAT Publishing, 1958.

"THE LAST OF THE BELLES" (STORY)

Reading Modern Fiction 30 Stories with Study Aids, ed. Winifred Lynskey. New York: Scribners, 1952.

Images of Women in Literature, ed. Mary Anne Ferguson. Boston: Houghton Mifflin, 1973.

"THE LONG WAY OUT" (STORY)

*The Realm of Fiction, ed. James B. Hall. New York: McGraw-Hill, 1965.

"LOOKING BACK EIGHT YEARS" (ESSAY)

Liberty/ Then & Now, I (Summer 1974).

"THE LOST DECADE" (STORY)

*31 Stories, ed. Michael R. Booth and Clinton S. Burhans, Jr. Englewood Cliffs: Prentice-Hall, 1960.

20th Century American Authors, ed. K. Ohashi and T. Koyama. Tokyo: Kinseido, 1964.

"MAGNETISM" (STORY)

Read With Me, ed. Thomas B. Costain. New York: Literary Guild of America, 1965.

"MARCHING STREETS" (POEM)

Nassau Lit 1842-1942, C (1942).

"MAY DAY" (STORY)

This Generation, ed. G.K. Anderson and E.L. Walton. Chicago: Scott, Foresman, 1939.

American Literary Masters Volume Two, ed. Charles R. Anderson. New York: Holt, Rinehart & Winston, 1965.

Short Story: A Thematic Anthology, ed. Dorothy Parker and Frederick B. Shroyer. New York: Scribners, 1965.

"MY GENERATION" (ESSAY)

Esquire, LXXX (October 1973).

Esquire The Best of 40 Years. New York: McKay, 1973.

"MY LOST CITY" (ESSAY)

"New York," *A Collection of Travel in America by Various Hands*, ed. George Bradshaw. New York: Farrar, Straus, 1948.

*Empire City, ed. Alexander Klein. New York: Rinehart, 1955.

The Best from Cosmopolitan, ed. Richard Gehman. New York: Avon, 1961.

The Personal Voice, ed. A.J. Guerard. New York & Philadelphia: Lippincott, 1964.

"THE MYSTERY OF THE RAYMOND MORTGAGE" (STORY)

Ellery Queen's Mystery Magazine, XXXV (March 1960).

"THE NIGHT BEFORE CHANCELLORSVILLE" (STORY)

The Bedside Esquire, ed. Arnold Gingrich. New York: Grosset and Dunlap, 1940; New York: Tudor, 1940; London & Toronto: William Heinemann, 1941; London: Arthur Barker, 1946; Sidney & London: Angus and Robertson, 1952.

Best of the Bedside Esquire, ed. Arnold Gingrich. New York: Bantam Books, 1954.

The Night Before Chancellorsville and Other Civil War Stories, ed. Shelby Foote. New York: New American Library, 1957.

MATERIAL FROM *THE NOTE-BOOKS (Crack-Up)*

"Fitzgerald's Recipes for Turkey from *The Crack-Up*," *Gourmet* (November 1959).

"From the Note-Books," *American Literature the Makers and the*

Making Volume II, ed. Cleanth Brooks, R. W. B. Lewis, and Robert Penn Warren. New York: St. Martin's, 1973, pp. 2315-2318. Excerpts.

"NOT IN THE GUIDEBOOK" (STORY)

Golden Book, IX (February 1929).

"OBIT ON PARNASSUS" (POEM)

Pocket Book of Humorous Verse, ed. David McCord. New York: Pocket Books, 1946.

What Cheer An Anthology of American and British Humorous and Witty Verse ..., ed. David McCord. New York: Coward-McCann, 1945; New York: Modern Library, 1955.

"ON A PLAY SEEN TWICE" (POEM)

"Past Poetic," *University*, VIII (Spring 1961).

"ONE INTERNE" (STORY)

Doctor's Choice; Sixteen Stories about Doctors and Medicine Selected by Famous Physicians, ed. Albert P. Blaustein and Phyllis Blaustein. New York: W. Funk, 1957; London: W. H. Allen, 1958.

"ONE OF MY OLDEST FRIENDS" (STORY)

Golden Book, IX (February 1929).

"THE PASSIONATE ESKIMO" (STORY)

Showpiece, I (July, August, September 1972).

"PASTING IT TOGETHER" (ESSAY)

The American Treasury 1455-1955, ed. Clifton Fadiman and

Charles Van Doren. New York: Harper, 1955, p. 955. Excerpt.

Esquire, LXXX (October 1973).

Esquire The Best of 40 Years. New York: McKay, 1973.

"A PATRIOTIC SHORT" (STORY)

Best Movie Stories, ed. Guy Slater. London: Faber & Faber, 1969.

"A PENNY SPENT" (STORY)

Modern Woman, CXI (September 1926).

"THE PIERIAN SPRINGS AND THE LAST STRAW" (STORY)

Washington Post (27 December 1964).

"PRINCETON" (ESSAY)

1917's 40th [Class of 1917, 1957].

The College Years, ed. A.C. Spectorsky. New York: Hawthorn Books, 1958.

1917's 50th, [Class of 1917, 1967]. Excerpt.

"THE PUSHER-IN-THE-FACE" (STORY)

Golden Book, VII (February 1928).

Recent Short Stories, ed. Margaret Pendleton and David Schermerhorn Wilkins. New York: Appleton, 1928.

"RAIN BEFORE DAWN" (POEM)

"Past Poetic," *University*, VIII (Spring 1961).

"Reade, Substitute Right Half" (story)

Princeton University Library Chronicle, XVII (Autumn 1955).

"The Rich Boy" (story)

Present-Day American Stories. New York: Scribners, 1929.

The Bedside Book of Famous American Stories, ed. Angus Burrell and Bennett A. Cerf. New York: Random House, 1936.

*Tellers of Tales, ed. W. Somerset Maugham. New York: Doubleday, Doran, 1939.

*The Golden Argosy, ed. Charles Grayson and Van H. Cartmell. Garden City: Garden City Publishing, 1947; New York: Dial Press, 1947.

The Greatest Stories of All Time, ed. W. Somerset Maugham. Garden City: Garden City Publishing, 1947.

The Pocket Treasury, ed. Louis Untermeyer, Philip Van Doren Stern, Eric Swenson, and Caryl Brooks. New York: Pocket Books, 1947.

*A College Book of American Literature; Briefer Course, second edition, ed. Milton Ellis, Louise Pound, G.R. Spohn, and F.J. Hoffman. New York: American Book Co., 1949. (First edition not seen.)

The Perma Week-End Companion, ed. Edwin Valentine Mitchell. Garden City: Permabooks, 1950.

A Quarto of Modern Literature, third edition, ed. Leonard Brown and Porter G. Perrin. New York: Scribners, 1950. (Earlier editions not seen.)

The American Twenties: A Literary Panorama, ed. John K. Hutchens. New York & Philadelphia: Lippincott, 1952.

An Anthology of Famous American Stories, ed. Angus Burrell and Bennett A. Cerf. New York: Modern Library, 1953.

The American Treasury 1455-1955, ed. Clifton Fadiman and Charles Van Doren. New York: Harper, 1955, p. 956. Excerpt.

The Golden Argosy, ed. Van H. Cartmell and Charles Grayson. New York: Bantam Books, 1956.

The American Literary Record, ed. Willard Thorp, Carlos Baker, James K. Folsom, and Merle Curti. New York & Philadelphia: Lippincott, 1961.

Major Writers of America II, ed. Perry Miller. New York: Harcourt, Brace & World, 1962.

Modern American Literature, ed. Bernard I. Duffey. New York: Holt, Rinehart & Winston, 1962.

An Approach to Literature, fourth edition, ed. Cleanth Brooks, John Thibaut Purser, and Robert Penn Warren. New York: Appleton-Century-Crofts, 1964. (Earlier editions not seen.)

Studies in Fiction, ed. Blaze O. Bonazza and Emil Roy. New York: Harper & Row, 1965.

An Anthology of American Literature, ed. Thomas M. Davis and Willoughby Johnson. Indianapolis & New York: Bobbs-Merrill, 1966.

The Literature of the United States, Volume Two, third edition, ed. Walter Blair, Theodore Hornberger, Randall Stewart, and James E. Miller, Jr. Chicago: Scott, Foresman, 1966. (Earlier editions not seen.)

The Short Story: An Introductory Anthology, ed. Robert A. Rees and Barry Menikoff. Boston: Little, Brown, 1969.

The Genius of American Fiction, ed. William Wasserstrom. Boston: Allyn & Bacon, 1970.

American Literature The Makers and the Making Volume II, ed. Cleanth Brooks, R.W.B. Lewis, and Robert Penn Warren. New York: St. Martin's, 1973.

"RING" (ESSAY)

New Republic (40th Anniversary Issue 1914-1954), CXXXI (22 November 1954).

Major Writers of America II, ed. Perry Miller. New York: Harcourt, Brace & World, 1962.

The Faces of 5 Decades, ed. R. B. Luce. New York: Simon & Schuster, 1965.

The Critic as Artist, ed. Gilbert A. Harrison. New York: Liveright, 1972.

"THE ROUGH CROSSING" (STORY)

Young Man Axelbrod & Other Stories, ed. Hiroshige Yoshida and Akio Maruta. Tokyo: Eihōsha, n.d.

"THE SCANDAL DETECTIVES" (STORY)

The Tehran [Iran] Journal (3 September 1957). Story was continued.

"THE SENSIBLE THING" (STORY)

Understanding Fiction, ed. Cleanth Brooks and Robert Penn Warren. New York: Appleton-Century-Crofts, 1959.

The Short Story: Ideas and Backgrounds, ed. Louis E. Glorfeld, Robert N. Broadus, and Tom E. Kakonis. Columbus, Ohio: Merrill, 1967.

"A Short Trip Home" (story)

Stories for Men, ed. Charles Grayson. Boston: Little, Brown, 1936; Garden City: Garden City Publishing, 1944.

World's Great Mystery Stories American and English Masterpieces, ed. Will Cuppy. Cleveland and New York: World, 1944.

Rex Stout's Mystery Monthly, No. 7 (December 1946).

A Little Treasury of American Prose, ed. George Mayberry. New York: Scribners, 1949.

Stories for here and now, ed. Joseph Greene and Elizabeth Abell. New York: Bantam, 1951.

"Show Mr. and Mrs. F. to Number———" (essay)

Abroad Travel Stories, ed. Alan Ross. London: Faber & Faber, 1958.

"Thousand -and-First Ship" (poem)

"There'd Be An Orchestra from 'Thousand-and-First Ship,' " *The Golden Journey Poems for Young People,* ed. Louise Bogan and William Jay Smith. Chicago: Reilly & Lee, 1955, p. 135. Excerpt.

"Three Acts of Music" (story)

The Armchair Esquire, ed. Arnold Gingrich and L. Rust Hills. New York: Popular Library, 1960.

"Three Hours Between Planes " (story)

Esquire, XXXIII (February 1950).

"TWO FOR A CENT" (STORY)

Short Stories for Class Reading, ed. Ralph P. Boas and Barbara M. Hahn. New York: Holt, 1925.

*Contemporary Types of the Short Story, ed. G.H. Gerould and Charles Bayly, Jr. New York: Harper, 1927.

Golden Book, XXI (February 1935).

"Birthplace," *The Fabric of Fiction*, ed. Douglas Bement and R. M. Taylor. New York: Harcourt Brace, 1946, pp. 352-354. Excerpt.

"VOYELLES" (POEM-TRANSLATION)

"Documentary: 'Voyelles,' by Arthur Rimbaud; 'Translation,' by F. Scott Fitzgerald; 'Notes,' by Paul Schmidt," *Delos: A Journal on and of Translation*, II (1968).

"WINTER DREAMS" (STORY)

*The Bedside Tales A Gay Collection, ed. Peter Arno. New York: William Penn, 1945.

Short Story Masterpieces, ed. Robert Penn Warren and Albert Erskine. New York: Dell, 1954.

*McLean's (50th Anniversary Issue) (15 October 1955).

American Literature A College Survey, ed. Clarence A. Brown and John T. Flanagan. New York: McGraw-Hill, 1961.

American Literature: Readings and Critiques, ed. R.W. Stallman and Arthur Waldhorn. New York: Putnam, 1961.

Twelve Short Stories, ed. Marvin Magalaner and Edmond L. Volpe. New York: Macmillan, 1961 (with *Teacher's Manual*).

American Literature Survey The Twentieth Century, ed. Milton R. Stern and Seymour L. Gross. New York: Viking Press, 1962.

The Modern Talent, ed. John Edward Hardy. New York: Holt, Rinehart & Winston, 1964.

The Short Story: Classic & Contemporary, ed. R.W. Lid. New York & Philadelphia: Lippincott, 1966.

The Art of Fiction: A Handbook and Anthology, R.F. Dietrich and Roger H. Sundell. New York: Holt, Rinehart & Winston, 1967.

An Introduction to Literature: Fiction, ed. Theodore L. Gross and Norman Kelvin. New York: Random House, 1967.

American Literature Tradition & Innovation III. Modern and Contemporary Writing, ed. Harrison T. Meserole, Walter Sutton, and Brom Weber. Lexington, Mass.: Heath, 1969.

The Literature of America: Twentieth Century, ed. Mark Schorer. New York: McGraw-Hill, 1970.

"THE WOMAN FROM TWENTY-ONE" (STORY)

Manhattan Stories from the Heart of a Great City, ed. Seymour Krim. New York: Bantam Books, 1954.

"A WOMAN WITH A PAST" (STORY)

"Josephine," *The Pleasures of the Jazz Age*, ed. William Hodapp. New York: Berkley, n.d.; New York: Farrar, Straus, 1948.

LETTERS

To Frances Scott Fitzgerald

18 November 1938; 5 October 1940. *The American Treasury 1455-1955*, ed. Clifton Fadiman and Charles Van Doren. New York: Harper, 1955, pp. 257, 28. Excerpts.

July 1937. *Authors on Film*, ed. Harry M. Geduld. Bloomington: Indiana University Press, 1972, pp. 223-224.

8 August 1933; Autumn 1937; Spring 1940; 12 April 1940, 12 June 1940; 18 July 1940; 29 July 1940; 3 August 1940; 12 August 1940. *A College Treasury: Prose, Fiction, Drama, Poetry*, I, ed. Paul A. Jorgensen and Frederick B. Shroyer. New York: Scribners, 1956, pp. 7-12.

8 August 1933. *Literature for Our Time*, ed. Harlow O. Waite, B.P. Atkinson, and L.S. Brown. New York: Holt 1947, pp. 581-582.

8 August 1933; Autumn 1937; 7 July 1938; Summer 1939. *Modern Prose Form and Style*, ed. William Van O'Connor. New York: Crowell, 1959, pp. 189-192.

8 August 1933. *A Quarto of Modern Literature*, fifth edition, ed. Leonard Brown. New York: Scribners, 1964, pp. 574-575. This letter did not appear in the 1940 or 1950 editions. (Other editions not seen.)

8 August 1933. *A Treasury of Great American Letters*, ed. Charles and Eleanor Hurd. New York: Hawthorn, 1961, pp. 265-266.

To Ernest Hemingway

December, 1927. *The Culture of the Twenties*, ed. Loren Baritz. Indianapolis & New York: Bobbs-Merrill, 1970, pp. 309-310.

To John Grier Hibben

3 June 1920. *The Culture of the Twenties*, ed. Loren Baritz. Indianapolis & New York: Bobbs-Merrill, 1970, 301-303.

To Marya Mannes

October 1925. *The Culture of the Twenties*, ed. Loren Baritz. Indianapolis & New York: Bobbs-Merrill, 1970, pp. 307-308.

To Frances Newman

26 February 1921. *The American Twenties: A Literary Panorama*, ed. John K. Hutchens. Philadelphia & New York: Lippincott, 1952, pp. 349-350.

To Maxwell Perkins

Before 16 April 1924. *The Culture of the Twenties*, ed. Loren Baritz. Indianapolis & New York: Bobbs-Merrill, 1970, pp. 305-307.

10 October 1924. *American Heritage/Special Issue: The Twenties, XVI* (August 1965) ed. Oliver Jensen. New York: American Heritage, 1965, p. 37. Excerpt.

To Edmund Wilson

May 1921; January 1922; Spring 1925. *The Culture of the Twenties*, ed. Loren Baritz. Indianapolis & New York: Bobbs-Merrill, 1970, pp. 303-305, 307.

Supplement: Letters in Books
and Journals that have not been examined.

Excerpts from letters. *Books and Bookmen*, IX (June 1964), 40-41.

Excerpts from letters. *London Sunday Times Colour Magazine* (3 May 1964), 16-17, 19-21, 23-24, 26.

To Frances Scott Fitzgerald: The Father, Letters to Sons and Daughters. New York: Rinehart, 1960.

"School Report," U. Mahoney. *New York Times Magazine* (12 September 1965), 59.

Patterns for Living, alternate edition, Part I, ed. O.J. Campbell, J. Van Gundy and Caroline Shrodes. New York: Macmillan, 1947, pp. 145-157; 1949, pp. 103-116.

Two letters. *This Week*, (19 June 1960), 2.

Worlds to Explore, ed. Matilda Bailey and Ullin Levell. New York: American Book Co., 1951, pp. 192-193.

LINDA BERRY

FITZGERALD

IN

TRANSLATION II

This list supplements "Fitzgerald in Translation" in the *1972 Annual*–L.P.B.

THIS SIDE OF PARADISE

[*This Side of Paradise*], trans. Sanaullah Nuri. Dacca, Pakistan: M/S Book Villa, 1970. Pak-Bengali.

THE VEGETABLE

Le Legume, trans. Jean Loup Dabadie. Paris: Laffont, 1972. French.

THE GREAT GATSBY

Der Grosse Gatsby, trans. M. Lazar. Berlin: Knaur, 1932. A reprint of the 1928 edition. German.

Den Gule Bil [The Yellow Car], trans. T. Thomsen. Oslo: Gyldendal, 1927. Norwegian.

TENDER IS THE NIGHT

Suave es la Noche, trans. Marcello Cervello. Barcelona: Plaza & Janes, 1972. Spanish.

THE LAST TYCOON

El Ultimo Magnale, trans. Cecilia Boissier and Antonio Skarmeta. Santiago, Chile: Ediciones Zig-Zag, 1972. Spanish.

FITZGERALD'S SHORT STORIES

"Bablyon Revisited," trans. Abbas Mahmoud el-Akkad. In *[Facets of the Short Story (Novellette) in American Literature]*. Cairo: Dar Akhbas el-Youm, 1954. Arabic.

*"Den Rige Dreng," trans. H. Lassen. In *Udenfor Saesonen og andre Amerikanske noveller*, ed. S. M. Kristensen. Copenhagen: C. Andersen Forlag, 1956. Danish.

Gekke zondag en andere verhalen, trans. Jean A. Schalekamp. Amsterdam: Contact, 1972. Dutch.

*L'Eta Del Jazz, trans. Domenico Tarizzo. Milan: Il Saggiatore, 1960. Italian.

[The Literature of Decay: A Study in F. S. Fitzgerald], trans. Ichiro Ishi. Tokyo: Nanwundo, 1958. Japanese.

Historias de Pat Hobby, trans. Alberto Luis Pérez. Barcelona: Luis de Caralt, 1970. Spanish.

FITZGERALD'S COLLECTED WORKS

Romanzi, trans. Fernanda Pivano and Domenico Tarizzo. Milano-Verona: Mondadori, 1972. Contains *This Side of Paradise, The Beautiful and Damned, The Great Gatsby, Tender is the Night,* and *The Crack-Up.* Italian.

[This Side of Paradise, Tender Is the Night, Short Stories] ("Babylon Revisited," "Family in the Wind," "Winter Dreams"), trans. Katsuji Takamura. In *[Collection of Contemporary American Literature]*, Vol. 3. Tokyo: Arachi, 1957. Japanese.

ZELDA FITZGERALD – SAVE ME THE WALTZ

Accordez-moi cette valse, trans. Jacqueline Remillet. Paris: Editions Robert Laffont, 1973. French.

MARGARET M. DUGGAN

FITZGERALD
CHECKLIST

This checklist omits all reprintings of Fitzgerald stories which are listed elsewhere in this number of the *Annual* in "Reprintings of Fitzgerald." Except for items of special interest, this list does not repeat entries listed in "Bruccoli Addenda," also in this issue of the *Annual*.

Anon. "Finding Fitzgerald," *London Times Literary Supplement* (30 March 1973), 360. Review of *F. Scott Fitzgerald: A Descriptive Bibliography*.

_____. "The Great Gatsby," *San Francisco Examiner* (11 July 1926), 7-8E. Notes the completion of the silent movie version of *Gatsby*.

_____. "Great Scott?," *Newsweek* (26 March 1973), 61. Impact of *Gatsby* movie on current fashion.

_____. " 'The Last Tycoon' To Be a Movie," *New York Times* (19 June 1973), 30-C.

_____. "Sheila Graham," *New Orleans Siempre* (20 May 1973), 9.

————. "To the Editor: 'Dear Scott/Dear Max,' " *London Times Literary Supplement* (18 May 1973), 546.

————. "The Writer's Vice," *Time* (5 October 1970), 59. Fitzgerald's alcoholism.

Albert, Hollis. "Scott, Zelda and the Last of the Southern Belles," *Saturday Review/World*, I (20 November 1973), cover, 52-54.

Barbour, Brian M. "*The Great Gatsby* and the American Past," *Southern Review*, IX (Spring 1973), 288-299.

Beer, Otto F. "Der Epiker des Jazz-Zeitalters," *Forum*, II (June 1955), 228-229.

Bigsby, C.W.E. "The Two Identities of F. Scott Fitzgerald," *The American Novel and the Nineteen Twenties*, ed. Malcolm Bradbury & David Palmer. London: Edward Arnold, 1971, pp. 128-149.

Boylan, James ed. *The World and the 20's*. New York: The Dial Press, 1973. Reprints 1927 Salpeter interview.

Bruccoli, Matthew J. *Apparatus For F. Scott Fitzgerald's The Great Gatsby [Under the Red, White, and Blue]*. Columbia: University of South Carolina Press, [1974]. Also 50 boxed copies in facsimile of original *GG* binding.

Bryer, Jackson R. "F. Scott Fitzgerald," *Sixteen Modern American Authors*, ed. Jackson R. Bryer. New York: Norton, 1973, pp. 277-321.

Buttitta, Tony. *After the Good Gay Times: Asheville—Summer of '35 A Season with F. Scott Fitzgerald*. New York: Viking, 1974.

Connolly, Cyril. "Drafts and Over Drafts," *London Sunday Times* (25 March 1973). Review of *Dear Scott/Dear Max*.

Cowley, Malcolm. "Fitzgerald: The Romance of Money," *A Second Flowering: Works and Days of the Lost Generation*. New York: Viking, 1973, pp. 19-47.

Crowther, Frank. "The Day I Didn't Have Cancer," *The Village VOICE* (25 October 1973), 19. Treats *GG*.

Eble, Kenneth E., ed. *F. Scott Fitzgerald: A Collection of Criticism*. New York: McGraw-Hill, 1973.

Fahey, William A. *F. Scott Fitzgerald and the American Dream*. New York: Crowell, 1973. Juvenile biography.

Farrell, James T. "F. Scott Fitzgerald and his Romanticism," *Thought* (5 May 1973), 15-17.

Finney, Jack. *Marion's Wall*. New York: Simon and Schuster, 1973, pp. 175-176. Novel which includes imaginative reconstruction of lost *Gatsby* film.

Fitzgerald, F. Scott. *The Basil and Josephine Stories by F. Scott Fitzgerald*, ed. Jackson R. Bryer & John Kuehl. New York: Scribners, [1973].

————— & Zelda Fitzgerald. *Bits of Paradise* ed. Scottie Fitzgerald Smith & Matthew J. Bruccoli. London: Bodley Head, [1973]; New York: Scribners, [1974].

Flandrau, Grace. "Fitzgerald Panegyric Inspires Some Queries," *St. Paul Pioneer Press* (9 September 1945), Magazine Section, 6. Rebuttal of Trilling's essay in *The Nation*, "F. Scott Fitzgerald."

Galey, Matthieu. "Une aimable sotie/Le Legume de Scott Fitzgerald," *les Nouvelles Litteraires* (16-22 October 1972). French production of *The Vegetable* reviewed.

Gidley, M. "Notes on F. Scott Fitzgerald and the Passing of the Great Race," *American Studies*, VII [1973], 171-181.

Gingrich, Arnold. "Scott, Ernest and Whoever," *Esquire*, LXXX (October 1973), 151-154, 374-380. Reprint.

Griffith, Ann. "Brick Top Shared Life with Famous," *Bergen (N.J.) Evening Record* (10 September 1973), A-14.

Hills, Rust. "Fiction," *Esquire*, LXXX (October 1973), 68P-74. Refers to *GG*.

Inge, M. Thomas. "Fitzgerald's *Great Gatsby*: It's THE Great American Novel," *Richmond Times-Dispatch* (24 June 1973), F-5.

Judge, Frank. "Judging It," *Detroit News* (25 June 1973) 12-A. Previews T.V. production of "The Last of the Belles."

Katkov, Norman. "In Reply to Grace Flandrau—Calls Fitzgerald 'A Great Writer,' " *St. Paul Pioneer Press* (30 September 1945), Magazine Section, 8

Larsen, Erling. "The Geography of Fitzgerald's Saint Paul," *The Carleton Miscellany*, XIII (Spring-Summer 1973), 3-30.

Lerman, Leo. "The *Gatsby* File," *Vogue*, CLXII (December 1973), 158-165. On the movie.

Lewis, William F. "Masculine Inferiority Feelings of F. Scott Fitzgerald," *Medical Aspects of Human Sexuality*, VII (April 1973), 60-73. Nonsense.

Lockwood, Allison. "A Day for Scott," *Princeton Alumni Weekly*, LXXIII (22 May 1973), 10, 14. Fitzgerald's burial and grave.

Maibaum Richard. "*Great Gatsby* Employs Two Generations of Farrows," *Los Angeles Times/Calendar* (15 July 1972), 14, 38-39, 41-42.

Mayo, Travis. "Monroe Native Author of Nostalgic Literary Work," *Monroe, Louisiana News-Star* (4 July 1973), 13-A. Forthcoming book by Anthony Buttitta.

McCooey, Meriel. "Gatsby the Third," *The London Sunday Times Magazine* (14 October 1973), 58-74. Color spread on the movie.

Miller, James E., Jr. *"The Great Gatsby* (F. Scott Fitzgerald),"
20th Century American Novel/Cassette Curriculum Series.
Deland, Florida: Everett/Edwards, 1970.

Monteiro, George. "The Limits of Professionalism: A Sociological
Approach to Faulkner, Fitzgerald and Hemingway," *Criticism*,
XV (Spring 1973), 145-155.

Nemy, Enid. "Those Extras on *Gatsby* Set Weren't Doing It for
the $20," *New York Times* (11 July 1973), 42-M.

Omarr, Sydney. "Libra Proper for Fitzgerald," *Washington Evening Star and Daily News* (26 May 1973), 18.

Raymond Landon. "A Fitzgerald Bibliography," *Princeton Alumni
Weekly*, LXXIII (22 May 1973), 11. Review of Bruccoli.

Rosenbaum, Ron. "The Corpse as Big as the Ritz," *Esquire*,
LXXX (August 1973), 57-61, 148-159. Suicide victim, David
Whiting, depicted as Fitzgerald worshipper.

Smith, Scottie Fitzgerald, Matthew J. Bruccoli & Joan P. Kerr,
eds. *The Romantic Egoists: A Pictorial Autobiography from the
Scrapbooks and Albums of Scott and Zelda Fitzgerald.* New
York: Scribners, [1974].

Starr, Roger. "F. Scott Fitzgerald and Robert Moses," *New York
Affairs*, I (1973), 60-69. Fitzgerald's treatment of "the Valley
of Ashes" and the revitalization of the area. Reprinted in
Intellectual Digest (October 1973).

Tillotson, Jery. "Some Call it Lousy . . . But Fans Cherish Zelda's
Art Works," *Montgomery Advertiser* (3 February 1973).

Vandersee, Charles. *"Gatsby* in Kiev," *New York Times Book
Review* (9 September 1973), Letter to the Editor.

[Warren, Robert Penn.] "Scott Fitzgerald (1896-1940)," *Ameri-
can Literature: The Makers and the Making*, Volume II, ed.
Cleanth Brooks, R.W.B. Lewis, and Robert Penn Warren. New
York: St. Martin's, 1973, pp. 2282-2318. Introduction essay.

Wells, Walter. "The Hero and the Hack," *Tycoons and Locusts: A Regional Look at Hollywood Fiction of the 1930's.* Carbondale and Edwardsville: Southern Illinois University Press, 1973, pp. 103-121.

Wenglin, Barbara. "Zelda's Montgomery," *Montgomery Advertiser-Journal/Alabama Sunday Magazine* (29 April 1973), 5, 14-15.

Wood, Rob. "USC Professor Probes Writer's Past," *Columbia, South Carolina State* (14 November 1972), 5-B. About *Fitzgerald/Hemingway Annual.*

Reviews of *The Basil and Josephine Stories:* Anon., "The Basil and Josephine Stories," *Publishers Weekly* (16 July 1973), 110; Nona Balakian, "Beautiful and Undamned," *New York Times,* (2 October 1973) 47-M; Bill Kastelz, "Early Fitzgerald," *Jacksonville, Florida Times-Union and Journal* (21 October 1973), Magazine Section, 9; Kathryn Morton, "Fitzgerald: Our Perpetual Boy Wonder," *Virginian-Pilot* (23 September 1973), C-6; Hoke Norris, "Out of a Dead Past, Fitzgerald's Glittering Boy-Girl Stories," *Chicago Daily News Panorama* (13 October 1973), 9; Phil Thomas, "The Basil Josephine Stories," *Columbia, South Carolina State* (4 November 1973), E-2.

MARGARET M. DUGGAN

HEMINGWAY
CHECKLIST

Anon. "Joan Hemingway Publishes Novel," *New York Times* (17 July 1973), 40-M. Hemingway's granddaughter.

_____. "Life A Struggle to Hemingway," *Greenville, South Carolina News* (8 July 1973), 9-C.

Ash, Agnes. "Keepers of the Key," *Women's Wear Daily* (15 June 1973), 2. Key West and Hemingway.

Baker, Carlos. "A Conversation with Edmund Wilson," *Princeton Alumni Weekly*, LXXVIII (26 September 1972), 12-13.

Bakker, J. *Ernest Hemingway: The Artist as a Man of Action.* Assen, The Netherlands: Van Gorcum, 1972.

Brasher, Jim. "Hemingway's Florida," *Lost Generation Journal*, I (Fall 1973), 4-8.

Brian, Denis. "The Hemingway Hunters," *Murderers and Other Friendly People; The Public and Private Worlds of Interviewers.* New York: McGraw-Hill, 1973, pp. 1-81.

323

Cowley, Malcolm. "Hemingway in Paris" and "Hemingway The Old Lion," *A Second Flowering: Works and Days of the Lost Generation.* New York: Viking, 1973, pp. 48-73, 216-232.

Ditsky, John M. "Professor Says Hemingway Fantisized Before Decline," *Lost Generation Journal,* I (Fall 1973), 30-31.

Fererro, Jim. "Two Reviewers Differ on Hadley Hemingway Book," *Lost Generation Journal,* I (Fall 1973), 33.

Gingrich, Arnold. "Scott, Ernest and Whoever," *Esquire,* LXXX (October 1973), 151-154, 374-380. Reprint.

Hemingway, Ernest. "A Canary for One" and "A Clean, Well-Lighted Place," *American Short Stories/Volume VI,* ed. Theodor Wolpers. Paderborn: Verlag Ferdinand Schoningh, n.d.

————. "Foreword," *Charles Ritz: A Fly Fisher's Life,* prepared in collaboration with John Piper. New York: Crown, 1972, p. 1. Revised and enlarged edition.

————. "The Killers," *Studies in the Short Story,* revised edition, ed. Virgil Scott. New York: Holt, Rinehart and Winston, 1966, pp. 382-392.

————. *The Nick Adams Stories* (Preface by Philip Young). New York: Bantam Books, 1973.

————. "On the Blue Water," *Esquire,* LXXX (October 1973), 140-142, 380-382. Reprint.

————. "The Short Happy Life of Francis Macomber"; "Old Man at the Bridge"; "Cat in the Rain"; "The Undefeated"; "In Another Country," *Selected Short Stories,* ed. P. Costa and D. Caldi. Torino: G.B. Petrini, 1973.

————. "The Snows of Kilimanjaro," *American Literature: The Makers and the Making,* Volume II, ed. Cleanth Brooks, R.W.B. Lewis, and Robert Penn Warren. New York: St. Martin's, 1973, pp. 2271-2282. With an introductory essay on Hemingway, pp. 2250-2270.

_____."The Snows of Kilimanjaro," *Esquire*, LXXX (October 1973), 143-147, 366-372.

_____. ALS to "Dear Matthew," L-T Ranch, Cooke Montana, 10 October 1930. #152, *Charles Hamilton*, Auction Number 71 ... 20 September 1973: " ... it looks as though Paramount would have to accept the power of attorney signature which is certainly legal and which they appear to have accepted in the case of Stallings ... Sorry the play did not turn out better. The easiest and simplest way is for Reynolds to send me the box office reports and checks for receipts ... $80,000 is a good sum, even with 10% off and divided by three. It is interesting to know that is the sum your office got for the *Journeys End* rights ... regret you should have been put to the trouble of trying to call long distance and other annoyances. The way things have gone with the critics there is probably no use discussing the matter of *The Sun Also Rises* dramatization possibilities ...." Facsimiles part of the letter.

_____. ALS to Nathan ("Bill") Davis, Finca Vigia, 12 April 1959. #39, *Goodspeed's Book Shop*, Catalogue 575 ... (1973): " ... cholesterol down to 286, kidneys including busted one functioning–liver functioning ...."

_____. ALS to "Muy Monique mio," Ketchum, n.d. # 241, *House of Books, Ltd.*, [Spring 1973]. See *Hemingway at Auction*, p. 246.

_____. 4 ALS and 4 TLS to Edward O'Brien, Paris, Toronto, Hendaye, and Spain, 21 May 1923 through 7 September 1927. #211, *Sotheby Parke-Bernet Galleries*, Sale 3476, 20 February 1973. See *Hemingway at Auction*, pp. 241-243.

_____. ALS to B.G. Rudd, Finca Vigia, 13 April 1956. #52, *Doris Harris Autographs*, Catalogue 15 ... (1973): " ... About the bartender; he never dropped me in Red Lodge nor anywhere else. But there are several phonies who go around using my name so give him the benefit of the doubt. My sister met one in Honolulu last winter who was signing books and have heard of three more this year ... if you ever run into ... anybody that lived at Crandal or up the Clark's Fork or Coolie

City before they built the road give them my best. It is a wonderful country but it got too over-run and we had to pull out . . . It will be fine to have a good book on Charlie Russell . . . ."

_____. *For Whom the Bell Tolls*, inscribed: "For Mrs. Timothy and Mrs. Ward with sincere good wishes always Ernest Hemingway July 11 1944". #229 *House of Books, Ltd.*, [Spring 1973].

_____. *in our time*, inscribed to Lewis Galantiere. #216, *House of Books, Ltd.*, [Spring 1973]. See *Hemingway at Auction*, p. 244.

_____. *in our time*, inscribed to Don Rafael Hemandey. #217, *House of Books, Ltd.*, [Spring 1973]. See *Hemingway at Auction*, p. 244.

_____. *The Old Man and the Sea*, inscribed: "In memory of Harriet Monroe and wishing all good things to Poetry, a Magazine of Verse. Best always. Ernest Hemingway. Finca Vigia, San Francisco de Paula, Cuba. 3/11/55." #30, *The Modern Poetry Association* . . . . 16 November 1973. One of the special copies prepared for Hemingway.

_____. Final corrected TS and corrected galleys of *In Our Time*. #6, *House of El Dieff*, "Treasures At Tokyo" Catalogue, 27 July 1973.

Hoffman, Frederick J. (Supplement by Melvin J. Friedman) "Ernest Hemingway," *Sixteen Modern American Authors*, ed. Jackson R. Bryer. New York: Norton, 1973, pp. 367-416.

Johnson, Robert O. "Hemingway's 'How Do You Like it Now, Gentlemen?': A Possible Source," *American Literature*, XLV (March, 1973), 114-117.

Kazin, Alfred. *Bright Book of Life; American Novelists and Storytellers from Hemingway to Mailer*. Boston and Toronto: Atlantic Little Brown, 1973, pp. 2-20. Includes "A Dream of Order/Hemingway" and passing references to Fitzgerald.

Kleinfield, N.R. "Man's Best Friend, A Bartender's Work Involves Much More Than Mixing Martinis," *The Wall Street Journal* (22 January 1973), 1, 21. Bartender John Gallagher remembers Hemingway.

Konopa, Charles. "Hemingway's Royal Cats," *International Cat Fancy*, XVI (Jan.-Feb. 1973), 6-7.

Kvam, Wayne E. *Hemingway in Germany; The Fiction, the Legend, and the Critics.* Athens: Ohio University Press, 1973.

Longyear, Christopher Rudston. *Linguistically Determined Categories of Meanings; A Comparative Analysis of Meaning in "The Snows of Kilimanjaro."* The Hague/Paris: Mouton, 1971. Comparison of English and German translations.

MacDonald, Scott. "The Confusing Dialogue in Hemingway's 'A Clean, Well-Lighted Place': A Final Word?," *Studies in American Fiction*, I (Spring 1973), 93-101.

Matthews, Herbert L. *Half of Sapin Died: A Reappraisal of the Spanish Civil War.* New York: Scribners, 1973.

McLendon, James. "Hemingway: Last Days in Key West," *Jacksonville, Florida Times-Union and Journal* (8 July 1973), Magazine Section, 6-10.

Monteiro, George. "The Limits of Professionalism: A Sociological Approach to Faulkner, Fitzgerald and Hemingway," *Criticism* XV (Spring 1973), 145-155.

Ross, Morton L. "Bill Gorton, the Preacher in *The Sun Also Rises*," *Modern Fiction Studies*, XVIII (Winter 1972-73), 517-527.

Rubin, Louis D., Jr. "A Portrait of Nick Adams and How He Happened," *Washington Star* (23 April 1972), C-6. Review.

Schneiderman, Leo. "Hemingway: A Psychological Study," *The Connecticut Review*, VI (April 1973), 34-49.

Sokoloff, Alice Hunt. *Hadley: The First Mrs. Hemingway*. New York: Dodd, Mead, 1973. Excerpted in *Cosmopolitan* (March 1973).

Stephens, Robert O. "Hemingway and Stendhal: The Matrix of *A Farewell to Arms*," *PMLA*, LXXXVIII (March 1973), 271-280.

Styron, William. "A Second Flowering," *New York Times Book Review* (6 May 1973), 8, 10, 12, 14; comments on Faulkner's debt to Hemingway's *DIA*. Ashley Brown, "Red Leaves," *New York Times Book Review* (1 July 1973), 24; refutes Styron's claim of Faulkner's use of *DIA*. William Styron, "Red Leaves (Continued)," *New York Times Book Review* (22 July 1973), 26; acknowledges Brown's correction and suggests Faulkner's use of Hemingway Spanish stories of the 1920's.

Sulzberger, C.L. *Unconquered Souls; The Resistentialists*. Woodstock, N.Y.: The Overlook Press, 1973. Study of three men, one of whom—Michel Dupont—was Hemingway's driver and bodyguard during WW II. Revised second edition after suppressed first edition.

Sutherland, Fraser. *The Style of Innocence; A Study of Hemingway and Callaghan*. Toronto/Vancouver: Clarke, Irwin, 1972.

Sylvester, Bickford. "Hemingway's Unpublished Remarks on War and Warriors," *War and Society in North America*, ed. J.L. Granatstein & R.D. Cuff. Toronto:Nelson, 1971, pp. 135-152. Based on Lanham correspondence.

Wagner, Linda Welshimer. "The Marinating of *For Whom the Bell Tolls*," *Journal of Modern Literature*, II (November 1972), 533-546.

Waldhorn, Arthur, ed. *Ernest Hemingway: A Collection of Criticism*. New York: McGraw-Hill, 1973.

Weber, Brom. "Ernest Hemingway's Genteel Bullfight," *The American Novel and the Nineteen Twenties*, ed. Malcolm Bradbury & David Palmer. London: Edward Arnold, 1971, pp. 150-163.

Young, Philip. " 'Big World Out There': The Nick Adams Stories,"
   Novel, VI (Fall 1972), 5-19.

MARGARET M. DUGGAN

GENERAL
CHECKLIST

Anon. "The Fitzgerald Hemingway Epoch," *Esquire*, LXXX (October 1973), 139.

Coben, Stanley, ed. *Reform, War, and Reaction, 1912-1932.* Columbia: University of South Carolina Press, 1972.

Dos Passos, John. *The Fourteenth Chronicle: Letters and Diaries of John Dos Passos*, ed. Townsend Ludington. Boston: Gambit, 1973. Includes letters and notes on Fitzgerald and Hemingway. Excerpted in *Works in Progress/Number Eight*, 1973.

Frank, Waldo. *Memoirs of Waldo Frank*, ed. Alan Trachtenberg. Amherst: University of Massachusetts Press, 1973. Passing references to Fitzgerald and Hemingway.

Geitz, Robert. "True Confessions: 'How I Learned to Stop Worrying and Enjoy Vomiting,' " *Yale Daily News Magazine* (31 October 1973), 2. Alcoholism and writers.

Jablonski, Edward & Lawrence D. Stewart. *The Gershwin Years*. Garden City: Doubleday, 1973.

Landsberg, Melvin. *Dos Passos' Path to U.S.A.* Boulder: Colorado Associated University Press, 1972.

Selznick, David O. *Memo from David O. Selznick*, ed. Ruby Behlmer. New York: Viking, 1972. Mentions Fitzgerald and Hemingway and the adaptations of *Tender* and *For Whom the Bell Tolls*.

Westcott, Glenway. "Memories and Opinions," *Prose*, V (Fall 1972), 177-202.

Wilson, Edmund. "Edmund Wilson's Princeton," *Princeton Alumni Weekly*, LXXVIII (26 September 1972), 14-15. Excerpts from *A Prelude*.

ANNOUNCEMENTS

Lowry on *Tender*

In 1951 Malcolm Lowry and his wife, Margerie Bonner Lowry, wrote a screenplay for *Tender Is the Night* as an expression of their admiration for the novel. *Notes on a Screenplay for Tender Is the Night* (Bloomfield Hills & Columbia: A Bruccoli Clark Book, 1975) publishes their 96 pages of explanatory and interpretive notes on the unproduced screenplay.

Gatsby Concordance

A computer-generated work compiled by Andrew Crosland, *Concordance to The Great Gatsby* (Detroit: Bruccoli Clark/ Gale Research, 1975) lists Fitzgerald's words both in order of frequency and alphabetically in context. A 450-page volume priced at $35, it is the first published concordance for an American novel.